Feminism in Russia, 1900–17

Feminism in Russia, 1900–17

Linda Harriet Edmondson

Stanford University Press
Stanford, California
1984

Stanford University Press
Stanford, California

Originating publisher: Heinemann Educational Books Ltd, London
First published in the U.S.A. by Stanford University Press, 1984
Printed in Great Britain
ISBN 0-8047-1212-3
LC 83-45338

To my parents

Contents

Preface

It was the original intention of this book to make a comparative study of feminism in nineteenth- and early twentieth-century Europe, focusing on two highly contrasted societies, Russia and Britain. With all the confidence of one who knows very little about a subject, I imagined that it would be a relatively simple task to account for the rise of feminism in the nineteenth century and find a common source of inspiration to explain its almost simultaneous emergence in two nations whose social and political cultures were otherwise so dissimilar.

I soon discovered some of the problems. Firstly, how was one to define the subject? Feminism as a term was not widely used by contemporaries. Supporters of female equality tended to refer rather vaguely to 'the women's movement' and 'the woman question'. Early in the twentieth century they called themselves 'suffragists'. In Russia particularly, feminism took on a pejorative meaning. Not only was it used by socialists (in Russia as elsewhere) as a term of abuse to dismiss the movement for women's equality as a diversion from the class struggle and a threat to the progress of the revolutionary movement. Even those whom we would now call feminists were apt to use the term disparagingly to denote 'fanatics of the woman question' who separated the struggle for women's rights from the broader problems of Russia's social and political life. When feminists in Russia began to demand political rights early in the twentieth century they called themselves 'equal-righters' (*ravnopravki*) and associated their own campaign for equality with the wider political campaign for the legal equality of all citizens, regardless of sex, religion, class or nationality.

But even if 'equal-righters' avoided the term feminism, there is no reason why we should do so, except for the fact that historians (and feminists) still disagree about its definition. At the risk of seeming to side-track the issue, I have chosen to use the term as a general description of a movement whose adherents believed (in the words of the first American declaration on sexual equality) 'that all men and women are created equal, that they are endowed by their Creator with certain inalienable rights: that among these are life, liberty and the pursuit of happiness . . .'[1] The declaration, composed in 1848, was as appropriate to feminists in early twentieth-century Moscow or St Petersburg as to their American predecessors.

However, if one can dispose of the problem of definition, it is much more difficult to find a satisfactory explanation of feminism as a historical phenomenon. Historians have tended, understandably, to be rather insular in their research – few have tried to study the growth of feminism in the mid-nineteenth century as an international movement, and those who have attempted to do so, by relating it to the growth of liberal individualism and the development of industrial capitalism, have had to confront the uncomfortable fact that their model does not fit a number of countries where feminist ideas flourished.[2]

Because the problem of interpreting the rise of feminism is still so far from resolution, I have chosen to devote the first part of Chapter 1 to a brief examination of the theories put forward by historians. It is no more than a brief sketch, but I hope that it will prompt others to examine more closely some of the theories in general circulation and to test them against the experience of countries outside western Europe and North America. Russia is a particularly good testing ground because feminist ideas which were current in mid-century Europe took root very rapidly in a society which, economically, was extremely backward compared with Britain or the United States and in which liberal individualism was far from being the ruling ideology.

So far there has been remarkably little published, either in the West or in the Soviet Union, on women's history in tsarist Russia, and what has been published has tended to focus on women as revolutionaries. There are now three full biographies of the Bolshevik, Aleksandra Kollontai, and almost nothing on women in the economy, or women in family life.[3] Nor has much attention been paid to 'bourgeois feminists'. Richard Stites has woven them skilfully into his book, *The Women's Liberation Movement in Russia* (Princeton: 1978). But his intention, in a book spanning the years 1860–1930, is to examine 'the origins of the communist variety of women's liberation in Russia'. His sympathies are quite clearly with the revolutionaries and he identifies with them in their suspicion of the feminists. I hope that my book will be read as a sympathetic, if critical, account of a movement for women's civil and political equality, whose supporters trusted that a better world could be created without resort to violence, and a constitutional solution be found to Russia's ills. That they ultimately failed is no reason for ignoring their existence or dismissing their efforts.

I should like to thank the library staffs of the School of Slavonic and East European Studies, the British Library, the London School of Economics and Political Science and the London Library for help and assistance. My thanks too to David Doughan at the Fawcett Library, City of London Polytechnic, for ferreting out information on the international movement, to Tom Nesmith in the Public Archives of Canada, Ottawa, for archival material on the International Council of Women, and to the staff of the Slavonic Section, University of Helsinki Library for their constant helpfulness and kindness during a six-week stay in 1977. I must also thank the Central Research Fund, University of London, for making that trip possible.

There is no room here to acknowledge all the assistance that I have had from friends and academic colleagues. But I should like to thank Professor Hugh Seton-Watson who supervised the thesis on which this book is based, Richard Stites for his advice and help in the early stages of the work, Rochelle Ruthchild (formerly Goldberg), Noralyn Neumark, Ruth Dudgeon, Amy Knight and Barbara Engel for their suggestions, references and ideas. A special word of thanks to Rose Glickman for reading and criticising the thesis, to Ruth Cohen and Tinch Minter for reading portions of the book and making helpful comments, to Hilary and Jeremy Barr for typing, tea and sympathy, and to Gary Marker for transatlantic exhortations in times of need. Finally, to my husband William I owe a debt that can never be repaid for his unfailing enthusiasm and encouragement and the generous donation of his own time, at every stage of the work.

London, October 1982

Notes

1 Declaration of Rights issued at the Seneca Falls Convention in 1848. Eleanor Flexner, *Century of Struggle. The Woman's Rights Movement in the United States* (New York: 1973), p. 75.

2 See Richard Evans, *The Feminists* (London: 1977). See also W.L. O'Neill, *The Woman Movement. Feminism in the United States and England* (London: 1969) and Olive Banks, *Faces of Feminism. A Study of Feminism as a Social Movement* (Oxford: 1981).

3 Rose Glickman's book, *Russian Factory Women: Workplace and Society, 1880–1914* will be published by University of California Press in 1983.

Note

Transliteration and dates

I have used the Library of Congress system of transliteration, minus most diacritical marks. Dates where they relate to Russia are given according to the Julian calendar, twelve days behind the western calendar in the nineteenth century, thirteen in the twentieth.

Abbreviations

ICW	International Council of Women
IWSA	International Woman Suffrage Alliance
RZhVBO	Russkoe Zhenskoe Vzaimno-Blagotvoritel'noe Obshchestvo (Russian Women's Mutual Philanthropic Society)
SRZh	Soiuz Ravnopravnosti Zhenshchin (Union of Equal Rights for Women)
SRs	Socialist–Revolutionaries
M	Moscow
Spb	St Petersburg

1 Origins

I wish to see women neither heroines nor brutes, but reasonable creatures.

Mary Wollstonecraft
A Vindication of the Rights of Women

No one who has studied the history of women's emancipation in the nineteenth and early twentieth centuries can have failed to notice the remarkable parallels which existed between women's movements in countries with profoundly differing social and political systems. It cannot be coincidence that women of good upbringing and genteel education, in England and Russia, Germany and the United States, Scandinavia and France, began to question a way of life which was highly circumscribed by law and custom and which offered them little outlet for their energies beyond domesticity and the diversions of a limited social life. In its place, women began to seek a full education, access to paid employment, greater rights within marriage and the family and, ultimately, the right to participate in the government of the nation. Despite numerous, and significant, national variations the pattern was broadly the same in all these countries and in the many others where feminism made its appearance. Quite why this phenomenon occurred, however, has not yet been adequately explained despite the recent revival of interest in the history of feminism.

Of all the intellectual influences leading to the development of feminism undoubtedly the most universally significant (and universally acknowledged) was the philosophy of the Enlightenment and, more particularly, the egalitarianism of the French Revolution. With that assault on the bastions of hierarchy and privilege came the first sustained questioning of the hitherto omnipotent convention that a man was the natural ruler of both home and nation. 'The divine right of husbands,' wrote Mary Wollstonecraft, 'like the divine right of kings, may, it is to be hoped in this enlightened age, be contested without danger.'[1]

Most obviously subversive of the status quo was the theory of the rights of man. If a man was no longer born to his station in life, but was judged to be a reasonable being capable of determining his own destiny without the direct supervision of temporal or spiritual authority, it required only a small leap of the imagination to dismantle the sexual hierarchy which denied that freedom to a woman and held her in a state of legal dependence on her husband or father. 'Either no member of the human race has real rights, or else all have the same,' wrote Condorcet, the most unequivocal of the *philosophes* in his support for female equality. 'He who votes against the rights of another, whatever his religion, colour or sex, thereby abjures his own.'[2]

The impact of this doctrine was, however, largely reserved for future generations; the imaginative leap was rarely made at the time. The Declaration of the Rights of Man and Citizen, like the American Declaration of Independence thirteen years earlier, spoke for mankind but ignored the female sex. Though Condorcet was not alone among the philosophers of the Enlightenment when he considered that women had an equal claim to human dignity, the politicians of the Revolution did little to advance that claim. Anti-feminism, in fact, grew with revolutionary extremism: at the height of the Terror, women were banned from the political clubs which they had joined during the preceding four years and the most outspoken advocate of female emancipation, Olympe de Gouges, went to the guillotine.[3] Outside France women, with the spirited exception of Mary Wollstonecraft, went generally unheard.

In terms of immediate benefit to the female sex, the French Revolution brought nothing. Indeed, as the rulers of Europe battened down the hatches against revolutionary turbulence, libertarian ideas of any sort became suspect. On France and on its military conquests abroad Napoleon imposed a law code which, for all its equalising tendency in other spheres, defined the subordination of women with even greater stringency than under the old regime. In strengthening the authority of husband over wife, children and property, and in narrowing the grounds for divorce, the *Code Napoléon* exerted a strong influence on the civil law of much of Catholic Europe for the whole of the nineteenth century.

If the Revolution itself could not serve as a successful model for female emancipation, it did bequeath to the nineteenth century concepts which were as significant for the emergence of feminism as for any other political philosophy of the time. Itself the product of a century and more of theoretical speculation into the place of the individual in society, the ideology of the Revolution exalted to the status of a religion the powerful doctrines of the inalienable rights of man and the sovereignty of the people. From these twin doctrines came the modern interpretation of democracy, the inspiration for every radical political movement of the succeeding century. From them also came the conflict between individual rights and the collective will, which no political philosophy was fully able to reconcile within itself, either in the nineteenth century or later.

It has become customary, with considerable justification, to treat nineteenth-century feminism as a manifestation of the tendency towards individualism, the epitome of liberal ideas, totally at odds with the collectivism of later socialist women's movements.[4] Both in its ideology and in the methods adopted to promote its aims, the women's movement bore many of the hallmarks of contemporary liberalism. Its point of departure was the equality of all citizens before the law and the right of the individual to self-fulfilment, provided that the interests of others were not harmed thereby. To achieve these goals it used the methods favoured by liberal reformers, preferring (at least before 1900) legal reform and personal achievement to an attempted reconstruction of society. It is no accident that the most celebrated and widely translated essay in support of women's rights in the second half of the century should have issued from the pen of John Stuart Mill.[5]

But there was another dimension to the women's movement, though one which became fully apparent only later. While feminist aspirations were founded in the first place on a theory of individual rights, there developed simultaneously a strong tendency to equate individualism with the inborn egotism of the male which, it was felt, had profoundly anti-social consequences for society. Women, by contrast, were seen as social beings, possessing qualities of co-operation and conciliation essential to civilisation but long undervalued. This aspiration to a collective consciousness became somewhat obscured by the growing rivalry, late in the century, between the established women's movement and the newly-emergent socialist women's organisations, which seemed to pit the individualism of the former against the collectivism of the latter. But that antagonism was not a simple conflict between individualist and collectivist solutions to the 'woman question'. It was as much an incompatibility between what could be called the 'moral collectivism' of the reformist women's movement and the socialist goal of economic and social revolution.

By no means all those who could be counted as feminists shared a conception of woman as a redemptive force, with power to restore to society a spirit of harmony to balance the harsh competitiveness of a world dominated by men. But even to those who did not take such a metaphysical view, the notion of sisterhood, of collective action by women, was attractive and to many was the dominant impulse for joining women's organisations. Here was another potent source of discord with the socialist movement, whose members rejected vehemently any attempt to undermine a class interpretation of society by appeals to female solidarity.

The importance of morality to the women's movement can hardly be exaggerated. It was expressed most forcibly in what may seem now to be a prudish attitude towards sexuality, but which is more fairly interpreted as one aspect of a movement to raise the standards of morality in every sphere. Undoubtedly, matters concerning sexual ethics (and pre-eminently the issue of prostitution) loomed larger than any other. Feminists were in the forefront of campaigns everywhere to suppress brothels, raise the age of consent and provide shelters for the fallen. But in some countries, notably the United States, the temperance cause proved to be as popular. In America the Women's Christian Temperance Union grew to be one of the largest organisations of the women's movement, claiming 200,000 supporters in the 1880s and actively participating in the campaign for female suffrage in later years. The union also established successful branches in Australia and New Zealand, and even in Russia, where the temperance movement was comparatively weak, many feminists supported its aims.

* * *

To trace the ideological roots of feminism is a comparatively simple task, but without some understanding of its social origins, any attempt to explain the rise of the women's movement is doomed to sterility. It is only when one begins to study the social and economic conditions obtaining in those countries where feminism developed that one appreciates the full complexity of the problem. A theory which fits conditions in Victorian England, for example, will not do for tsarist Russia, and one begins to wonder whether the search for a common denominator is not in fact the pursuit of a red herring. Yet it is difficult not to look for some common source where there were such striking similarities in form and chronology between the various women's movements.

An excellent illustration of the problem is provided by the role of economic change. This is, regrettably, an aspect of the women's movement (and of women's history generally) which has only recently begun to receive the attention it deserves. Given the present state of research it is not possible, with any precision, to account for the economic motivations of feminism in any one country, still less to make useful comparisons between differing economic systems. But it is worth taking a brief look at the one country, Great Britain, for which an adequate body of literature already exists.

In discussing the women's movement in Britain, historians have tended to assign much of the responsibility for the awakening consciousness of women's subordination to the changes wrought by the industrial revolution. It is indeed hard to see how such a profound transformation of social relations and methods of production (combined with an unprecedented growth in population) could have been without significance for the history of feminism, though it is still not clear quite where that significance lay.

It has been argued that, with the shift from a predominantly agricultural economy to one based on commerce and industry, the economic roles of women were forced to undergo two major adjustments.

The first affected women of the middle classes. Instead of contributing to the maintenance of the household through their own labour, women began to withdraw from productive work. Their husbands' incomes rose, goods could be bought rather than made and a growing army of servants became available to take over domestic chores from their mistresses. Thus, it is suggested, the middle-class woman became economically as well as legally the dependant of her husband. Her functions were to produce children, supervise the servants and create a warm but refined atmosphere in the home. If she was unfortunate enough not to have secured a husband, the middle-class woman had few outlets for her energies besides religion and charitable works. If she lacked private means there was little alternative but to seek a post as governess or companion.[6]

The second adjustment concerned working-class women and was a more complex one. On the one hand it has been shown that the mechanisation of industry brought women (and children) into the new industrial towns as a source of cheap labour for the textile mills. By the middle of the nineteenth century, however, heavy industry (in which men predominated) began to outstrip the lighter industries to which women had been recruited. Though the proportion of women in Britain working outside the home remained fairly constant throughout the century, the focus of work shifted away from manufacturing: girls went increasingly into domestic service, making it an overwhelmingly female occupation.[7] As men's wages rose, married women (like their middle-class counterparts) became housewives taking outside work only in times of their husbands' unemployment, illness or death.

Thus a paradox emerged. A 'cult of domesticity', which worshipped the woman as a homemaker and the home as a refuge from an unkind world, developed alongside women's recruitment into a number of economically important industries and services. Women continued to form 30 per cent of the total labour force working outside the home in a society which viewed the separation of men's and women's work, the separation of workplace from home, as an essential element of a civilised world. While working-class girls were expected to earn their living, at least before marriage, girls of genteel upbringing and adequate means were effectively barred from employment.

The implications for the development of feminism of women's changing economic role within the family are still somewhat obscure, however. It has been argued, for example, that by their participation in an industrial wage economy, working-class women were freed from the bonds of tradition; with their independent income they acquired an independence of spirit and a political consciousness which they had earlier lacked. The thesis rests on the well-documented role which women played in radical political movements such as Chartism, especially in the textile towns of northern England, where they formed a high percentage of the permanent workforce.[8] Elsewhere, however, the employment of women (and especially married women) in large-scale industry was not so extensive, nor was their involvement in trade union or political activities. Moreover, the participation of working-class women in public affairs declined everywhere after 1850, at the very point when the women's movement was coming to life. Although working-class women (again notably in the north–west) took up the suffrage campaign, along with other social issues, in the 1890s and 1900s, they had virtually no interest in, or direct influence on, the earlier development of the women's movement in England.

It may well be, however, that they exerted an indirect influence, undermining a traditional attitude towards paid employment for women. In a pre-industrial economy, women generally worked as part of a family unit, within the home and for no payment. It was only with the mechanisation of industry that large numbers of women began to work for wages and, in the case of unmarried girls, outside the home. Thus the Victorian idealisation of the home (and woman's place within it) can perhaps be seen as the anxious reassertion of a previously unchallenged assumption in the face of unprecedented social and economic change, rather than as the creation of a new norm. If this was so it helps to explain why women of the middle classes began to chafe against restrictions which earlier generations of well-to-do women had taken for granted (or had suffered without protest) and why they were ultimately successful in establishing for the female sex what G.M. Young calls a 'conception of autonomous personality'.[9]

The astonishing changes which took place in Britain between 1750 and 1850 may, therefore, have been significant for the women of the rapidly expanding middle classes less by imprisoning them in the suffocating environment of the home than by creating conditions and attitudes in which women could begin to choose an alternative existence.[10] For, whatever the 'rough equality' at work which women shared with men in a pre-industrial economy, there is no evidence to suggest that such equality gave women a higher status or greater freedom. The legal impediments to female autonomy which the women's movement everywhere helped to demolish were (with the notable exception of laws on prostitution) almost entirely the product of earlier centuries, and it is surely not irrelevant to the discussion to note that only in the nineteenth century were consistent attempts made to dismantle them. Even the sentimental cult of woman as 'the angel in the house', so repugnant to later generations and to feminists at the time, may have had its benevolent aspect when compared with the disregard or contempt which is all too often to be found in the works of earlier writers.[11]

If a causal relationship between industrialisation and the women's movement may be shown to exist in Britain, there remains the problem of accounting for the rise of feminism in countries which did not experience such rapid industrial expansion or which did so much later. Nowhere is the inadequacy of a theory which sees feminism as a product of an industrialising society more evident than in the case of Russia, where industrial power began to have a notable effect upon the economy a full twenty years after the 'woman question' first became a burning topic and where the peasant population still formed 80 per cent of the total in 1917. Even if industrialisation was further advanced before the emancipation of the serfs than has commonly been supposed, no one would argue that Russia was on the way to establishing a predominantly industrial economy as Britain was by 1850. Evidently, if one wishes to find sources of inspiration for the women's movement common to Britain and Russia, one must look elsewhere.

Demographic change has often been invoked as an explanatory factor. By 1850 the number of females in the population was exceeding the number of males almost everywhere in Europe. The excess was most marked in England (where there were 1,042 females to 1,000 males in 1851, rising to 1,064 by the turn of the century) but figures for other countries were comparable.[12] The reasons are still not fully understood, but a relatively higher male mortality and increased emigration seem to have been chiefly responsible. Whatever its cause, there is no question that the presence of 'surplus women' was highly disturbing to contemporaries, who saw it as depriving thousands of women of the fulfilment and economic security which they were brought up to expect in marriage, prompting them to look for employment outside the home. It was clear to many observers that this state of affairs had contributed in no small measure to the rise of the women's movement.[13]

The hypothesis is difficult either to prove or disprove. Certainly, by making marriage a statistical impossibility for a significant number of young women, the sexual imbalance may have stimulated the exploration of new areas of female employment, accompanied by a demand for economic and legal independence. But there is no evidence to show that women's numerical superiority alone was responsible for changing attitudes. From the experience of the women's movement, one has more reason to believe that to be in a minority was of greater advantage, since it was precisely in those regions where women were in short supply that equal rights were most easily attained.

The first countries in the world to grant female suffrage were New Zealand in 1893 and Australia in 1902, both of which had more male than female inhabitants. Similarly, in the United States, Wyoming, Colorado, Utah and Idaho adopted women's suffrage before 1900, while the older established communities of the eastern seaboard held out. However, in all these instances (as in Siberia, where colonists were more progressive towards sexual equality than in the older parts of the Empire) the unequal sex ratio may have been far less significant than the fact that in a pioneering community, tradition will be sacrificed to the needs of the moment.

A more promising clue to the origins of the women's movement may be found within the family. This social institution, whose structure and development remained largely untouched by historical research until recently, has been subjected to intense scrutiny over the past two decades. The most controversial area of research has focused on the transition of the family from an extended to a nuclear structure, a question which is still far from resolved. Upsetting the long-held view that the nuclear family was a product of industrialisation and urbanisation, a new orthodoxy has pushed back the emergence of the nuclear family, in the West at least, to the sixteenth and seventeenth centuries. Such a development, it has been argued, combined with a tendency to late marriage, 'sharply differentiated pre-modern [sic] English and western European society from its neighbours in eastern Europe and Russia . . . where large joint and complex family households predominated and marriage was early and virtually universal.'[14]

Obviously the history of the family, and of woman's role within it, cannot be divorced from the question of economic and social change in society at large. The objection could be raised that if one is incapable of establishing a clear link between the development of industrial capitalism and the rise of feminism in countries outside western Europe, then there is not much point in looking at the family for an explanation of the women's movement. The objection is reinforced by the very marked differences in family structure and function between, for example, western and eastern Europe, or between urban and peasant, or middle-class and working-class communities.[15]

However, regardless of the differing forms and functions of the family, there is no doubt that everywhere it was heavily patriarchal. Equally evident was the fact that by the middle of the nineteenth century it had begun to seem a constricting and oppressive institution to many of its dependent members. The family, according to its contemporary panegyrists, was the linchpin of society, yet in the West its structure was increasingly at odds with the prevailing social ethos. The nuclear family of mid-century Europe, as Eric Hobsbawm notes, 'was both a patriarchal autocracy and a microcosm of the sort of society which the bourgeoisie as a class (or its theoretical spokesmen) denounced and destroyed: a hierarchy of personal dependence.'[16] Within that hierarchy the female members inevitably assumed a subordinate and dependent role. It is in the persistence, even the entrenchment, of a hierarchical and patriarchal family structure, in an age which was painfully yielding to the forces of democracy, that it may be possible to find a common cause of the women's movement overriding the wide divergencies in economic development, social organisation and religion between the various countries.

This is a hypothesis which, paradoxically, would be highly relevant to Russia. There the patriarchal family was not in conflict with the official ideology: quite the opposite. Not only was it enshrined in law and custom, but its continuance was regarded by tsarist rulers as essential to the survival of autocratic government. The family, ordained Pobedonostsev, was 'the spiritual and cultural nursery for citizens', whose functions were to maintain tradition, ensure social stability and control man's instincts. The family was 'the foundation of the state'.[17]

It was, however, this very connection between the absolutism of the state and that of the family which made the latter so odious to the Russian radical intelligentsia, which took up the cause of women's emancipation with an enthusiasm and unanimity unmatched by male radicals anywhere else in Europe. Granted, the Russian intelligentsia owed an immense debt to Fourier, Saint-Simon and George Sand for its ideas. But the leading publicists (Chernyshevskii, M.L. Mikhailov, Lavrov, Pisarev, Dobroliubov and others) surpassed even Engels and Bebel in their attachment to the cause. In Russia no radical would have dared, as Proudhon did in France, to give vent to misogynist sentiments in public.[18]

From the very beginning of the women's movement in Russia a close association was established between the personal liberation of women and the liberation of society, which distinguished it from feminist movements in other countries and which was to influence its further development to a profound degree. In the West, rebellion against parental authority and social mores was a personal one. Although it often required tremendous perseverence on the part of the young women involved to overcome the opposition of their families and the derision of society, their actions had no obvious political connotations. In Russia, defiance of parental authority was quickly linked in official eyes with political subversion. Girls who had successfully broken away from their families to pursue the right to study or take up an occupation were frequently drawn into nihilist and radical circles, where abolition of the family (or at the very least its total transformation) was preached as gospel.

Many women soon abandoned the world of communes and collective workshops which flourished in the early 1860s, to seek their emancipation within established society. One of them, Anna Shabanova, who had begun her adult life in an illegal sewing workshop and spent some months in prison as a result, left her radical youth far behind her and became one of the leading moderates in the feminist movement.

But many more stayed in the radical camp. For them, the liberation of women shrank to secondary importance besides social revolution, and rebellion against the patriarchal family yielded to rebellion against the state.[19]

But it must not be inferred that in Russia the 'woman question' was the exclusive preserve of the radical wing of the intelligentsia. Radical writings, communal workshops and young women sporting tinted spectacles and cropped hair were only the most provocative manifestation of a movement towards female emancipation which had begun to stir the whole of educated society in the late 1850s. This movement was clearly stimulated by the first examples of feminist organisation abroad and still more by the highly polemical literature which was now occupying the pages of the European press. But it was also a response to circumstances at home, and particularly to the transformation of political conditions after 1855, without which even the most fertile ideas from abroad would have fallen on barren soil. And it is just when one examines the particular political and social environment in which the women's movement in Russia developed, that one is forced to question the helpfulness of a general theory of feminism. For not only was the experience of women in previous centuries unique in many respects to Russia but so were the conditions in which the 'woman question' became a pressing social issue in the middle of the nineteenth century.[20]

* * *

The 'woman question' arose in a society just beginning to recover from the horror and humiliation of the Crimean War and the conclusion of Nicholas I's inglorious reign. For a generation, intellectual life had been blighted by an autocrat whose realisation of the need for change had been more than matched by his dread of it. Severe censorship and the assiduousness of the secret police had sent many of the educated élite abroad or into exile, the victims of a policy aimed at the suppression of any new ideas. But Nicholas was unable to stifle the energies of his country's educated youth. Military defeat in the Crimea and the accession of a new ruler, Alexander II, who at once conceded the inevitability of reform, ushered in a decade of intense intellectual activity and unlimited hopes for the regeneration of society.

At the heart of the debate was the question of serfdom, an institution which permeated the whole social structure of Russia. Abolition of the serf system had already been the subject of discussion in government circles for half a century, and some minor reforms had been made in the law. But whereas the primary considerations of the government were economic efficiency, protection against peasant unrest and the integrity of the state, the overriding concern of the intelligentsia in the late 1850s was for the moral consequences of a system in which one man was the property of another. Radicals and liberals alike believed passionately that serfdom was an evil which degraded the serf-owner even more than his serfs and ultimately corrupted the entire society in which it was practised. To both wings of the intelligentsia equality in human relationships was a sacred principle; the quarrel between them lay in its interpretation, not in its validity.

A society whose bureaucracy admitted the need for reform, and whose intelligentsia was passionate for change, was one in which ideas of women's liberation found a ready audience. The obvious parallel between the subjection of the peasant to the serf-owner and that of a woman to her father or husband was quickly drawn and the emancipation of the serfs encouraged demands for female emancipation too.[21]

The legal position of Russian women in the middle of the nineteenth century, though heavily restricted, was in fact no worse than that of women abroad. In one respect it was better: married women of the non-peasant estates had a right to their own property.[22] This freedom was, however, largely negated by provisions of the civil code which obliged a woman to obey her husband and reside with him in a place of his own choosing. Since arranged marriages were common (and the norm among the peasantry) and divorce all but unobtainable, a woman generally had little control over her destiny while her husband was alive. An unmarried woman over the age of twenty-one was in some ways more fortunate, since she could obtain her own internal passport without her father's consent, but there was little that she could do with such freedom outside the family circle: the universities were closed to women, likewise the professions and public service. The fact that some women achieved an independent existence is a testimony more to their perseverence than to the opportunities available to them.[23]

As for peasant women, it is difficult to generalise. Peasant life in Russia was regulated by customary law which differed from region to region, and from the established legal code. The concept of individual rights was inapplicable: the peasants' responsibilities were to the village community and (when they were serfs) to their feudal landlord. However, in the peasant community at least as much as in gentry circles or among the urban merchant class, women were considered subordinate. Even though their status and authority generally (but not invariably) improved as they grew older, men took the decisions for the village, and both taxation and the redistribution of communal land were reckoned according to the number of male 'souls'. Right up to the 1917 Revolution a man was expected to be master in his own household. Though personal relationships between husbands and wives were undoubtedly more complex than the stereotype suggests, the symbol of male authority and coercion – the practice of wife-beating – was still sanctioned in peasant households long after it had been prohibited in statute law.

But the women's movement in Russia did not originate simply in an awareness that the subordination of one sex to another was as indefensible as the subordination of serf to serf-owner. It owed at least as much to two other major factors: the economic effects of the emancipation of the serfs in 1861 and the upsurge of interest in education which followed the Crimean débâcle. The former is by far the more difficult to unravel. The economic history of women in Russia (even more than in other countries) is an almost totally neglected field: if one can make only tentative conclusions about the inter-relationship of feminism and women's economic roles in the West, in the case of Russia one can do little more than guess.[24]

Although statistical material is still lacking, however, the observations of contemporaries and circumstantial evidence suggest that the abolition of serfdom and the accompanying decline of the gentry may have played as decisive a role in the development of the women's movement as industrialisation appears to have done in Britain. Before 1861, it has been argued, a family of the gentry class was usually able to provide economic security for its unmarried daughters and other female relatives. In those cases where it was not, a woman could take a post as governess in a more prosperous gentry or merchant family, a step which undeniably exposed her to personal humiliations and discomforts but did not entirely deprive her of social status. However, with the breakdown of the serf system, the poorer gentry tended to sell their land and migrate to the rapidly expanding cities, while changing fashions in education and the reduced economic circumstances of the gentry as a whole restricted the demand for governesses. The result, it would seem, was a superfluous urban population of women lacking any visible means of support.

However, an alternative hypothesis has been put forward. Instead of uprooting the gentry family, it is suggested, the emancipation of the serfs had the effect of removing members of the gentry from state service in the capital and returning them to their estates. Gentry wives, accustomed to enjoy responsibility for the running of the estate and household while their husbands were away, found their role reduced on their husbands' return. The result was a growing frustration on the part of female members of the household and the stimulation of feminist aspirations.[25]

Whichever was the general pattern, there is no doubt that in the larger cities (and particularly St Petersburg) the problem of female unemployment among the genteel population was a real one, and the first feminists in Russia were quick to recognise its importance. Mariia

Trubnikova, one of the leading figures in the women's movement at this time, wrote to her English counterpart, Josephine Butler, that in the middle ranks of society 'men find work and independence by means of intellectual and craft work,' but that meanwhile 'the number is growing yearly of married and unmarried women equally in need of work if they wish to avoid either dying of hunger or prostituting themselves.'[26]

Some found work in the cities as translators, book-binders and typesetters, as stenographers and telegraphists. But openings for women with some education were meagre, as were their earnings. It was for such women that Trubnikova and her colleagues set up a publishing workshop in 1863, run on co-operative lines and paying reasonable wages to its workers. The workshop was strikingly successful until the early 1870s, publishing a number of textbooks and children's books (including a censored version of Hans Andersen's tales) but despite repeated efforts it failed to gain official recognition and was finally disbanded in 1879.[27]

Even at the height of its success the publishing workshop was providing no more than a hundred jobs for women (and probably far fewer). In an attempt to widen the sphere of female employment, a more extensive project was proposed in 1863. This was the Society for Women's Work, which was to act as a type of employment exchange, making accessible to women jobs normally reserved for men and thus providing society with 'moral and intellectual forces' which were at present being wasted. The project was not realised, succumbing to the accumulated antagonism between moderates in the feminist movement (like Trubnikova and her collaborator Anna Filosofova) and the radical wing of 'nihilists', who dismissed their opponents as 'aristocrats' and objected to both the style and the content of their activities.[28]

Although the plight of women from the poorer gentry, clergy and urban middle classes was an obvious inspiration and focus of feminist activity, it would be quite misleading to suggest that the principal figures in the women's movement were themselves motivated by need. It is true that large numbers of the women who were supporting themselves in the city led a financially precarious existence – hence much of the appeal of communes and workshops – but as often as not they had accepted penury when they left home, preferring it to the security of an arranged marriage, a comfortable home and years of child-bearing. These women, in any case, were not the leaders of the women's movement. By and large the leadership, and much of its support, were drawn from ranks of society whose fortunes were still intact and whose female members had no need to earn a living.

Trubnikova and her sister, for example, were brought up in the home of a wealthy aunt and inherited a fortune. Although Trubnikova was later obliged to find work as a translator after separating from her husband (who had mishandled the fortune entrusted to him) her feminism long antedated this personal crisis. Filosofova was born into an old-established family, the Diagilevs, and made a good match. Her husband was, at the time of his wife's first involvement in feminist organisations, a high official in the War Ministry and spent all his working life in the upper echelons of the bureaucracy. Nadezhda Stasova, the third member of what became known as the Triumvirate, was the daughter of a court architect and the sister of the celebrated art and music critic, Vladimir Stasov.

It was not their own straitened circumstances but the perception of the needs of others which propelled the Filosofovas, Stasovas and Trubnikovas into the women's movement. If the breakdown of the serf system had not greatly altered their own way of life, they could not ignore the effects which it was having on others. Not only the poorer members of the gentry but also, in far greater numbers, migrating peasants were making claims on housing and employment which the cities were ill equipped to meet. Even before 1861, the population of St Petersburg was rising sharply in the first stages of the city's industrialisation, and existing charitable works were clearly insufficient to meet those claims.

Trubnikova's circle had in fact addressed itself to this problem before any other, drawing up plans for a philanthropic society to provide those in need with accommodation at a low rent. The scheme was remarkable for its time in that it specifically rejected the strict regulations and supervision characteristic of most charity organisations, aiming instead to help its beneficiaries 'to stand on their feet'. Launched in 1861, the Society to Provide Cheap Lodgings and Other Assistance to the Needy Population of St Petersburg proved a considerable success, expanding over a twenty-year period into a major charity whose facilities included not simply rooms and apartments, but workshops, canteens and even schools.[29]

However successful it later became, the society was at first able to make only a tiny dent in the number of homeless people in the capital. By 1869, no more than 400 were being accommodated. Its real value at this stage was to the feminists themselves, who gained immeasurably from the experience of organising and administering a public concern. As comparable ventures did for women abroad, the Society to Provide Cheap Lodgings proved both to itself and to an often sceptical public that women could be entrusted with responsibilities beyond the management of their households. The importance of this initial 'consciousness-raising' to the further development of the women's movement cannot be over-stressed. In a social environment where it was still daring for a young lady to go about unchaperoned, and most unladylike for her to make a speech in public, the demonstration of a businesslike approach to problems of social welfare had an immense psychological significance quite distinct from its practical benefits.

Important though these early activities were, they were soon eclipsed by what was to become the major focus of the Russian feminist movement for the remainder of the century. This was the protracted battle to get women admitted to the institutions of higher education, and the equally sustained endeavour to obtain professional recognition and status. These twin goals, shared by feminists throughout the world, proved to be the most substantial and ultimately the most fruitful area of activity in Russia before 1917.[30]

* * *

Although efforts to open higher education to women did not gain momentum until the end of the 1860s, the issue of female aptitude for learning had arisen fifteen years earlier, at a time when the whole educational edifice of the nation was being subjected to close scrutiny. Despite the educational innovations of Catherine the Great and the continued expansion of schools and universities in the first part of the nineteenth century, academic standards (particularly of the nation's future ruling elite) had begun to arouse acute concern by the 1850s. The accession of Alexander II in 1855 inaugurated a spate of reforms which touched every level of the educational hierarchy. Hampered though they were by the government's all too justified fear of creating demands incompatible with the preservation of autocracy, the reforms established a system which, in structure if not breadth, closely resembled those being created in the West at the same period.

Educational reforms, and the intense debates which accompanied them, naturally affected women. Since it was they who were responsible for the early upbringing of the next generation of citizens, it was inevitable that any re-evaluation of the role and content of children's education would raise the question of the education of women themselves. There was, as yet, little question of higher education for a career; what was at issue was the training of young women to be intelligent mothers and sympathetic wives. As Nikolai Pirogov wrote in his highly influential 'Questions of Life': 'the early development of thought and free will is as important for a woman as for a man.' Both were essential to make her a companion to her husband and to give her 'a clear and lucid idea of the purpose of children's upbringing.' Pirogov did not feel that girls' education should be identical to boys': their vocations were different. A woman could feel proud that she did not know everything; she had no need to pursue a career outside the home. But her present education did not fit her for her vital role as the mother and educator 'of the whole of mankind'.

Let the idea of educating herself for this goal, of living for the inevitable struggle and sacrifice, penetrate the whole moral being of a woman and sanctify her will – then she will know where she must seek her emancipation.[31]

Even in the context of its time this prescription was not a radical one. But the practical changes which resulted from the debate, notably the authorisation of a new type of girls' secondary school open to all classes, were far-reaching in their effects. With the establishment of the girls' gymnasium in 1858, most of the real and formal obstacles to higher education were removed, and with them the logical barrier to employment in the professions and public service.[32]

It did not follow, however, that if girls could now be educated to a level at which they might aspire to higher things, they were to be encouraged to do so. For a brief period after 1859 women were admitted to lectures in a number of universities, but the outbreak of political demonstrations among students two years later (during which one woman was arrested) was used as a pretext to bar their future admission. Although a large number of progressive academics in St Petersburg continued to champion their cause, it was not until the late 1860s that the question was taken up in a more systematic fashion by the feminist movement. In the meantime those wishing to study, and possessing the financial resources to do so, went abroad, and above all to Zurich, which by the early 1870s contained a sizeable colony of Russian students of both sexes. Many of them had by this time begun to take an active role in radical politics.[33]

The feminists' new interest in higher education arose directly from their activities over the previous decade. Concerned both to prove women's equal worth to society and, more practically, to create a wider range of female employment, they rapidly became aware that opportunities for expansion were blocked by women's own lack of qualifications. The initiative for reopening the question lay with Evgeniia Konradi, editor of a progressive journal, who in 1867 petitioned a congress of natural scientists to lend its support to women's higher education. This was soon followed by a petition, drawn up by Konradi, Trubnikova and Stasova and signed by 400 women, to the rector of St Petersburg University, requesting lectures and courses at university level and on university premises.

The university announced its 'full sympathy' with the proposal, but the government offered little encouragement. Only by dint of continued petitioning and the persuasive powers of well-placed feminists like Filosofova and the wife and daughter of the War Minister, did the Minister of Education eventually agree in 1869 to a course of academic lectures open to the public of both sexes. This was very much less than the campaigners had aimed for and provoked much acrimonious dispute between the 'aristocrats', who believed that the offer must be accepted as a first step towards the ultimate goal of a women's university, and their 'nihilist' opponents. The latter had, in any case, decided that the immediate need was not for university-level education but for preparatory courses to narrow the gap between girls' and boys' secondary schools.[34]

Although they were acrimonious, the disagreements did not significantly weaken the movement for higher education. Indeed, they may be taken more as a sign of its lively diversity than as an indication of feebleness; this was certainly how they appeared to sympathisers all over Russia. Despite restrictions on publicity and fund-raising, well-wishers sent messages of support and private donations. More importantly, all the courses, both at intermediate and at higher levels, were quickly oversubscribed. Their fame soon spread across Russia's borders: before the courses were even instituted, John Stuart Mill sent a letter addressed to 'the lady organisers of higher education in St Petersburg' congratulating them on their endeavours and noting that success in this field 'would be proof that comparatively new civilisations sometimes anticipate the old in great ideas of improvement.' The French feminist André Léo, a well-known novelist of the period, wrote that 'your glory will live after you for establishing in Russia what we are now only dreaming of,' and Josephine Butler invited the Russians to contribute to an international journal that she was planning to publish in London.[35]

The public lectures open to men and women soon became established as the Vladimir Courses, existing on an insecure basis of student fees and private donations (advertising was not permitted), and subject to periodic attacks from influential quarters. Nor were their organisers content with what had been achieved, hoping that the courses would be allowed to grow beyond the limits prescribed by the education ministry. A dissident group, led by Konradi, soon came to the conclusion that the money would be better spent on stipends for women to study abroad, and abandoned the courses after a row over student fees.[36]

The greatest threat to their existence was the widespread conviction in conservative circles that political radicalism and women's emancipation were two sides of the same coin. The burgeoning populist movement in which women (worse still, former students) took a prominent role, could not fail to reinforce the view that higher courses were a breeding ground for revolution. It was, however, precisely this misgiving which in the end saved the courses. Since the most conspicuous group of female radicals were studying not in Russia but abroad, in Zurich, feminists could argue that it was not education *per se* but the seductive influence of revolutionaries upon young women away from home that was to blame. If women could be educated in their own country under proper supervision, those most susceptible to radical ideas could be diverted by thoughts of useful study and the possibility of a career.

The argument was one which appealed to the Minister of Education, who used his influence within the government to press for an extension of women's education. In 1872, less than three years after the Minister's grudging permission for public lectures, the first full-time higher courses were opened in Moscow, under the direction of a university professor. In the same year the War Ministry sponsored medical studies for women at the Medical Surgical Academy in St Petersburg, the first anywhere in Europe. Initiated as four-year courses for 'learned midwives' they were extended in 1876 to give women the same education as men, bestowing on graduates the right to treat women's and children's diseases. In return for these concessions the government ordered women students in Zurich to leave, or otherwise forfeit all right to education and employment in Russia.[37]

The government's desire to bring women's higher education under bureaucratic control was revealed the same year (1873) when it established a commission to consider the future of the courses. The outcome, to the surprise and relief of the feminists themselves, was a considerable victory for their cause. A statute published in 1876 authorised higher educational institutes at university level, subject to ministry supervision but publicly funded. The first of these new establishments, modelled on the Moscow courses, opened in St Petersburg in 1878. They were known popularly as the Bestuzhev courses, after their first director, the historian K.N. Bestuzhev-Riumin.

Thus by 1880 the women's movement, measured by its educational achievements, could quite reasonably claim to be in the vanguard of feminism throughout Europe. Hundreds of women could now study a wide range of subjects to an advanced level, with expanding opportunities (regulated by government edict) for professional employment on graduation. By that time, yearly enrolments at the Bestuzhev courses had reached about 1,000; by the mid-1880s about 700 women had graduated from the medical courses. Permitted at last to practise under the title of 'woman doctor', they found employment mainly in the rural zemstvo and the town duma (elective institutions of local government, created by the reforms of Alexander II, and resembling English county and borough councils, though with far less autonomy). These new institutions employed increasing numbers of men and women as doctors, teachers, agronomists, statisticians and so forth.[38]

These achievements were a tribute to the perseverance and faith of the early feminists, a demonstration of 'the remarkable force of public initiative, the power of public opinion, and the sense of social consciousness among the educated classes in Russia as well as their willingness to work for reform through legal channels.'[39]

However, victory was not secure. None of the gains had been won without a fight, finance proved to be a constant source of anxiety and each fresh wave of political radicalism put the courses in jeopardy. Moreover, the courses were established on temporary regulations and therefore doubly at risk when the political climate deteriorated. Their vulnerability was soon to be tested.[40]

The assassination of the tsar in 1881 and the accession of Alexander III brought an abrupt change of fortune. The sympathetic War Minister, Miliutin, lost his post and the government announced the closure of the medical courses supervised by his ministry, conceding only that students already enrolled might complete their studies. A reshuffle in the Ministry of Education resulted in the dismantling of higher courses in Moscow, Kiev and Kazan, leaving the Bestuzhev courses in St Petersburg as the sole institution of higher education for women in Russia for the next fifteen years. Even they came near to permanent closure, but were saved by the strong ties which had been created between the university and feminist organisations in St Petersburg and by their access (though now limited) to those with influence in higher circles.[41]

The attack on higher education in the 1880s had profound significance for the future of the women's movement in Russia. To disrupt the progress of women's education was, to a much greater extent than elsewhere, to undermine the whole foundation of the movement, since the one had become virtually synonymous with the other.[42] This was not simply because of the enormous prestige of education among the Russian intelligentsia, which saw its duty to society in terms of study and work. It was also a reflection of the Russian movement's failure to develop a broader character, to move beyond education and philanthropy to other questions relating to women's role in society, notably their civil and political status.

The reasons for this are not difficult to find. The institutional structure of the country not only inhibited but actively forbade the formation of political pressure groups outside ruling circles. Difficult as it was to petition for schools and lecture courses, even in a period of relative enlightenment like the 1860s, it was well-nigh impossible to argue for political change and remain within the law. In Britain and the United States, those who saw politics as the key to the further emancipation of women could invest their energies in women's suffrage societies (though admittedly with negligible results before 1900). More radical women, in Britain at least, found a home in the non-revolutionary socialism of left-wing parties like the Independent Labour Party. Similar options were closed to Russian feminists.

Organised political life in Russia had no place for women. At a national level there was no forum for debate (and focus for campaigning) such as the British Parliament or the United States Congress provided. At provincial level the elected local government institutions of zemstvo and duma came under attack by central government during Alexander III's reign. In striking contrast to the position in western countries, where women were gradually being admitted to the local government franchise, the very limited voting rights of Russian women were actually narrowed in this period. Before 1890, a woman with sufficient property had the right to nominate as her proxy any male person whom she chose. In 1890 this right was redefined to include only close male relatives. The distinction, it is true, was not of major significance, since few women possessed enough property to qualify, but it was symptomatic both of the government's determination to curb the zemstvos' freedom of action and of its reluctance to entrust women with a greater role in social management.

As a result of these external circumstances, feminism in Russia remained largely apolitical until the end of the century. Women either abandoned all thoughts of structural change and concentrated on preserving what gains they had already made, or they abandoned feminism altogether, as hundreds of radicals had done in the 1870s, and as they were to do later, in the second wave of revolutionary activity from the 1890s.[43]

* * *

The reign of Alexander III from 1881 to 1894 marked a low point in the history of the women's movement. Beset by public discouragement and personal misfortune, many of the leading feminists of the 1860s and 1870s withdrew from an active role in its affairs. Filosofova, already suspect in the late 1870s because of her alleged sympathies with the terrorists, temporarily resigned from the committees which she had helped to establish; Konradi went abroad and Trubnikova finally succumbed to the insanity which had been threatening her for over a decade. Others naturally took their places, but even the most optimistic feminists experienced periods of doubt and disillusion in an environment hostile to their aspirations.

This situation endured until the early 1890s. Then, in the aftermath of the catastrophic famine of 1892–3, with the revival of social initiative and the first stirrings of a new wave of political opposition, feminism also began to seek new directions. In October 1893, a tentative notice appeared in the conservative daily newspaper *Novoe Vremia* inviting women in St Petersburg to form a mutual aid society modelled on women's clubs in the United States. This modest proposal met a sympathetic response from a small group which included Filosofova and Stasova, and the latter was unanimously chosen as its president. Even now, however, bureaucratic suspicion of social organisations hampered the new enterprise. The organisers were informed by the Ministry of the Interior that women were barred from membership of societies which lacked a specifically philanthropic or educational purpose and that the statute which they had submitted must be redrafted. As a result, the new society found itself with a cumbersome administrative structure and an unwieldy and unappealing name, the Russian Women's Mutual Philanthropic Society (*Russkoe Zhenskoe Vzaimno-Blagotvoritel'noe Obshchestvo* or RZhVBO). This compromise was won only through the personal influence of a maid of honour to the empress.[44]

If this had been all the society had had to endure, the organisers might have counted themselves fortunate. The very existence of the society was no mean achievement: in Moscow, the draft statute of a parallel society was rejected just a year after the St Petersburg society's formation and nothing similar was founded before the end of the century. But from its very inception the society's council had to meet stern criticism from those who believed that it was hamstrung both by its bureaucratic constitution and by its fear of police interference. Not long after the society's establishment the more radical and politically conscious members left.[45]

Nonetheless, the Mutual Philanthropic Society could boast some minor triumphs. Many were due to Anna Shabanova, one of the first generation of medical students in the 1870s and now a respected pediatrician, who became president on Stasova's sudden death in 1895. Thanks to her persistence the society was allowed to open a library and reading room on its premises and to hold seminars and lectures for its members. But these gains also proved tenuous; the 'home reading circle' was closed in 1899 and the seminar group two years later. Most of its other activities were of a directly philanthropic nature: a hostel and refectory for educated women, an employment service, a kindergarten and sundry facilities for poor mothers and their children.[46]

Despite the setbacks and frustrations which feminists encountered in the 1890s and the loss of that enthusiasm which had been so striking a generation earlier, there was no question that the movement was enjoying a revival. If the government still frowned on women's clubs and associations, it had become more appreciative of female skills in under-staffed professions like medicine and education. Consequently, the 1890s saw a renewed expansion of opportunities for women to study and to take up employment on graduation. In 1897 the first medical school for women was inaugurated in St Petersburg and the next year women were given greater rights to practise. The Bestuzhev higher courses were expanded, and voluntary 'collective lessons' authorised in Moscow and elsewhere. In 1900 the Moscow Higher Women's Courses reopened under their former director. Although many restrictions on employment and status remained in force, women found that they were at last achieving social recognition, if not as men's equals then as intelligent individuals who could make a worthwhile contribution to the nation's economy. The fact that at the same period the number of working-class and peasant women employed in large-scale manufacturing industries was rising rapidly could not fail to reinforce a new perception of women's social and economic functions. By 1885 women already formed 30 per cent of the manual workforce. In 1899 the proportion had risen to 44 per cent, 660,000 out of a total of one and a half million. Russia was now well into the industrial revolution which had barely begun when feminism first made its appearance forty years earlier.[47]

* * *

It is impossible to estimate the degree to which the feminist movement, as a cohesive force of individuals conscious of the need for change, was responsible for the transformation of women's lives in the second half of the nineteenth century. One might well argue that the movement was only a reflection of shifting attitudes and new social and economic relationships which would, regardless of personal initiatives, inevitably alter the position of women in society. If, however, the movement was the product of a particular set of social conditions, it is equally clear from the course of events that without the conscious intervention of feminists in St Petersburg and Moscow (as in London, Berlin and New York) the changes which took place would have occurred later, and in different forms. Impersonal forces may have dictated that in the long run women would be admitted to medical schools and be employed as zemstvo doctors, that they would become teachers and scholars, postal workers and stenographers. In the short term it required the persistent efforts of women themselves to overcome strong opposition and entrenched prejudice. They had largely succeeded in the sphere of education and employment: what remained was to attack the numerous inequalities in women's civil status and to tackle the highly contentious issue of political rights. Not until the political crisis which led up to the 1905 Revolution did this begin to happen.

Notes

1 Mary Wollstonecraft, *A Vindication of the Rights of Women* (1792), Everyman edition (London: 1970) p. 46.

2 'Sur l'admission des femmes au droit de cité' (1790) *Oeuvres de Condorcet* 12 vols. (Paris: 1847) vol. x, p. 122. Condorcet appreciated the danger of depriving women of freedom; 'The more women have been enslaved by the laws the more dangerous has been their empire . . .' It would diminish 'if it were less to women's interest to maintain it, if it ceased to be their sole means of defending themselves and escaping from oppression.' *Ibid.* p. 127. The same line of thought was pursued by Wollstonecraft in her *Vindication*.

3 Though not for her feminist ideas. Her crime was to issue a plea for the life of the king.

4 See Evans, *The Feminists* pp. 18–19.

5 Within a year of the publication of *The Subjection of Women* in 1869 it had been translated into six or more languages. In that time four Russian editions had appeared. Stites, *The Women's Liberation Movement* p. 74.

6 See Ivy Pinchbeck, *Women Workers and the Industrial Revolution 1750–1850* (London: 1930) pp. 315–16; Wanda F. Neff, *Victorian Working Women* (New York: 1929) ch. 6; J.A. and Olive Banks, *Feminism and Family Planning in Victorian England* (Liverpool: 1964) p. 12. The concept of middle-class idleness has been assailed by Patricia Branca. Though she fails to analyse sufficiently the many gradations of income and status within the middle ranks, she demonstrates that the stereotypic bored young lady and middle-aged matron were not representative of the new urban bourgeoisie. Nor were they the exclusive product of industrialisation, as any cursory reading of seventeenth- and eighteenth-century literature will show. Patricia Branca, *Silent Sisterhood. Middle-Class Women in the Victorian Home* (London: 1975).

7 Louise A. Tilly and Joan W. Scott, *Women, Work and Family* (New York: 1978) pp. 66, 69.

8 Jill Liddington and Jill Norris, *One Hand Tied Behind Us. The Rise of the Women's Suffrage Movement* (London; 1978) pp. 47–63; Dorothy Thompson, 'Women and Nineteenth Century Radical Politics: A Lost Dimension' in Juliet Mitchell, Ann Oakley (eds.) *The Rights and Wrongs of Women* (Harmondsworth: 1976) pp. 112–38. Thompson notes that the independence of working women has been exaggerated by some historians.

9 G.M. Young, *Victorian England. Portrait of an Age* (Oxford: 1960) p. 91. This would apply equally to Russia, where the disintegration of feudalism was at least as traumatic as the industrial revolution in Britain.

10 Branca points out that most middle-class women did not choose that alternative, but she underestimates the contribution of the minority to the modification of social attitudes. *Silent Sisterhood* pp. 10–19.

11 Mill certainly had no patience with the writers of the eighteenth century 'when satires on women were in vogue, and men thought it a clever thing to insult women for being what men made them.' But he was equally critical of the 'tiresome cant' of his own times when 'we are perpetually told that women are better than men, by those who are totally opposed to treating them as if they were as good.' *Subjection*, p. 258.

12 Constance Rover, *Women's Suffrage and Party Politics in Britain 1866–1914* (London: 1967) p. 15. In Russia there were 1,023 women to every 1,000 men in 1858. In 1897 the ratio was 1,042 to 1,000. A. Rashin, *Naselenie Rossii za sto let (1811–1913gg.)* (M: 1956) pp. 258, 261.

13 See W.R. Greg, 'Why are women redundant?' *Literary and Social Judgments* (London: 1868) pp. 44–90.

14 David L. Ransel (ed.) *The Family in Imperial History. New Lines of Historical Research* (Urbana–Chicago–London: 1978) p. 2. For the genesis of the new orthodoxy see Peter Laslett, *The World We Have Lost* (New York: 1960); Peter Laslett and Richard Wall (eds.) *Household and Family in Past Time* (Cambridge: 1972).

15 For a thought-provoking analysis of current perceptions of the family see L.J. Jordanova, 'The History of the Family' in The Cambridge Women's Studies Group *Women in Society* (London: 1981).

16 Hobsbawm emphasises that this was an ideal type rather than a universal pattern. E.J. Hobsbawm, *The Age of Capital 1848–1875* (London: 1975) pp. 237–40.

17 Robert F. Byrnes, 'Pobedonostsev on the Instruments of Russian Government' in E.J. Simmons (ed.) *Continuity and Change in Russian and Soviet Thought* (Cambridge, Mass.: 1955) p. 127.

18 See Stites, *The Women's Liberation Movement* pp. 38–47; 89–105; Barbara Alpern Engel, *From Feminism to Populism: A Study of Changing Attitudes of Women of the Russian Intelligentsia 1855–1881* (Ph.D. University of Columbia: 1974).

19 For the role of women in radical politics see Vera Broido, *Apostles into Terrorists* (New York: 1977); Amy Knight, 'The Fritschi: A Study of Female Radicals in the Russian Populist Movement' in *Canadian-American Slavic Studies* vol. ix, no. 1 (Spring 1975) pp. 1–17; R.H. McNeal 'Women in the Russian Radical Movement' *Journal of Social History* vol. v, no. 2 (Winter 1971) pp. 143–61; Stites *The Women's Liberation Movement*, Engel, *From Feminism to Populism*.

20 For a tentative description of women's changing fortunes in Russia over the centuries see Dorothy Atkinson, 'Society and the Sexes in the Russian Past' in Atkinson *et al*. (eds.) *Women in Russia* (Stanford: 1977) pp. 3–38.

21 The same connection was made by women in the United States, where women became actively involved in the movement to abolish slavery during the 1840s. That experience prompted those who had worked in the abolition movement to question their own lack of emancipation. In Russia women played virtually no role in the emancipation debate, except in private.

22 In Britain, the Married Women's Property Acts of 1870 and 1882 were a triumph of the feminist movement, giving married women the right to keep their earnings and own property separately.

23 It was not the case that 'legally both sexes were nearly equal'. Cynthia Whittaker, 'The Women's Movement during the Reign of Alexander II' *Journal of Modern History* vol. xlviii, no. 2 (June 1976) On Demand Supplement, p. 36. Women's position was defined by their position in the family and that was explicitly subordinate. See Atkinson, 'Society and the Sexes' pp. 29–33.

24 For the sole contribution by contemporary historians to the study of Russian working women, see Rose Glickman, 'The Russian Factory Woman 1899–1914' in Atkinson *et al*. (eds.) *Women in Russia* pp. 63–83, also her forthcoming book on the same subject. There is no adequate work on peasant women, in Russian or English.

25 Roberta Manning cited by Stites, *The Women's Liberation Movement* pp. 56–57.

26 Vladimir Stasov, *Nadezhda Vasil'evna Stasova. Vospominaniia i ocherki* (Spb: 1899) p. 215.

27 *Ibid.* pp. 120–48.
28 *Sbornik pamiati Anny Pavlovny Filosofovoi* (Petrograd: 1915) vol. i, pp. 125–34. A close parallel, the Women's Employment Bureau, was set up in Britain in 1858. Ray Strachey, *The Cause: A Short History of the Women's Movement in Great Britain* (London: 1928) pp. 94–8.
29 Stasov, *Stasova* p. 71; *Sbornik pamiati A.P. Filosofovoi* vol. i, p. 124; James Bater, *St Petersburg. Industrialization and Change* (London: 1976) p. 181.
30 See Ruth Arlene Fluck Dudgeon, *Women and Higher Education in Russia 1855–1905* (Ph.D. George Washington University: 1975).
31 N.I. Pirogov, 'Voprosy zhizni' *Morskoi sbornik* no. 9 (1856) pt. 3, pp. 595–7; E. Likhacheva, *Materialy dlia istorii zhenskago obrazovaniia v Rossii* 2 vols. (Spb: 1899, 1906) vol. ii, pp. 1–20. Likhacheva, one of the leading figures in the women's movement up to her death in 1904, compiled a history of women's education in Russia between 1086 and 1880 which has not been rivalled since.
32 The curriculum differed in certain respects from that of the boys' gymnasia, notably in the absence of the classics, a prerequisite for university entrance.
33 See J.M. Meijer, *Knowledge and Revolution. The Russian Colony in Zurich 1870–1873* (Assen: 1955).
34 The Alarchin preparatory courses, given by university teachers, were inaugurated in 1869. Similar courses in Moscow were opened the same year. For an almost identical disagreement in the English campaign for female education, see Strachey, *The Cause* pp. 144–54.
35 See Stasov, *Stasova* pp. 203–36. In Britain, Girton and Newnham colleges were founded in 1870 and 1871 respectively and the first students examined unofficially in 1873. In London, Bedford College opened in 1849, but no degrees were awarded until 1878. Strachey, *The Cause* pp. 159–65, 255. In America, Vassar opened in 1865, Smith and Wellesley ten years later, 'Harvard Annexe' in 1879 and Bryn Mawr in 1885. Eleanor Flexner, *Century of Struggle*. p. 36.
36 *Sankt-Peterburgskie vysshie zhenskie kursy za 25 let, 1878–1903* (Spb: 1903) pp. 50–51.
37 The text of the government's circular is in Stasov, *Stasova* pp. 288–9.
38 Barbara Alpern Engel, 'Women Medical Students in Russia, 1872–1882: Reformers or Rebels?' *Journal of Social History* vol. xii, no. 3, pp. 407–8; Christine Johanson, 'Autocratic Politics, Public Opinion and Women's Medical Education during the Reign of Alexander II, 1855–1881' *Slavic Review* (September 1979) p. 435. The right of women to enter state and public service was strictly limited by a decree of 1871 to telegraphy and certain branches of medicine and education. By 1889, twenty-three exceptions had been made and the list grew over the next twenty years. The prohibition did not cover zemstvo and municipal employment. 'Ustav o sluzhbe po opredeleniiu ot pravitel'stva' arts. 156, 157, *Svod zakonov Rossiiskoi Imperii* (Spb: 1896) vol. iii, pt. 1, cols. 1589–91.
39 Whittaker, 'The Women's Movement' p. 63. Richard Evans accuses her, on no evidence, of 'a fundamental misunderstanding of the nature of Russian politics and society in the mid-nineteenth century.' Evans, *The Feminists* p. 112. While not sharing Whittaker's belief in the uniqueness of the Russians' concentration on education and employment, I have no reason to question her assessment of its successes.

40 Dudgeon, *Women and Higher Education* pp. 184–6; Whittaker, 'The Women's Movement' pp. 61–3.

41 The Bestuzhev courses were suspended from 1886 to 1889. They reopened with a curriculum pruned of natural sciences, reduced in numbers (a maximum of 400) and deprived of their autonomy. Stasov, *Stasova*, pp. 373–4; *Sbornik pamiati A.P. Filosofovoi* vol. i. p. 364.

42 Dudgeon, *Women and Higher Education* pp. iii–iv. Even the philanthropic side of the movement was now concentrated on aid to women students. As all the higher courses were financed mainly by fees and public donations, a great deal of the feminists' energies went into fund-raising. See *Sbornik pamiati A.P. Filosofovoi* vol. i, pp. 298; 320–21, for the Society to Obtain Funds for the Higher Women's Courses, founded on Filosofova's initiative in 1878.

43 Mariia Tsebrikova's letter to Alexander III, pleading for an end to tyranny and corruption, was a rare example of political protest from women outside the populist movement. It earned her a prison sentence and an extended period of exile. *Pis'mo Imperatoru Aleksandru* (London: 1894).

44 Stasov, *Stasova* pp. 438–40; *Sbornik pamiati A.P. Filosofovoi* vol. i, p. 378.

45 *Ibid*. pp. 379–80; N. Mirovich, 'O pervom s"ezde russkikh deiatel'nits po blagotvoreniiu i prosveshcheniiu' *Russkaia mysl'* no. 5 (1905) pt. 2, p. 134.

46 *Trudy 1-go vserossiiskago zhenskago s"ezda pri Russkom Zhenskom (Vzaimno-Blagotvoritel'nom) Obshchestve v S-Peterburge 19–16 dek. 1908 goda* (Spb: 1909) p. 586.

47 M. Sobolev, 'Zhenskii trud v narodnom khoziaistve XIX veka' *Mir bozhii* no. 8 (1901) p. 73.

2 From Small Deeds to Suffrage

It has been observed that women have tended to become radicals on behalf of their own sex in times of social upheaval, even when those upheavals have led to no improvements in women's rights and social status. The French Revolution was a notable example, similarly England during the Interregnum and Germany in 1848. The 1905 Revolution in Russia was another such case. For the first time in its history, the feminist movement adopted the goals of political liberation and the tactics of political groups. This is not to say that hitherto women had taken no part in politics. Although women in liberal circles had had little to say in public (and left only isolated records of what they said and thought in private) the striking role played by women in the revolutionary movement from the 1870s, female participation in Marxist circles from the 1890s onwards and the sporadic disturbances in female student circles throughout the period, all indicated that women as individuals were far from apolitical. But they rarely classed themselves as feminists and shunned the idea of separate political activity on behalf of one sex alone. Indeed, radical antipathy towards female separatism became one of the most contentious issues dividing revolutionary women from feminists between 1905 and the 1917 Revolution.

The years between 1900 and the outbreak of Russia's disastrous war with Japan in 1904 saw a steady growth in the political opposition to autocracy. The nation's first Marxist political organisation, the Russian Social-Democratic Labour Party, took shape (and survived the major crisis of the Bolshevik–Menshevik schism), populism re-emerged in the form of the Socialist Revolutionary Party (the SRs) and terrorist activity was resumed. In non-revolutionary circles too, a coherent opposition to the government was being welded together, an uneasy coalition which included moderate liberals who wished to see a relaxation of autocracy, more radical liberals whose vision of the future was a western parliamentary democracy, and even non-party socialists who hoped to achieve a peaceful transition to a socialist society.

In this coalition (known then and since as the 'liberation movement') women were often to be found in supporting activities, but were not prominent propagandists of their own rights, and the development of the women's movement did not match the expansion of political activity in society at large. The reason for this emerges when one considers the concentration of the liberal opposition within Russia in local government and professional circles from which women were largely excluded. Women were not practising lawyers, professors in universities or elected representatives of zemstvo assemblies. Their opinion was rarely sought and they tended to be diffident in offering it. It was only when a left wing gained strength in the liberation movement and emancipated itself from the hegemony of the moderates that women were drawn in; and only when this happened, early in 1905, did the women's movement begin to make demands for those political rights which radical thinkers had added to their armoury in the 1860s.

By 1904 the women's movement seemed to be reaching a dead end. Those of the enthusiastic young activists of the 1860s who had survived were now old ladies. Some had deserted the cause, others had grown complacent or were fully occupied in administering the network of women's educational and philanthropic institutions which were the visible product of the earlier agitation. There was no general organisation of women in Russia to compare with the National Councils of Women to be found in Europe, North America, Australia and the Argentine. The nearest equivalent was the Russian Women's Mutual Philanthropic Society. Its membership, which had reached a peak of 1,600 in 1899, had been dropping steadily since the turn of the century and numbered only 716 by 1905. Outside St Petersburg few people knew of its activities, or even its existence. In the capital itself, the society continued to be the butt of criticism and failed to attract many of those women who were later to become prominent in the campaign for women's rights. One of the prime charges made against it was, as a disenchanted member declared, that it had become

> . . . excessively taken up with the philanthropic side . . . There is no doubt that philanthropy, aid to the needy, is a fine thing: nevertheless one cannot but observe that it is rather like a patch on an old dress. The time has come to sew a new one.[1]

The society had failed to come up to the expectations even of some of its founders. Anna Filosofova, the last remaining member of the 'Triumvirate' of the 1860s, felt that the society lagged behind in propaganda work and that even its philanthropy had disappointing results, since it did not lead to 'a free association of people founded upon love and self-help'.[2] The personality of Shabanova, a woman whose obvious energy and determination were apparently accompanied by an exaggerated opinion of her own achievements and a reluctance to accommodate the opinions of others, did not increase the popularity of the RZhVBO. The 'autocratic' way in which the society was run was particularly out of place in an intellectual environment which worshipped democratic procedure and co-operative endeavour, but more than anything else it was the leaders' insistence on working within the existing political structure and their dependence on personal petitions to ministers and bureaucrats that guaranteed its failure to gather a wide following. The society, continued the critic quoted above, 'has set fast and it will be very hard to change the regime which prevails there.'[3]

In the meantime those dissatisfied with the Mutual Philanthropic Society had begun to move out of its orbit. One of the first signs that the women's movement was becoming more self-assertive was the establishment of a new journal *Zhenskii vestnik* (*Women's Herald*) in September 1904. Hitherto no journal devoted to the women's cause in Russia had managed to survive, a deficiency which was in itself a symptom of the movement's failure to develop an organisational basis. A number of publications had been launched at various times from the 1860s onwards, but only one had kept afloat for more than two years and it too disappeared in 1891. There was no reason at the outset to believe that the new journal's fate would be different, but it proved to be more durable than any of its predecessors, thanks largely to the single-minded dedication of its editor, Mariia Ivanovna Pokrovskaia.

Like Anna Shabanova, she was a doctor who had graduated from the St Petersburg women's medical courses. For the past fifteen years she had been working as a duma doctor in the city, observing daily the close relationship between poverty and sickness in an urban environment. Simultaneously she had become involved in the international campaign against state-regulated prostitution. She did not abandon these interests when she launched her journal. Instead she fused them into an uncompromising attack on society as she perceived it, a society corrupted by the arrogant domination of men and maintained only by greed, selfishness and physical force. She was convinced that it must be radically transformed in order to survive and, like many feminists in the West, felt that the participation of women in the government of nations was the indispensable factor. 'The spiritual forces of any people,' she observed, 'its creativity, its energy, are to be found not in the male half of the human race alone, but also in the female.' Unless the subjugation of women disappeared the 'perpetual struggle between the sexes' would continue to poison the atmosphere, with unhealthy consequences for both the family and society.[4]

Such sentiments were part of the standard rhetoric of the women's movement. Most feminists in Russia, however, felt that the woman question, although urgent, was only one of the many problems besetting society and were not happy with Pokrovskaia's attempt to elevate it above all others. Her suspicion of men as collaborators in feminist organisations and her aloofness from the mainstream of the liberation movement (combined, perhaps, with her heavily moralising tone) resulted in the failure of *Zhenskii vestnik* to become the flagbearer for the new women's movement, either in 1904 or later.

On the other hand, the journal shared many of the concerns of the non-revolutionary intelligentsia, male and female, particularly in the realm of social reform. Pokrovskaia was fully alive to the economic hardships endured by peasant women, factory workers and domestic servants and *Zhenskii vestnik* espoused a broad programme of reform, with a strong feminist slant. It insisted that peasant women must be included in any future land settlement and it championed women workers' rights to equal pay as well as welfare provisions, including unemployment, sickness insurance and maternity benefits. The motivations behind such a programme of reform were mixed: partly the desire of a social reformer to eradicate poverty and partly propaganda to recruit women from the lower orders into the feminist movement. It was the professed aim of *Zhenskii vestnik* to attract not only the intelligentsia but also the 'women of simple rank', the latter receiving help and encouragement from the former in the struggle for equal rights and opportunities. Pokrovskaia's sympathy for the poor and downtrodden was expressed in a rather vague socialism combined with an interest in philanthropy reminiscent of the much-maligned Mutual Philanthropic Society, to which she belonged. Her socialism was, however, only conditionally extended to men. She felt that divisions based on sex tended to override class divisions and she rarely lost an opportunity to publish instances of men's selfishness as, for example, when they demanded that women be sacked in a time of high unemployment, or continued a strike in the face of their wives' opposition.[5]

In the absence of circulation figures it is difficult to assess the value of *Zhenskii vestnik*. It certainly did not transform the women's movement and its impact on the general public appears to have been negligible. But the journal, for all its shortcomings, was a symptom of change, and if it did not mould opinions it undoubtedly reflected them.

Like most of the international women's movement (and like much of the liberal and socialist intelligentsia in Russia and abroad until the outbreak of the First World War), *Zhenskii vestnik* was vigorously anti-militarist and preached peace and harmony between nations. When it came to particular military conflict, however, the journal displayed all the ambivalence of those who deplore war yet cannot accept the prospect of their country's defeat. At the time that *Zhenskii vestnik* was launched, Russia had been embroiled in the war with Japan for eight disastrous months, and the government's military performance had become the target of increasingly virulent attacks. Pokrovskaia's journal had little to say on this issue. Instead it was concerned to refute allegations that Russian women were failing in their duty to the nation.

Women, as Pokrovskaia pointed out, contributed to the war effort both as nurses and doctors at the front and by sewing for the wounded in their free time. She demolished the contention of a male critic that women's opposition to war arose out of pure envy of men, which rendered them helpless to do anything but weep in the privacy of their homes. If it came to a last-ditch defence of Russia against an invader, she declared, women's courage in arms would not fail them. However, women's first duties lay elsewhere. It was women who were left to support their children and keep the national economy functioning when their husbands went to fight.

> What would become of the country if married women, like married men, went off to war, abandoning children and household to the mercy of fate?

However, women were not only patriots. They were also natural pacifists:

> Female soldiers do not serve human progress . . . Women long ago renounced such murderous squabbling and now put all their energies into persuading men to renounce it as well. Let us hope that success will come soon.[6]

Such comment was typical of the journal, combining moral righteousness with the total absence of a clear political line. This may be ascribed partly to the censor, whose authority Pokrovskaia seems to have respected at a time when others were risking the lives of their publications. But *Zhenskii vestnik* resembled feminist journals throughout Europe, in that events were interpreted predominantly in moral rather than political terms, and exclusively in terms of their effect on women.

Zhenskii vestnik was an encouraging development in the movement, but it was a propaganda weapon only and made no attempt at that juncture to build an organisation to further its aims. It was, however, not the sole indication that women were beginning to voice their discontent with the status quo. In a number of provincial towns, such as Kharkov and Saratov, small 'women's mutual aid societies' and educational or philanthropic associations had been established over the course of the past few years. While these societies did not usually initiate political protest, many of their members were very keen to establish a national women's organisation and hoped to reap some benefit from the changed political mood of late 1904.

By this time the non-revolutionary opposition was openly demanding constitutional change and even moderates were now prepared to defy government prohibitions on meetings and congresses. A number of women came to St Petersburg in November in search of active women's groups which would serve as a nucleus for a political union. They must have been sorely disappointed. All they found there, as one feminist noted dismissively, was the Mutual Philanthropic Society, 'on which they could place few hopes.'[7]

The major congress of those weeks, an unofficial gathering of zemstvo representatives, had nothing to offer, and women were to find at most a very grudging support in zemstvo circles for their own political rights. This was only to be expected. Though zemstvo representatives were often enthusiastic supporters of the liberation movement in the years up to 1905, conservative influence at local government level was still strong. Even by the end of 1904 there was still intense disagreement over the form which a future national assembly should take – whether it should be a consultative or a legislative assembly and whether it should be elected on universal male suffrage. In such an environment the issue of women's suffrage predictably aroused little interest.[8]

Women also encountered less than total commitment to their interests in the more radical wing of the liberal opposition, the alliance known as the Union of Liberation. The union was generally bolder in its demands and its campaigning than the zemstvo liberals, and in the autumn of 1904 organised a series of banquets as part of its political campaign. These were attended by women, but besides signing declarations and approving resolutions they made little impact on the proceedings. With the exception of Ekaterina Kuskova, a left-wing Liberationist and former Marxist, they were hardly to be found among the leadership and they rarely made speeches.

One exception was revealing. The banquet of 20 November was typical of the campaign in its demands for free speech and the right of assembly; for 'actual equality of all before the law'; the immediate summoning of a legislative assembly of 'freely elected representatives from the whole population of the Russian state' and a full political amnesty. Speakers eloquently proclaimed the rights of all classes, nationalities and religions, but no one referred to restrictions based on sex, until one Zinov'eva rose and attracted 'considerable attention' by her defence of women's rights and her attack on political activists for ignoring them.

> The time may soon be here . . . when spies will be given the vote and made eligible for election while women, who languish in prison for the cause of freedom, are disqualified and put on a level with the Chukchi and Iakuts. Follow the example of our youth, who do not neglect to specify male and female citizens in their resolutions – those same young people who will sacrifice their life blood to win the rights which we can only talk about.[9]

Any response from the audience to these provocative words went unrecorded and the proposed resolution of the banquet was passed without any amendment in favour of women.

But if women were still ignored by the mainstream of the constitutional movement there were two areas where their involvement in the opposition to the authorities was conspicuous. One was in student circles, where women took an active and hazardous part in student meetings and demonstrations. Towards the end of 1904 these were becoming more frequent and more outspoken; meetings passed uncompromising resolutions calling for an end to the war and for universal suffrage (not excluding women), whilst marches often ended in violent confrontations with the police. One demonstration in St Petersburg on 28 November 1904 was treated with more than usual force and prompted a collective protest from 120 well-known liberals and socialists, among whom were about a dozen women. Several of them were active participants in the liberation movement and later became involved in the women's rights campaign.[10]

The second area where women were becoming more assertive was in the factories. The female proletariat had long been dismissed for its backwardness and ignorance: rarely in the past forty years had revolutionary propaganda (either populist or Marxist) been directed specifically at women factory workers, despite their increasing participation in the industrial labour force. In the early 1870s a few populist women themselves went to work in factories in Moscow and elsewhere in an attempt to reach working-class women. But their experiences did not encourage others to follow suit, and in any case the experiment came to a premature end with the mass arrests of radicals in 1874. Not for another two decades were consistent efforts made to attract factory women into political action.

By the early 1890s, however, a number of women who had become involved in Marxist revolutionary circles turned their attention specifically towards the female factory worker. In some instances women workers themselves took the initiative in organising circles for their fellows, on other occasions the lead was taken by Marxist students or intellectuals. Few of these groups had any long-term success – all too often they were broken up by the police. Moreover, despite the theoretical commitment of Marxists to the emancipation of women (economic, social and political), in practice, women's groups were regarded with suspicion or indifference by many social–democrats, particularly by working-class men. Though women had participated in strike action during the 1890s (and had initiated at least forty strikes of their own over the decade) the revolutionary potential of the female proletariat was not yet felt to be very significant.[11]

Since this was the case, the participation of women in Father Gapon's Assembly of St Petersburg Factory Workers during 1904 was quite remarkable. The assembly had been officially sanctioned by the police early in the year as a workers' mutual aid society, one of whose aims was to keep workers away from trade unionism and revolution. By the autumn its membership had risen to about 9,000 (with support from over half the factory workers in St Petersburg) and, although still nominally supervised by the police, it had become increasingly susceptible to radical propaganda. Towards the end of the year, as public discontent with the government mounted, it became a major focus of working-class activity in the city.

The statutes of the assembly permitted women as members, though not as elected representatives. Gapon himself was no ardent feminist (apt on occasion to quote the old proverb, 'Long in hair, short in brains') but he was readily persuaded that the presence of women in the assembly would do no harm and might even be beneficial: 'If women are not drawn into the movement,' he is reported to have stated, 'if they do not help it then they will only interfere with it.'[12]

The leading role in attracting female support was taken by Vera Karelina, a weaver and a former social–democrat who, with her husband, worked closely with Gapon during 1904. By the end of the year she had succeeded in setting up a separate women's organisation within the assembly which held meetings and study groups catering for about a thousand women, both factory workers and workers' wives. Besides working-class women, the assembly attracted a number of individuals who, in the coming months, took an essential part in the women's rights movement. One of them was Liubov' Gurevich, a writer on the left wing of the liberation movement and Karelina's collaborator in running women's meetings.

Gurevich, who was sympathetic to Marxist ideas, was also a committed feminist and believed that the struggle for social and political liberation must include a campaign for women's rights. Unlike her sister Anna, a Bolshevik who became heavily involved in the socialist women's movement, Liubov' Gurevich believed that working women could and must be drawn into a liberation movement which cut across class barriers, and she saw Gapon's assembly as one means of doing so. Another of Karelina's middle-class supporters was Varvara Avchinnikova-Arkhangel'skaia, a journalist whose activities during 1905 included the establishment of a short-lived Union of Working Women in St Petersburg. With her husband, also a journalist, Arkhangel'skaia began to attend the assembly's meetings at the end of 1904 and helped to foster its links with the liberation movement.[13]

* * *

Nonetheless it is clear that even by the end of 1904 women were taking only the most hesitant steps into the political arena and could not yet be regarded as a serious force. The situation began to change in the New Year. The contradictory policy of the government continued, having failed to stop the zemstvo congress and the banquets whilst maintaining that they were illegal, and minor concessions on civil liberties, made by the tsar in December, served only to increase the impatience of the opposition.

Meanwhile, labour unrest was beginning to disturb the authorities. A strike at the Putilov ironworks (in which members of Gapon's assembly were involved) rapidly spread to other factories in St Petersburg, until by 7 January 1905 about 85 per cent of the city's workforce was on strike. Simultaneously, the assembly's leaders took up a proposal to draft a petition to the tsar. Couched in the most respectful language, the petition nonetheless contained demands for basic economic and political reforms which were bound to be considered provocative by the authorities. This would be presented to the tsar by Father Gapon on Sunday 9 January, the culminating event in a day-long procession of workers and their families to the Winter Palace. Thoroughly alarmed, the government ordered out the troops. Last-minute efforts to avert the procession and to persuade the authorities to compromise failed totally and the lamentable result was the massacre of Bloody Sunday. Official estimates of the dead and wounded were around 430, unofficial estimates suggested ten times that number.[14]

The response in society was predictably one of outrage. A wave of strikes swept through the Empire, protest meetings were held, petitions were signed and organisations which were only tentatively being initiated at the end of 1904 now began to take concrete form. The events of Bloody Sunday and continued military disaster in the Far East were the catalysts which brought hostility towards the government to a head.

By this time women were beginning to organise their own protests. Two days after the massacre in St Petersburg a private meeting took place in Voronezh at which 150 women signed a memorandum to the provincial zemstvo, urging it to petition for female suffrage 'without distinction of class, nationality or religion'. It seems that this was the first of what later became a flood of demands by women for political rights. A few weeks later the leading liberal newspaper in Russia published a declaration from 468 Muscovites, which protested in the name of Russian women against 'the untimely death of their sons, brothers, husbands killed on the distant field of a country which is foreign to us and in the deep waters of the ocean which washes its shores . . .' They went on to express their horror at the 'events in St Petersburg the news of which made the whole world shudder' and at the repression of student disorders:

> We hope that those measures . . . which over the course of many years have brought such misfortune and grief to Russian families, will not be tolerated again.[15]

The declaration was in no way a radical statement; it was a plea from wives and mothers for the safety of their loved ones, not a demand for rights. Yet the women who signed it were engaging in a political act, namely the public criticism of government. The response from other cities was even bolder. Letters published in the same newspaper expressed solidarity with the Moscow women and went on to call for an end to the war and the summoning of a national assembly. A Kiev statement with 207 signatures declared that women would feel secure only 'when in place of the bureaucratic regime a fundamental legal order has been created which guarantees freedom of the person, the press, speech, conscience, association and assembly.'[16]

It was in these weeks that over a dozen political unions came into existence, representing various interests in society. Besides nine professional unions (including lawyers, doctors, engineers and writers) a union of zemstvo representatives was formed, a union of railway workers, a union of clerks and book-keepers and a union to defend the rights of Jews. Later in the spring, all these unions would agree to affiliate to form an umbrella organisation, grandiosely named the Union of Unions, whose aim was to force the government to grant a constitution.

As women's dissatisfaction with the government became more vocal, so did their desire to create a new organisation, one which would draw the existing feminist societies and circles together. Towards the end of February, a group of about thirty women in Moscow decided to follow the example of the professional unions and establish an All-Russian Union of Equal Rights for Women. They immediately came up against a problem which was to bedevil the whole of the union's existence, namely, to what extent it should align itself with the liberation movement. Some feared that unless it maintained a certain isolation from male-dominated organisations it would lose sight of its feminist aims, while others emphasised the indissoluble links between the women's movement and the wider social movement against autocracy. The issue was soon decided, not without misgivings, in favour of the 'broad path': membership would be open to men as well as women, and it would apply to join the Union of Unions, which was just then in the process of formation.[17] The underlying conflict between 'pure' feminism and the aspirations of the liberation movement in general did not, however, disappear and proved to be a major source of friction in later months.

Though none of the women who came together in the spring of 1905 had taken a leading role in the liberation movement, many had established careers in literary and professional fields and were not unknown to the educated public. Very few could remember the 'glorious sixties', though generally they were past their first youth. Anna Miliukova was born in 1861, Liubov' Gurevich in 1866, Mariia Chekhova (who became the union's first and only secretary) was born the same year, Zinaida Mirovich in 1865. One member of the older generation was

Anna Evreinova, who as a young woman had escaped from her parents to study in Leipzig. She had the distinction of being the first Russian woman to acquire a doctorate in law (in 1878) and, though barred from practising in Russia, had made good use of her knowledge by giving lectures at home and abroad. For several years she had edited the journal *Severnyi vestnik* (*Northern Herald*) and she remained a familiar figure in literary and political circles in St Petersburg and Moscow.

No one in the union besides Evreinova had a legal training, but many were graduates of the women's higher courses. Both Miliukova and Ekaterina Shchepkina, graduates of the Moscow courses, were historians by profession, though the former had given up her own research to help her husband. Shchepkina had taught at the Petersburg higher courses and was the author of several historical works. Mirovich had also studied in Moscow, and made a career for herself as a writer. Until 'censorship problems' intervened, she had specialised in the period of the French Revolution. Since then she had translated several of Ibsen's plays, written prolifically on education in Russia and abroad and in recent years had been taking a close interest in women's movements in western Europe. The teaching profession was represented by Chekhova and her husband, both founder members of the teachers' union, and there was at least one doctor, Ol'ga Klirikova, in the union's central bureau.[18]

It was not entirely by chance that the inspiration to launch the women's union should have come from Moscow: this stronghold of liberalism in Russia was also the home of a number of the most committed suffragists in the movement, notably Chekhova and Mirovich, whose section remained relatively unaffected by the internal wrangling that later undermined its counterpart in St Petersburg. The initiative of the Muscovites was critical in mobilising the energies of women all over Russia and the fledgling union rapidly gathered recruits. In the two months up to the end of April the Moscow group managed to establish contact with eighteen other groups around the country.[19]

In these same weeks the first mass meetings of women in Russia's history were taking place, clearly inspired by the tsar's decree in February which conceded the right of petition. In Saratov on 12 March the newly-established Society for Mutual Aid to Working Women held a meeting of 1,000 people, which passed a resolution (later sent to the local zemstvo) calling for equal suffrage:

> Both as members of families and as citizens, women must take an active part in deciding questions of war and peace.

Refuting the common objection that women were politically immature, the resolution pointed out that the very same objection had been made by the government to the demand for universal male suffrage. Besides, it continued, 'political freedom is not a reward for maturity and skill,' but rather the 'sole means' by which a social system could be created where people could develop their potential.[20]

In St Petersburg a month later, a speech by Anna Evreinova attracted an audience of similar magnitude to a meeting which turned out to be far more contentious than its organisers had anticipated. Evreinova's speech was not so much propaganda for women's rights as a critical analysis of the recently-published draft Civil Code as it affected women. Far from liberalising Russian law, Evreinova argued, the code would remove those vestiges of equality between spouses which existed in old Russian and Slavonic law, particularly the separation of property. It reinforced the husband's control over the upbringing of their children, and it obliged a woman to support her husband even if she had been granted legal separation on the grounds of his adultery. Evreinova argued that the draft code was totally out of step with the trend towards greater equality and 'reduces the woman question to a question of pure slavery'. She called on the meeting to protest against the code, and she endorsed the creation of the Union of Equal Rights.[21]

However academic Evreinova's speech, it sparked off a debate which went right to the heart of the contemporary women's movement. This meeting, at which the vice-president of the Mutual Philanthropic Society found herself in the same company as Aleksandra Kollontai and a number of male social–democrats, created the prototype for later confrontations between reformists and revolutionary feminists, where a vociferous group (mainly of social–democrats, but also including socialist–revolutionaries and others) would challenge the aims and methods of the other speakers, sometimes with the sole intention of disrupting the meeting, but more often in the hope of radicalising it. On this occasion the political resolution proposed by social–democrats 'on behalf of working women' was passed, after much bickering and heckling; at the same time Evreinova's protest against the draft Civil Code and her call for the establishment of a women's political union were unanimously approved.[22]

The Union of Equal Rights (known by its initials SRZh) eventually published a draft statute on 24 April and called its founding congress for a fortnight later. Besides the original Moscow members, thirty-one delegates from eighteen towns in Russia travelled to the city for the occasion. Even at this inaugural congress, the conflict between separatist feminism and the demands of the Russian liberation movement was already in evidence. Although most groups were as committed to the liberation movement as to women's rights and demanded the inclusion of a political programme, a significant number were quite apolitical in composition and 'had united only under the slogan of "equal rights for women".' These groups objected to the demand for a political platform: it would fatally narrow the union's appeal, since 'it would be impossible to unite everyone on one platform.' Their opponents replied that in the current political climate 'a union which locked itself up in the narrow bounds of feminism risked being extremely unpopular and would not succeed in drawing members.' While the union must not neglect its task of spreading feminist propaganda, they argued, political involvement was essential.

The union, in seeking to represent women all over the Empire, had naturally to appeal to nationalities other than Russian. In doing so it was confronted with an issue which was being furiously debated among (and within) all the opposition factions in 1905 – the question of national self-determination and cultural autonomy for the non-Russian peoples of the Empire. Polish, Belorussian and Jewish delegates to the women's congress made it a condition of their co-operation that the union recognise the right of national and cultural self-determination, a demand which was vigorously contested.

It was a measure of the union's radicalism that no one opposed autonomy on principle, but some delegates objected to its inclusion in the programme, again on the grounds that it would prove divisive and that the union would lose sight of its primary aim. There was, however, never any doubt that the 'politicals' would prevail. 'To the oppressed nationalities,' they declared, 'the question of national freedom is closer than any other and it is impossible to exclude it from the platform.' The congress voted by thirty-nine to seven for a political programme and thirty-nine to three (four abstaining) for the inclusion of the demand for national autonomy.[23]

Yet those favouring a political stance were not in agreement over the feminist content of the platform. Radicals (who included a number of social–democrats and SRs) were extremely critical of the moderates' attempt to limit its social and economic demands. To do so, they said, would be to restrict the union's popular appeal and give it a 'philanthropic and bourgeois air.' They were successful in getting factory legislation and compulsory insurance included in the programme, but not the standard social–democratic formula of the eight-hour day.[24]

The statute and platform which were finally hammered out betray the union's origins, infused as they are with the rhetoric of the liberation movement. Declaring that 'under the present regime woman exists totally without political rights', the platform went on to state that 'the struggle for women's rights is indissolubly linked with the political struggle for the liberation of Russia'. It called for the 'immediate summoning of a constituent assembly on the basis of universal, direct, secret suffrage without distinction of sex, nationality and religion, with the preliminary establishment of personal immunity and the inviolability of the home, freedom of conscience, speech, the press, assembly and association, the restoration of their rights to all those suffering for their political and religious beliefs.' It included the controversial formula stipulating political autonomy and cultural self-determination for the nationalities within the Empire, and rounded off with the demand for an end to the war.[25]

Its feminist demands included (besides labour legislation): 'the equalisation of peasant women's rights with men's in all future agrarian reforms; the admission of women to all occupations and offices; co-education of men and women in lower, middle and higher schools, both general and specialist; the abolition of all exceptional laws relating to prostitution, which offend the dignity of women.' To leave women without rights while liberating men would be to hold back 'both the economic development of the country and the growth of the nation's political awareness.'

The four-day congress was held in some secrecy and no press reports of its sessions emerged. But on the second evening the union held a public meeting which was attended by several hundred women and chaired by Miliukova. Like the meeting in St Petersburg on 10 April, it was a gathering of the principal activists in the Russian women's movement, representing widely differing views. But it did not produce the violent controversies of the Petersburg meeting and concluded with a unanimous resolution calling for an end to the war, a constituent assembly, civil liberties and social reforms. It also sent a telegram to the National Union of Women's Suffrage Societies in London, regretting the recent rejection of a women's suffrage bill in the House of Commons, and expressing the hope that this was 'the last echo of ancient prejudice'. The telegram was the inspiration of Zinaida Mirovich, who had close contacts with feminists in western Europe, and in England particularly, and was an indefatigable propagandist for the international women's movement.[26]

Besides building up its influence within the women's movement, the Union of Equal Rights was also involved in the creation of the Union of Unions, although the relationship was not totally harmonious. The issue of women's equality had not generated much enthusiasm among liberals, and the establishment of a political union of women produced some condescending smiles and the occasional ribald comment. Few of the constituent unions had hitherto paid much attention to the question of female suffrage and did not always react favourably when feminists tried to get women included in the suffrage formula. With the arrival on the political scene of each new union, women activists within that union and outside would pressurise it to adopt the amendment 'without distinction of sex'. Their campaign eventually yielded results, but they met strong opposition on some occasions as, for example, at the founding congress of the Union of Writers in April.[27]

Nonetheless the SRZh joined in the preparatory conferences of the Union of Unions and attended its founding congress on 8–9 May, towards the end of the women's congress.[28] The feminist leaders had agreed among themselves not to insist that a vote be taken on women's suffrage until the constituent unions had been persuaded to change their own platforms, for fear of precipitating a hostile verdict. As a result it was not until July that the Union of Unions formally recognised the demand for women's rights (with the liberal Miliukov the only dissenter). In fact, however, the contentious formula began to creep into the public pronouncements of the Union of Unions weeks earlier. In an appeal to society following the catastrophic naval defeat at Tsushima, an emergency congress called for the creation of a constituent assembly elected on a seven-point suffrage 'to bring the war and political regime which has prevailed up to now to an end as soon as possible.'[29]

The feminists' campaign would have had little chance of success without the activities of the revolutionary and left-wing liberation groupings which were intent on radicalising the political unions from within. Shchepkina noted that 'with the support of the extremists women succeeded in getting amendments to all the platforms,' and the growing influence of the left wing in the Union of Unions was critical. But the SRZh's dependence on radical support from outside for its suffrage demands (and the presence of revolutionaries within its own ranks) did not automatically put it in the radical camp. On non-feminist issues, SRZh members often took a noticeably more moderate stand than the majority in the Union of Unions. At the emergency congress at the end of May, for instance, they forcefully opposed a majority resolution which stated that, in the struggle against autocracy, 'all methods are legal, all must be tried.' The two SRZh delegates (plus one from the teachers' union) protested that such a resolution sanctioned the same arbitrary methods which the government was now employing against the people, and contradicted 'elementary feelings of morality'.[30]

The victory of the SRZh in the Union of Unions was in fact less impressive than at first sight, since by this time the liberation movement had split decisively into two wings, and the least radical unions (and those most opposed to women's suffrage) had defected from the Union of Unions. Nevertheless one should not belittle the achievements of the SRZh. Though the union may have owed its existence to the advance of the radicals after January, political radicalism was not synonymous either in theory or in practice with support for the feminist campaign. This was particularly true of the social–democrats' response. Individual social–democratic women who became involved in the union's activities in 1905 soon found themselves at odds with their party organisations, which feared the lure of feminism over impressionable working-class women.

The principle of women's suffrage had now been recognised by the left wing of liberal opposition and the socialists. The next step was to get more moderate opinion committed to the principle. This understandably proved difficult, not least because moderate liberals had doubts about the advisability of universal male suffrage, let alone female. By the end of May, when it became clear that the tsar was prepared to offer the concession of a national consultative assembly (the so-called 'Bulygin Duma'), the moderates were increasingly concerned to damp down the radical fire which was threatening to jeopardise the liberal campaign.

The initiators of the SRZh had appreciated the importance of winning moderate opinion to their cause very early on. Even before the union was officially constituted, the Moscow group had organised petitions to the city duma and the provincial zemstvo in support of women's suffrage, a tactic which was being adopted by numerous women's groups throughout the country. The public meetings of women which were held in the spring frequently ended with the passing of a resolution on women's suffrage, which was then presented to the local duma or zemstvo with a list of signatures (usually a few hundred, but occasionally well over a thousand). It is hard to say how much of this activity was co-ordinated. It seems probable that until the middle of May (that is, until after the founding congress of the SRZh) there was little co-ordination and that individual circles of women were emulating local branches of the liberation movement. After the May congress the links between the circles were strengthened. Nevertheless, the union was in no position to impose uniformity on its local sections, nor did it seek to do so. The sections were guaranteed autonomy and they made full use of it.

The response from the zemstvos and dumas was mixed. A considerable number of assemblies received the petitions sympathetically and resolved to submit the request for a seven-part franchise to the Council of Ministers. Some accepted the principle while objecting to its implementation for 'practical reasons', and others rejected the petitions or ignored them altogether. Unfortunately for the women's cause, among the least enthusiastic assemblies were those with the most influence. They included the Moscow city duma, whose commission on the organisation of the proposed national assembly briefly discussed women's suffrage. The commission's report was revealing, more for what it omitted to say about the question than for its final pronouncements.

The commission had reviewed all the principles upon which national representation might be based. It rejected out of hand any proposal for an assembly which would deny the legal equality of all citizens; it also rejected qualifications of education or property. Universal suffrage, it declared, was 'a powerful weapon for developing the popular masses and inculcating in them a feeling for legality and respect for the law.' It denied that the people were 'unprepared' and it quoted approvingly the 'wise Bulgar Slaveikov':

> There is no greater stupidity than to imagine oneself to be wiser than all the rest and to lay claim to the leadership of others . . . Sirs, have greater faith in the people.

Having convincingly argued the case for universal suffrage, the commission went on to list 'the usual exceptions': women, children, lunatics and criminals. It concluded by noting that a minority of its members had found no objection in principle or practice to the admission of women to the electoral register, but had not insisted on that view being debated.[32]

This judgment was naturally a severe disappointment to feminists, coming as it did from a centre of liberal opinion. Pokrovskaia, whose journal had been following the suffrage campaign with passionate interest, reacted with angry sarcasm. Clearly, she observed, women are insufficiently violent. If they had used 'sabres, guns and bombs' to demonstrate their equality, instead of petitions and persuasion, they would have won their case. She predicted that a continued denial of female suffrage would lead to a new fighting spirit among women, a prospect which she abhorred. The battle between the sexes which would ensue would have no benefit for the country, but instead would exhaust those energies needed for 'the rebirth of Russia':

> Let Russian men consider all this and put the welfare and the regeneration of their fatherland before their own egoistic interests and conveniences.[33]

The Union of Equal Rights, meanwhile, had carried the battle for zemstvo opinion to the centre. The opposition of the zemstvo and academics' unions had been the principal obstacle hindering the adoption of the seven-point formula in the Union of Unions, and it came as no surprise when the zemstvo congresses treated the issue with indifference. The subject was first raised at the zemstvo congress in April. The bureau of the SRZh despatched a petition which the congress agreed to 'take into consideration' but refused to debate. After this unpromising beginning (which coincided with a setback in the Union of Unions) the bureau broadened its attack by arranging for seventeen sections of the SRZh to submit separate petitions to the July congress of zemstvo and duma representatives. One came from Polish, Jewish and Lithuanian women and was presented personally by a representative from the Lithuanian section. The congress refused to hear her and none of the petitions were read. In its resolution on women's suffrage, the congress recognised that 'the political equality of women was desirable in the future legal system of Russia' but believed that any decision should be postponed (along with 'other essential reforms') until that system had been established.[34]

An influential opponent of the feminists in the zemstvo debates was Fedor Kokoshkin, a young lecturer in law at Moscow University and a future Kadet deputy to the Duma. At the April zemstvo congress he had submitted a report on the proposed national assembly, which considered at some length the question of the franchise. Kokoshkin's reasons for opposing the immediate concession of women's suffrage were those frequently encountered by feminists during 1905: that the principle was not yet generally accepted either in Russia or 'in the more cultured states' of the West; that women's greater illiteracy rendered them more susceptible to irrational judgments; that an imbalance might result if women voted more heavily in the towns than in the villages and in Christian areas than in Muslim regions. Like so many liberals, not only in Russia but throughout Europe and North America, he argued that women's suffrage should be 'tried out' first in local government and extended only gradually to national elections.

But Kokoshkin's principal (though unstated) argument against female enfranchisement was the simple fact that women, as a separate social group, presented no threat to the stability of the state. Elsewhere in his report he had made it quite clear that the only way to avert the danger of an uprising among the peasantry was to draw them into the political process, regardless of their widespread illiteracy. It was, he said, a question of *force majeure*. Women (even peasant women) posed no such threat. On this point Kokoshkin and Pokrovskaia were in agreement: women would have to become more militant before they would get a hearing – numerical strength alone was not enough.[35]

The Union of Equal Rights did not take the zemstvos' opposition lightly. It believed that there had been a slight shift of opinion in favour of women's suffrage between April and July and it decided to exploit the shift. The bureau sent a stiff reply to the congress bureau, pointing out that its resolutions were not legislative acts, but 'principles which should serve as the basis of the future state system of Russia'. If, therefore, the congress failed to recognise women's equality as one of those principles, 'what guarantee do women have that their equality will be recognised by the majority in a future representative assembly from which women are excluded?' Was it not more likely that the majority would oppose emancipation as 'untimely'?

Untimeliness is the usual refrain of monarchs depriving their people of freedom, the refrain of slaveowners refusing to free their serfs, of the ruling classes withholding rights from the oppressed classes.

The declaration went on to criticise the proposed 'Bulygin Duma' for excluding large sections of the population, and it ended with a threat:

> If the electoral law for the national assembly leaves [women] in their disfranchised state they will have only one recourse – to join those parties and groups which, like themselves, are not satisfied with this law . . . we request an answer: are you our friends or our enemies?[36]

Simultaneously the union prepared a questionnaire which it sent to 169 zemstvo and duma representatives. They were asked whether they felt that women should receive equal rights, and if so, whether they should be eligible to vote for the first constituent assembly. As Shchepkina later noted, the very wording of the questionnaire was bound to alienate the more conservative representatives, assuming, as it did, the immediate goal to be a full constitution. Of the 169 approached, sixty-three replied, sometimes at length. Half answered in the affirmative and only four were unconditionally opposed.[37]

The fears expressed in many replies were commonplace enough: that the family would suffer if women involved themselves in the hurly-burly of politics; that a falling birth rate would jeopardise the future of the race. Women's supposed ignorance of politics and their constitutional inability to make detached judgments, were also cited as reasons for encouraging women to keep out of political life and devote themselves to their families instead. One correspondent conceded women's right to active suffrage, which he held to be a 'general' right. The right to be elected, however, he claimed to be a 'personal' right requiring 'particular individual qualifications' which he judged men to possess, but not women: the 'freedom from personal and family ties, the capacity for dispassionate thought, the gift of reticence, a knowledge of popular feelings.' Those who accepted the principle of women's suffrage but opposed its implementation for 'practical considerations', cited the probable opposition of peasant men, the mass illiteracy of peasant women and their subjection to men (especially in non-Russian areas) and the need to proceed gradually (either from local to national suffrage or from male to female).[38]

The letters from unconditional supporters of women's suffrage were generally shorter, some restricted to a simple affirmative. Others replied in more detail. One articulated a widely-held view:

> Yes, yes, yes! I regard it as extremely illogical and inconsistent to vote in favour of granting the suffrage to Kirghiz, Votiak or Chukchi men, but refuse the same right to the educated Russian woman.

Others argued, as the Union of Equal Rights did, that it was neither equitable nor practicable to exclude half the population from the reconstruction of society and its political system. Other supporters insisted that suffrage was a basic human right: 'Women must have equal rights with men simply because they too are people.'[39]

The questionnaire was followed by a renewed campaign of petitioning. At the congress of zemstvo and duma representatives in September, a motion to debate the issue was narrowly defeated (seventy-two to sixty-three); the minority quickly issued its dissenting opinion, protesting against the majority verdict. But by this time the congress bureau itself had changed its mind, apparently overwhelmed by the flood of protests and declarations which had been arriving from all over the country. Soon after the September meeting, the bureau voted to include female suffrage (active and passive) in the draft election regulations which were to be presented to the next zemstvo congress. In November the regulations were approved.[40]

The zemstvo campaign took up a substantial portion of the SRZh's energies and was fiercely criticised by radical members, especially in St Petersburg, who insisted that the union must not neglect propaganda among the masses for the sake of nurturing what at best could only be a small party of supporters from among the liberal bourgeoisie. Their criticisms were particularly apposite at that moment, when the popular movement seemed to be taking the initiative from the liberals.[41]

There were, however, good reasons for this preoccupation. Firstly, the campaign was important as a public relations exercise. Propaganda in local government institutions was vital for the realisation of the Union's immediate goal, which was the franchise. Before the inauguration of the State Duma the zemstvos and municipal dumas were the only elected public institutions in the country and also the principal legal channel through which proposals for a national representative assembly could be directed. Zemstvo opinion (and, to a lesser extent, opinion in the dumas) was hostile or indifferent to female suffrage throughout most of 1905. It was therefore important to win them over. How far the SRZh succeeded is open to doubt; in the political reaction which followed the October Manifesto, zemstvo radicalism gave way to a more conservative outlook less favourably disposed towards women's equality.

Meanwhile the SRZh had not neglected its other concerns, which were propaganda and the expansion of the union's membership. After the first congress in May, the central bureau sent out congress reports and general information to contacts in ninety-seven towns in Russia. Members of the bureau travelled round the country delivering exhortatory speeches and helping to set up local sections. By the autumn, sections had been established in fifty-four localities, including the principal cities, and the union had close links with women's unions in Poland, Lithuania and Finland. Its membership was now several thousand and it was continuing to grow.[42]

Surprisingly, the union issued little printed propaganda during the year, and not until March 1906 did it establish a publications commission. It had not yet learnt to appeal to a mass audience. Hitherto it had been so preoccupied with recruiting members from the ranks of the intelligentsia and campaigning in the zemstvos and professional unions, that it had paid insufficient attention to the factory workers and peasant women whose interests it aimed to promote. This was a charge levelled at the union by its more radical members, whose influence grew as the year progressed.

The criticism was not entirely just, however. Towards the end of the summer, a number of peasant women's groups were formed in Moscow and Voronezh provinces, as a result of the efforts of individuals in the union; and in other regions, union members found that their propaganda did not fall on deaf ears. They also made good use of the newly-established Peasants' Union, an uneasy amalgam of radicals from the professional intelligentsia (who dominated the leadership) and rank-and-file members from the peasantry. Members of the SRZh joined the Peasants' Union and persuaded its 'agitators' to incorporate feminist slogans into their propaganda.[43]

Despite some strong opposition, the Peasants' Union adopted the seven-point suffrage formula at its founding congress. Peasants supporting female suffrage pointed out that men in many villages had had to go away in search of work, leaving their wives to look after the affairs of the village. In such circumstances it was illogical and unjust to deprive women of the vote. More persuasively, speakers argued that enfranchised women would form a 'second army', strengthening the forces of the peasantry. In the subsequent ballot, the congress voted unanimously for women's active suffrage, and by a large majority (three opposed) for passive rights. The vote was confirmed at the union's second congress in November. On that occasion a small group of peasant women from Voronezh made a prepared statement, evidently the work of the SRZh. It rejoiced in the existence of the Union of Equal Rights, since 'even those close to us often do not regard us as human beings, they look on women as beasts of burden'. It complained that women not only worked and suffered, but had to live without rights. They needed literacy, land and the vote.[44]

The women's union also made some converts among factory women and domestic servants in the larger cities, though it found itself highly susceptible to competition from local social–democratic organisations. In Kharkov, for example, the local SRZh section had established a sub-commission on servants during the summer which collaborated with a workers' rights group, held meetings and drew up a draft statute for a Union of Domestic Servants. No sooner had it done so than it came into conflict with members of the Kharkov social–democratic party, who took over the campaign and made it their own.[45] Such rivalry was common and did not improve the position of radicals within the Union of Equal Rights itself. Social-democrats in particular were becoming increasingly impatient with its 'bourgeois' ideology and tactics, and were naturally more inclined to draw their working-class converts into the party than to encourage their feminism.

The conflict between the 'bourgeois' and the revolutionary wings came into the open at the union's second congress. It was held in Moscow on 8–11 October in the midst of a turmoil of meetings, conferences and demonstrations and the wave of strikes which had already paralysed the Moscow railway network, and was spreading rapidly to other regions and occupations. Of the fifty-four sections of the SRZh now in existence, forty-four sent delegates, most of the remainder having been prevented from attending by the railway strike.

The main issue on the agenda was the union's attitude to the 'Bulygin Duma' and the policy to be adopted on the strike movement. In contrast to liberals such as Miliukov, who had greeted the Bulygin electoral law as the first step on the road to constitutionalism, members of the SRZh were overwhelmingly ill-disposed towards it, both for its neglect of women's suffrage and for its limited powers. They were, however, at odds over the question of a boycott. The left wing, dominated by social–democrats and SRs, demanded an unconditional boycott of the elections; their opponents advocated the exploitation of the election campaign 'for the political education and unification of the masses'.

The boycotters argued that to accept the Duma in its proposed form would be to accept the continuation of the old regime, and to lose the support of working-class women who would desert to the revolutionary parties. It would also be to uphold the continued disfranchisement of women.

> Before us are two roads: one to the Duma without the people, the other to the people. This Duma has trampled on all our ideals. We cannot recognise it; we cannot be the accomplices of those men who enter the Duma, nor can we assume responsibility for any decisions which they may take. This responsibility will be on our conscience if we reject a boycott. The people have made us responsible.[46]

Opponents of the boycott stated that it was doomed to failure because it would not find favour with the peasants. Moreover, they argued, the tactics to be employed by the boycotters (including an armed insurrection) would alienate the 'average citizen'. If, on the other hand, the Duma were allowed to assemble, the more radical elements could disrupt it from within by stating their demands and issuing an ultimatum which the government would not dare to reject. Public opinion within and without Russia would be on the side of the radicals. In the unlikely event of the government ignoring public opinion, the dissolution of the Duma would be 'the signal for a revolutionary uprising which would unite everyone'. It can be seen from the debate the extent to which the SRZh was dominated by the radicals in these weeks and how intoxicated it was by the utopian mood of the moment. The vote resulted in a victory for the boycotters of fifty-four against twenty-nine.[47]

On the second issue, that of the political strike, the radicals dominated almost without a fight. The congress voted to support the strike by all the means at its disposal, and declared that it must be total, joined by lawyers and even doctors.

> If society does not wish to place the whole burden of the struggle for freedom on the shoulders of the proletariat it must bear all the inconveniences of a political strike and support it in every possible way, as a powerful weapon in the struggle.

Virtually the only speakers to oppose a total strike were non-voting delegates from the lawyers' and doctors' unions. As a gesture of its support the congress allocated 1,000 roubles to the strikers and 'other political organisations'. The union's amended programme was a further demonstration of the radicals' influence during this period:

> If our union wishes to get close to life and to the battle, if it wishes to be a women's and not a ladies' organisation . . . it must learn how to extend the limits of its work and go out to meet the woman worker.[48]

Undeniably, the domination of the congress by the left wing was facilitated by the political chaos of these weeks, when the country was in the grip of what seemed to be a bloodless rebellion. There was, however, another reason why union members leaned towards the left. This was the invaluable support which the suffrage campaign had mustered from the radicals at a time when liberal zemstvists and professionals had emerged as doubtful allies and, on occasion, opponents. Feminists therefore found themselves drawn towards the left, even when they were unsympathetic to other socialist goals. If additional proof were needed of liberal unreliability, it was provided only days after the women's congress, at the foundation of the Constitutional–Democratic Party in Moscow.

The Kadet Party was forged from two distinct groups, the more radical wing of the zemstvo organisation on the one hand and a majority of the Union of Liberation on the other. Despite strong differences between the two groups, they shared a lack of interest in the question of women's suffrage during 1905. The indifference of the zemstvo congresses has already been described; the Union of Liberation was hardly more encouraging, despite pressure from its radical minority. Liubov'

Gurevich had discovered this at first hand, at the March congress of the union, when many of her male colleagues treated the subject of women's suffrage with levity, and mocked her when she advocated the inclusion of women in the suffrage formula. After a stormy debate the congress had finally voted for female suffrage, but with a majority of only one and an exemption clause making it non-binding on members.[49]

This performance was repeated seven months later at the Kadets' first congress. Gurevich was joined by Miliukova, who had been in the forefront of the suffrage campaign throughout the year and who now came into open conflict with her own husband, to the amusement of many of the spectators. Miliukov had opposed women's suffrage at earlier meetings of Liberationists and at the congresses of the Union of Unions, and he continued to oppose it on the grounds that it would lose the new party many votes and that peasant women's illiteracy would have a deleterious effect on the level of debate. One cannot help feeling, however, that personal antagonisms must have played their part for him to have risked an embarrassing scene of marital discord in public. The incorporation of the seven-part formula into the Kadet programme was hardly likely to drive away potential voters in their thousands. The principle could have been admitted and quietly buried thereafter. Instead Miliukov preferred to alienate his well-wishers among the feminists and tarnish his liberal reputation. He was, however, in good company. Miliukova's resolution was passed by only two votes and her husband successfully moved an amendment making support of female suffrage non-mandatory on the party.[50]

The result was profoundly discouraging for moderates in the Union of Equal Rights. The decision made it impossible for them to join the party which reflected most closely their political outlook. Even if they had been willing to compromise they were prohibited from doing so by a resolution passed during the SRZh congress itself, which prevented union members from belonging to any party not recognising women's equality.[51] For the time being the only acceptable parties were those on the left. This the moderates felt to be a highly undesirable situation and they were determined that it should not last. In the months following the congress they put heavy pressure on the Kadets to get the non-binding amendment removed and were finally rewarded at the party's second congress in January.

In the intervening period the union immersed itself in the political concerns of the moment. The national political crisis came to a head in the middle of October. Faced with the disruption of transport, telephone communications and the electricity and water supplies, and the apparent determination of all parties to support the nation-wide strikes until the government gave in to their demands, the tsar was reluctantly persuaded to make major concessions. On 17 October a manifesto was issued which promised civil liberties, including freedom of the press and assembly, and a State Duma which (unlike the 'Bulygin Duma') would enjoy extensive legislative powers and would be elected on a wide male franchise.

The effect of the manifesto was to split up the constitutionalist coalition which had already been put under great strain during the year. The more conservative accepted the manifesto in its entirety, the Kadets and non-revolutionary socialists saw it as only a first concession towards their ultimate demands. As for the revolutionary parties, they rejected its terms outright, while using it as a breathing space for a further assault on autocracy.

However, all parties were at one in using the concession of free speech to their own advantage. The 'days of freedom' which the manifesto ushered in were filled with meetings, marches and demonstrations. Not all were anti-government: the manifesto encouraged extreme right-wing nationalist groups (the Black Hundreds) to attack students, liberals and non-Russians, especially the Jews, with no fear of retribution from the authorities. These pogroms only stiffened the resistance of the opposition: in Moscow the funeral procession for a Bolshevik killed by the Black Hundreds turned into a massive demonstration of about 100,000 people.

Members of the Union of Equal Rights participated in all this activity to the hilt. They raised funds for the political Red Cross (which gave aid to political prisoners and exiles), established canteens for strikers and signed protests against the Black Hundreds, capital punishment and so on. In all this activity there was often little time for feminist propaganda, although union banners were to be seen on all the major political demonstrations. Meetings organised by the union sections were often very successful (in Moscow, attracting 2,500 people) but at these events general political demands for a constituent assembly and a boycott of the Duma took pride of place.

It is easy to see how feminist energies were diverted at this critical juncture: indeed, many of the women who joined the Union of Equal Rights late in 1905 may have done so less because of its particular feminist demands than because it was a political organisation accessible to them as women, in the way that other local associations were not. Though women joined professional unions (especially the teachers' union) they were always in a minority and rarely assumed a position of leadership in them. In the Union of Equal Rights they could feel at home. This is not to say that they did not share the feminist aspirations of the union, but to suggest instead that their enthusiasm for women's liberation was fired by their realisation that it was part of a broader liberation movement. This was doubly true of women's groups among the non-Russian nationalities, like the Georgians who established their own Union of Equal Rights in 1905.[52]

Meanwhile the conflict between revolutionary and reformist members of the union remained unresolved. It could hardly have been otherwise. Despite the radicalism of the October congress, most union members never supported the most extreme demands of the revolutionaries, in particular the call for an armed insurrection. In the excitement of the October days they could envisage a national revolt against an intransigent government, but at no time would they lend their support to a planned uprising. The furthest they would go, when violence finally erupted in Moscow early in December, was to help man the first aid posts set up by the Union of Unions.[53]

For their part, the socialists in the union felt that it catered too much to the interests of middle-class women, to the exclusion of the working class. This was undoubtedly true, but even if it had not been, the position of revolutionary socialists in a 'bourgeois feminist' organisation would still have been ambiguous. Ideologically they were committed either to take it over or destroy it. They could not remain in the union as it was constituted and still be faithful to their revolutionary beliefs. A schism was inevitable and in the spring of 1906 a number of the most active socialists left the union, either to set up their own working women's clubs or to devote more time to party work.[54]

The divisive tendencies of the Russian women's movement were not manifested in the Union of Equal Rights alone. The Russian Women's Mutual Philanthropic Society also suffered. The society had not been inactive during 1905, despite its early hesitancy. In May it petitioned the government to include women in the assembly promulgated under the February rescript, and sent requests for support to 108 towns and 398 zemstvo boards. In addition, it petitioned eighty governors and forty-six marshals of the nobility, five governors-general and the Council of Ministers. The society adopted the same tactics to campaign for the admission of women to universities, for extended employment opportunities in public service and for coeducation in schools. It also planned a national congress of women to discuss education and philanthropy (the only subjects permitted by the Ministry of the Interior) but this was cancelled at the last moment.[55]

Nonetheless it had not corrected any of the defects for which it had been criticised in 1904. It deliberately eschewed popular appeals and relied on personal approaches to officials and organisations, as it had done in earlier years. Moreover, its bureaucratic structure was left intact. At a meeting of the society in December 1905, Pokrovskaia (who had continued to be a member even while criticising it in *Zhenskii vestnik*) announced the formation of a new organisation, the Women's Progressive Party. Her aim was to attract dissidents not only from the

RZhVBO, but also from the Union of Equal Rights, which she deemed to be orientated too far towards the left and insufficiently feminist.[56]

Pokrovskaia's decision reopened the debate over the priorities of the women's movement. The formation of the SRZh had raised the question of how much feminists should isolate themselves from (indeed, set themselves against) the male-dominated liberation movement. In the spring of 1905 it was almost a foregone conclusion that politically conscious feminists would refuse to detach themselves from the general struggle. Eight months later, many women felt less well-disposed towards the new political parties whose leaders had so conspicuously failed to advance the emancipation of women. Pokrovskaia's party was intended to attract those who believed in the necessity for political action but were reluctant to join any of the established parties. Its platform did not differ substantially from that of the Union of Equal Rights, except that it favoured a constitutional monarchy. But its tone was more hostile to the male sex; men were held responsible for the worst evils in the world and were excluded from membership. Unhappily, the party suffered a schism at its inception. One faction believed that it should concentrate entirely on feminist goals, to the exclusion of general (*obshchechelovecheskiia*) concerns, and refused to participate in the new party. Instead it established an All-Russian League of Women, of which little was heard for another three years.[57]

The schism was naturally a great setback to the new party, but did not extinguish it. Lacking the union's close links with radical politicians, it was better suited to the sober realities of life in the political reaction which followed in the wake of the revolution's defeat. The party soon applied for legal status (which the union never did) and was eventually permitted to open a club in St Petersburg. It also had the advantage of the monthly (though unofficial) journal, *Zhenskii vestnik*, which, until the middle of 1907, was the only feminist journal in Russia. Still edited by Pokrovskaia, it kept up a barrage of propaganda on behalf of women's rights and monitored the progress of the movement.

* * *

The existence of *Zhenskii vestnik* as the only source of feminist propaganda and information throughout 1905 and 1906 highlights a serious weakness in the Russian women's movement: its failure to re-establish the 'woman question' as one of the burning issues in Russian life. The woman question had been greatly discussed in the 1860s; it acquired a new importance in early Soviet society. But in 1905 there was a curious absence of debate.

Though feminists were fully involved in all the activities of the opposition, their participation and their specific demands merited only the most abbreviated reports in newspapers and journals, and virtually no analysis. Despite the fact that the Union of Equal Rights had a substantial membership and successfully influenced other unions and organisations to support women's suffrage, little of this was reflected in the press.

This was undoubtedly due in part to the continued domination of journalism by male writers, for whom women's emancipation was largely a matter of indifference or, sometimes, a positive threat. It was also a result of women's near-exclusion from the moderate wing of the liberation movement (the zemstvo and duma organisations, the unions of lawyers and academics) a situation which was governed by their continued exclusion from local government representation, from the legal profession and the universities.

But it was also a result of women's reluctance to 'make a scene' in public. With a few exceptions they were reticent at the political banquets of November and December 1904 and did not push themselves forward in the radical groups which sprang up after Bloody Sunday. Their success in forcing the seven-part suffrage formula on the Union of Unions owed much to the activities of the extreme left wing, for whom female equality was an inalienable principle if not always a fact. Although women's groups, and especially the Union of Equal Rights, became more demanding during the year, they tended to be most vocal at meetings of women themselves where they were generally preaching to the converted. Their failure to convince by peaceful means did not provoke them to step over the bounds of decorum to break up meetings, chain themselves to railings or attack public property, as the suffragettes were just beginning to do in Britain. This was not simply because the physical penalties for violent behaviour in Russia were far more savage and the fear of anarchy greater. It was also because women continued to identify with the general aims of the liberation movement and found it harder to separate their own demands from that of society. This was true even of the 'separatists' in the movement, despite their greater antagonism towards men.

It could, of course, be argued that the absence of debate in the press was an indication that women's equality was already fully acknowledged and that there was no longer anything to debate. This was far from the case, as the chronicle of the women's movement in 1905 amply demonstrates. Women had made notable advances over fifty years, and public attitudes (at least in educated circles) had changed dramatically. They had now begun to fight for political equality 'in the future state system'. Their halting progress illustrates how far the woman question still was from a satisfactory solution.

Notes

1 *Zhenskii vestnik* no. 3 (1904) p. 84; *Zhenskoe delo* no. 1 (1899) p. 135;

N. Mirovich, 'O pervom s"ezde russkikh deiatel'nits' p. 134.
2 *Sbornik pamiati A.P. Filosofovoi* vol. i, p. 383.
3 *Zhenskii vestnik* no. 3 (1904) p. 84.
4 *Ibid.* no. 1 (1904) p. 1; P.N. Ariian (ed.), *Pervyi zhenskii kalendar' na 1905g.* (Spb: 1905) pp. 394–6 (hereafter cited as *PZhK*).
5 *Zhenskii vestnik* no. 6 (1905) pp. 190–91; no. 9 (1905) pp. 286–7. For Pokrovskaia's full economic programme see no. 1 (1906) p. 28.
6 *Ibid.* no. 1 (1904) p. 22.
7 (E. Shch.) *Zhenskoe dvizhenie v otzyvakh sovremennykh deiatelei* (Spb: 1905) p. 1.
8 *Zemskii s"ezd 6-go i sl. noiabria 1904g. Kratkii otchet* (Paris: 1905) p. 30. Some zemstvo assemblies had proposed a limited female franchise as early as 1902, impressed by women's reliability as zemstvo doctors and teachers. *PZhK na 1904g.* pp. 402–404.
9 *Listok osvobozhdeniia* no. 19 (1904) p. 4; no. 21 (1904) p. 4.
10 The signatories included Anna Miliukova (wife of the liberal leader Pavel Miliukov), Aleksandra Kollontai, Ekaterina Kuskova and the writer Zinaida Gippius. *Ibid.* no. 22–3 (1904) p. 7.
11 Glickman, 'The Russian Factory Woman' pp. 79–80; Amy Knight, *The Participation of Women in the Revolutionary Movement in Russia from 1890 to 1914* (Ph.D. University of London: 1977) pp. 77–88; 130–32.
12 L. Gurevich, *9-e ianvaria. Po dannym anketnoi komissii'* (Spb: 1905) p. 6; Walter Sablinsky, *The Road to Bloody Sunday* (Princeton: 1976) p. 138.
13 *Ibid.* pp. 106–107, 129, 138; [L. Gurevich] *Zhenskoe dvizhenie poslednikh dnei* (Odessa: 1905) pp. 10, 14–16; *Pravda* no. 6 (1905) pp. 273, 282.
14 Sidney Harcave, *The Russian Revolution of 1905* (London: 1964) p. 93; Lionel Kochan, *Russia in Revolution* (London: 1970) p. 92.
15 *Russkiia vedomosti* 4 February 1905, p. 3; *Zhenskii vestnik* no. 4 (1905) pp. 121–2; no. 12 (1905) p. 366.
16 *Ibid.* no. 4 (1905) p. 115.
17 N. Mirovich, *Iz istorii zhenskago dvizheniia v Rossii* (M: 1908) p. 5; *Ravnopravie zhenshchin: otchety i protokoly 1906g.* (Spb: 1906) pp. 2–3.
18 A. Zhikhareva, 'Anna Sergeevna Miliukova. Zhiznennyi put'' *Posledniia novosti* 5 April 1935, p. 2; 7 April, p. 2. For Shchepkina see *Ents. slovar' Brokgauz-Efron* vol. xl, p. 60; 'Pamiati dvukh zhenshchin-vrachei' *Obrazovanie* no. 5–6 (1896) pt. 1, pp. 92–104. For Mirovich see *Sbornik na pomoshch' uchashchimsia zhenshchinam* (M: 1901) p. 242; A. Kizevetter, 'Pamiati Zinaidy Sergeevny Mirovich' *Russkaia mysl'* no. 9 (1913) pt. 2, pp. 140–41; *Jus Suffragii* October 1913, p. 4. For Chekhova see *PZhK na 1912g.* pp. 8–11. For Gurevich see *Ents. slovar' Granat* 7th ed. vol. xi col. 634.
19 *Ravnopravie zhenshchin* p. 2; *Protokoly zasedanii delegatov vserossiiskago soiuza ravnopravnosti zhenshchin* (unpublished report in London Library collection) p. 1.
20 *Zhenskii vestnik* no. 5 (1905) pp. 143–4.
21 *Pravo* no. 16 (1905) cols. 1324–5; *Zhenskii vestnik* no. 6 (1905) p. 189. The draft Civil Code (2nd ed.) came out in 1904; the subject of prolonged debate, it was never enacted. A woman would have gained a little by its provisions (no longer obliged to offer her husband 'unlimited obedience') but she would have remained subordinate within the family, especially in

decisions relating to children. Evreinova heavily criticised its proposal that a woman sacrifice her independent income to support her husband if in need (art. 109). See I.M. Tiutriumov (ed.) *Grazhdanskoe ulozhenie* 2 vols. (Sbp: 1910) vol. i, pp. 224–5, 230, 336.

22 *Pravo* no. 16 (1905) cols. 1325–9; Aleksandra Kollontai, 'Avtobiograficheskii ocherk' *Proletarskaia revoliutsiia* no. 3 (1921) p. 268. An assessment of Kollontai's role in 1905 is dependent on her own memoirs. Judging by other reports, she overrated her contribution to this meeting.

23 *PZhK na 1907g.* p. 356; *Protokoly zasedanii delegatov* pp. 1–2.

24 *Ibid.* pp. 4, 5.

25 Mirovich, *Iz istorii* pp. 6–10. Mirovich quotes the revised version of October 1905.

26 *Russkiia vedomosti* 8 May 1905, p. 3. Most published accounts at the time reported only this public meeting, confirming the impression that the congress itself was kept quiet. See also *Novoe vremia* 9 May 1905, p. 1; *Slovo* 7 May 1905, p. 2, 9 May, p. 1, 10 May, p. 3.

27 *Novosti* 26 April 1905, p. 2. Many of the battles within the liberation movement in 1905 centred on the suffrage formula. Often the four-part formula ('universal, direct, equal, secret') caused less controversy than the three additional 'tails' ('without distinction of sex, religion or nationality').

28 *Zhurnal soveshchaniia delegatov 14 vserossiisk. prof. soiuzov, proiskhodivshago v g. Moskve 8 i 9 maia 1905g.* (unpublished report in London Library collection).

29 N. Cherevanin, 'Dvizhenie intelligentsii' in L. Martov *et al*, (eds.) *Obshchestvennoe dvizhenie v Rossii v nachale XX-go veka* (Spb: 1909–14) vol. ii, pt. 2, p. 182; *Ravnopravie zhenshchin* pp. 3–4.

30 *Zhurnal soveshchaniia delegatov 14 vserossiisk. prof. soiuzov proiskhodivshago v Moskve 24–25 maia 1905g.* (unpublished report in London Library collection); (E. Shch.) *Zhenskoe dvizhenie* p. 2.

31 *Zhenskii vestnik* no. 4 (1905) pp. 122–3; no. 5 (1905) p. 144; no. 12 (1905) pp. 366–7.

32 *Novosti* 3 June 1905, p. 4.

33 *Zhenskii vestnik* no. 7 (1905) pp. 206, 210.

34 Mirovich, *Iz istorii*, pp. 12–13.

35 F. Kokoshkin, *Ob osnovaniiakh zhelatel'noi organizatsii narodnago predstavitel'stva v Rossii* (M: 1906).

36 Mirovich, *Iz istorii* pp. 13–16.

37 *Ibid.* pp. 16–17; (E. Shch.) *Zhenskoe dvizhenie* p. 4.

38 Mirovich, *Iz istorii* pp. 7–11.

39 *Ibid.* p. 13.

40 Mirovich, 'S"ezdy zemskikh i gorodskikh deiatelei' *Russkaia mysl'* no. 12 (1905) pt. 2, pp. 168, 169.

41 *Rus'* 9 October 1905, p. 4.

42 *Russkiia vedomosti* 9 October 1905, p. 14; *PZhK na 1907g.* pp. 358–60. By the end of 1905 it had 80 sections in 69 towns. Membership figures are elusive. The union estimated 8,000 in May 1906. *Ravnopravie zhenshchin* p. 7. S.D. Kirpichnikov in *Soiuz soiuzov* (Spb: 1906) p. 24, gives 6,000.

43 *Ravnopravie zhenshchin* p. 2.

44 *Soiuz zhenshchin* no. 1 (1907) p. 9; V. Groman (ed.) *Materialy k krest'ianskomu voprosu* (Spb: 1905) pp. 37–8.

45 *Ravnopravie zhenshchin* pp. 23–24.

46 *Biulleten' no. 3–i* (London Library collection) p. 2, a leaflet put out by the union soon after the congress. Passages are reproduced in Mirovich, *Iz istorii* pp. 19–23. Bulletins were apparently being issued monthly. *Vserossiiskii soiuz ravnopravnosti zhenshchin* (leaflet issued in November 1905, n.d., n.p. in London Library collection).

47 *Ibid.* Moscow recorded 46 for the boycott, 2 against; Saratov voted 34 to 2 in favour; Kaluga, by contrast, voted 17 to 14. *Novosti* 11 October 1905, p. 3; *Russkiia vedomosti* 11 October 1905, p. 3.

48 *Biulleten'* pp. 2, 4.

49 Ariadna Tyrkova, 'Pervyi zhenskii s″ezd' *Zarnitsy* no. 2 (1909) pt. 2, p. 184. Text in *Osvobozhdenie* 7 May 1905. The exemption clause was superfluous, as the Union of Liberation's programme was adopted as a non-binding manifesto because its members could not agree on basic issues. Shmuel Galai, *The Liberation Movement in Russia 1900–1905* (Cambridge: 1973) pp. 244–5.

50 A. Tyrkova-Williams, *Na putiakh k svobode* (New York: 1952) p. 239; Tyrkova, 'Pervyi zhenskii s″ezd' p. 185. Two of his potential allies, I.V. Gessen and V.D. Nabokov, had left the hall during the debate and failed to vote. They were greeted by an angry Miliukov on their return. I.V. Gessen, 'V dvukh vekakh: zhiznennyi otchet' *Arkhiv russkoi revoliutsii* (Berlin: 1937) vol. xxii, p. 205.

51 There was some controversy over the legality of the resolution. *Novosti* 11 October 1905, p. 3; *Russkiia vedomosti* 10 October 1905 p. 3.

52 Mirovich, *Iz istorii* pp. 56–9. See *Soiuz zhenshchin* no. 1 (1907) p. 5, no. 7–8 (1909) p. 7, for examples of feminist activity after the October Manifesto.

53 *Ravnopravie zhenshchin* p. 11.

54 Kollontai, 'Avtobiograficheskii ocherk' pp. 270–271; *PZhK na 1907g.* pp. 373–4.

55 *PZhK na 1906g.* pp. 326–8.

56 *Zhenskii vestnik* no. 3 (1906) pp. 90–91.

57 *Ibid.*; *Ravnopravie zhenshchin* p. 30.

3 Political Rights and Political Realities

It may be reasonable to doubt whether a political crisis whose outcome left the tsar on the throne and in control of the government can really be called a revolution. Yet the name sticks. The assault on autocracy had been only partially successful and the gains precarious. Nevertheless, the tsar had been forced to concede something which hitherto he had dismissed as an impossibility, namely a national representative assembly with a degree of legislative power. At the beginning of 1906, liberals and moderate socialists could look back on a year in which the autocracy's favoured methods of dealing with political unrest had failed to quell an opposition whose left wing had become more daring with each victory, before fragmenting in the face of the tsar's concessions. Notwithstanding the increased violence from both extremes of the political spectrum and the government's resort to repressive measures in violation of the promises made in October, the moderate opposition now looked forward to the convocation of the First State Duma to lay the foundations for what they hoped would be a constitutional government in Russia.

As 1906 progressed, the government regained the whip hand. The extension of martial law, the punitive expeditions and the premature dissolution of two Dumas came near to breaking the back of the opposition. The history of the following decade showed that the apparent victors of 1905, the liberals and moderate socialists, were in fact the losers. 1905 was their year of promise; thereafter, hopes for a reformist solution to Russia's problems became progressively dimmer. But autocracy's strength faded correspondingly. The tsarist regime had been shaken to its core and lacked the resilience to weather the next onslaught, which came twelve years later.

Even at its most savage, the reaction did not restore the balance of political forces to the status quo before 1905. The Duma survived attempts to destroy it (and reports of its debates could be read in the daily press). Political parties enjoyed a semi-legality; suppressed periodicals resurfaced with new titles; meetings and conferences withstood police interference; and organisations established during 1905 lived on into the less optimistic times that lay ahead.

At the beginning of 1906 the women's movement found itself in a mood of chastened expectation characteristic of the opposition in general. The movement had made undeniable progress during 1905, but its achievements fell far short of those for which they hoped. While feminists could congratulate themselves on their victories over male intransigence in the Union of Unions, municipal dumas, zemstvos and political parties of the left, they were obliged to recognise that their successes were limited entirely to the ranks of the opposition. From the government there had come no hint whatsoever that women were henceforth to be regarded as equal citizens of Russia. Indeed they had been specifically excluded from the franchise by the electoral laws.[1] Moreover they could not regard their victories as secure: given that support for women's suffrage had so often been rendered grudgingly by men in the liberation movement, women could feel no confidence that it would not be withdrawn in the future. 'Will the zemstvo, in common with other forces in society, support the demands of the majority of the population and breathe life into the principle of women's political equality with men?' asked Mirovich.[2] Even if the zemstvists were to adhere to the recently conceded principle, would the government pay any attention?

Awareness that the political status of women had changed significantly after the October Manifesto was an important factor in the development of the movement during 1906. It had become a commonplace of the women's movement that men and women in Russia shared an equality not to be found in the West. The sexes in Russia, it was held, were 'equal in their lack of rights' and as a result respected each other's aspirations to political self-determination.[3] There was undoubtedly an element of self-deception in this view. Not only was Russian society still heavily patriarchal in structure, power at all levels being held exclusively in the hands of men, but the experience of 1905 had shown women the strength of men's opposition to their political emancipation. Nevertheless, it was true that before 1905 the sexes had shared a greater political equality than elsewhere in Europe. This came to an end with the October Manifesto. With the opening of a new era a definitive change was wrought in what one might call the balance of power between the sexes, and politically active women felt themselves to be at a serious disadvantage. Pokrovskaia, in *Zhenskii vestnik*, claimed that women had participated in the liberation movement, even fighting on the barricades, in the conviction that 'the struggle would lead to the liberation of the whole Russian people, including women . . .' The victims had been many, the sufferings great and to what avail? The electoral law excluded women from the franchise and posed the 'surprising question: do women count as citizens or not?' The census regarded them as part of the population, they were citizens for the purposes of taxation and general responsibilities, but not for rights. Women, she declared, must protest.[4]

Although Pokrovskaia, with her undisguised antipathy towards men, never exercised an influence over Russian women remotely comparable to that wielded by the Pankhursts over the English suffrage movement, she was expressing a sentiment that in 1906 was not confined to those intransigent feminists who grouped themselves around *Zhenskii vestnik*. It was accepted by almost all the women's rights groups that the most urgent task before them was to get the State Duma to introduce legislation granting women the vote. If they allowed the Duma to give priority to other business the moment would be lost, and a principle which had been generally conceded by the opposition only after a year of active campaigning would become a dead letter.

A quick glance at the new political parties' programmes was enough to demonstrate how slender was the feminists' support in society. Predictably, none of the parties of the extreme right was prepared even to entertain the idea, but in the First Duma this would not have been an obstacle had the suffragists been able to depend on the moderate conservative and centre parties. Instead they found at best a distinct ambivalence which, although it came as no surprise, was not encouraging.

The largest of the moderate groups in the Duma, the Octobrists, simply ignored the issue, making no reference at all to women in any of their statements of policy. But their generally conservative outlook towards female emancipation was made quite clear during the election campaign for the First Duma. An Octobrist pamphlet attacking the policy and tactics of the Constitutional–Democratic Party, dismissed the Kadets' support of female suffrage as a 'jesuitical' election manoeuvre, and went on to assail the whole basis of the women's movement in language typical of anti-feminists the world over:

> When people fight for women's equality, they always leave out of account the essential psychological distinction between the two sexes. This distinction consists in the elevation of feeling over reason in woman's nature. A woman may have a greater mind, but feeling always predominates in it. This development of feeling in the various manifestations of her life makes her both a heroine and a cruel tyrant.[5]

But the targets of this attack, the Kadets, were themselves sorely divided over the issue of women's suffrage, and the second congress of the party was the scene of renewed confrontation between the suffragists and their opponents, led by Miliukov. The first congress in Moscow had left support of the seven-point formula non-binding on members of the party, and women in the suffrage movement, such as Mirovich, Liubov' Gurevich and Anna Miliukova, were concerned to reverse that decision at the earliest opportunity.

At the second congress they were joined by a newcomer. This was

Ariadna Tyrkova, who used the occasion to make her debut in the women's movement and in Kadet politics. She was not new to the liberation movement, however. After the breakdown of her first marriage she had worked as a journalist for liberal newspapers in the provinces, before being arrested in 1903 for attempting to smuggle the émigré opposition paper *Osvobozhdenie* (*Liberation*) into Russia. After three months in prison she was released on bail and escaped to Europe, and had since become fully involved in the émigré political world. She returned from her eighteen-month European exile after the October Manifesto, and consequently did not discover the women's suffrage campaign until late in 1905. An encounter with Ol'ga Vol'kenshtein, an SR and an outspoken member of the Union of Equal Rights, did nothing to draw her closer to the movement, but she changed her mind when she attended the Kadets' congress in St Petersburg the following January.[6]

As in October, Miliukov and his wife found themselves on opposing sides. On this occasion, Miliukov's opposition was reinforced by Peter Struve, who regarded the issue as irrelevant at such a critical juncture in the nation's history, and by the influential leader of the Volga Tatars, Akchurin, who was openly hostile:

> We Muslims are against women's equality. It does not accord with either our law or our customs. Our women do not wish for equality. If you put into your programme that women too must vote, thirty million Muslims will not give you their votes. I am against.[7]

His words provoked Tyrkova to make her first speech, not notably original but effective nonetheless, in defence of women's rights. Rejecting the notion that the rights of Russian women should be 'equalised' with those of the subjected Muslims, she asked how suffrage could be regarded as universal if half the adult population were excluded. No one, she argued, could be deprived of the franchise on the grounds of his or her political maturity, for who was politically mature in Russia? Women had gone to prison and to their death in the liberation struggle. 'Does this mean together to prison but not to the representative assembly?'

Miliukov rather lamely replied that in a constituent assembly the non-binding amendment would disappear of its own accord (a claim that no doubt left some of his audience wondering why it could not be allowed to disappear from the Kadet programme too). The issue, which was threatening to become a bone of contention in a congress whose purpose was to achieve unity, was finally settled in women's favour by the persuasive speech of Lev Petrazhitskii, professor of jurisprudence and a man widely respected in liberal circles. The offending amendment was at last excised from the programme, if not without some subsequent protests from leading figures such as Struve.

Kadet supporters in the Union of Equal Rights were pleased with the vote, which removed the ban on membership of the party imposed by the last union congress in October. Nevertheless the debate reinforced their suspicions of Kadets as allies. The practical value of the vote was limited. Leaders of the party continued to be lukewarm or disdainful towards the campaign for women's suffrage and did little to advance it when the First Duma met. But Kadets were not averse to using their formal commitment to women's rights to win converts. An appeal from the party during the election campaign called on women to persuade their male relatives to vote for the Kadets:

> Citizen-mothers, wives and daughters! You are deprived of the vote. Parties such as the Union of 17 October, the Commercial–Industrial Party and others do not recognise you as citizens of Russia. Only the Party of National Freedom has resolved to struggle for your equal rights. Persuade your sons, husbands and fathers to vote for the friends of freedom. The triumph of the party of national freedom will be the triumph of the whole of Russia and your triumph. May the time come when you also will sit in the Russian parliament and dictate just laws to our great and troubled land.[8]

Like political parties in the West, the Kadets were quick to appreciate the value of women in the party organisation as propagandists and secretarial help. Women took an active part in the Kadets' election campaign, producing literature, raising money and generally doing the 'unskilled labour' of the campaign. Women also went along to Kadet election meetings, although their presence was frowned upon by the authorities. More than one such meeting was closed by the steward before it had a chance to begin, because men in the audience refused to heed his demand that women be ejected.[9]

One indication that the Kadets, if unenthusiastic, were serious in their commitment to women's rights came just before the opening of the Duma. Along with her Muslim opponent, Akchurin, Tyrkova was co-opted on to the central committee, one of ten members brought in to broaden the regional basis of the committee. This was a significant appointment, taking her to the heart of the party's work both in and out of the Duma. But her new position also illustrates the profound discrepancy which existed between the role of the Kadets in Russian politics and that of a liberal party in a western parliamentary system. Just as it was possible for Miliukov to hold the leadership at a time when he was officially disqualified from standing for the Duma, it was possible for a women without a vote to be admitted to the inner councils of the party. It would have been unthinkable in the West (or in Russia) before 1918 for a woman to achieve such a status in a party which wielded real power. The Constitutional–Democratic Party had no responsibility for government even when its members held over one-third of all Duma seats. Power in Russia remained with the tsar's government and women had no share in it.[10]

Despite their difficulties with the Kadets, the suffragists undoubtedly found more supporters within the party than anywhere else in the constitutional camp, and they could cite the party programme whenever they suspected their colleagues of backsliding. Other more moderate parties took a very cautious line, limiting female suffrage to local government.[11]

The parties to the left of the Kadets were, by contrast, unconditional advocates of women's rights, but social–democrats and, to a lesser extent, SRs looked with suspicion on 'bourgeois feminism', and the Radical Party, which proposed socialist legislation without socialist revolution, was too tiny to be of any account. There remained the Trudoviks (the 'Labour Group') an *ad hoc* coalition of peasant deputies who, with the Kadets, were the most substantial block in the First Duma. Though the Trudoviks had no official programme, they proved to be the most reliable group in the Duma in their support of women's equality. The Union of Equal Rights rapidly established friendly relations with the group, hoping to use it not only as a lever in the Duma but also as a propaganda weapon among the peasantry.

Despite the political parties' ambivalent response to the women's movement there is no question that the Duma elections were critical for the continued momentum of the suffrage campaign. For this reason the Women's Progressive Party which Pokrovskaia had founded at the end of 1905 was more than just an expression of dissatisfaction with existing women's organisations. It was also a response to what seemed to be the new political realities in Russia.

Pokrovskaia believed that the salvation of Russia lay in a democratic parliament committed to basic social reforms. If the country was now to have a parliament representing a range of political parties it seemed a logical step for women too to have a party which would lobby the Duma to grant women's suffrage. Once women were admitted to the Duma on an equal footing it would become possible to embark upon a programme of social legislation directly and indirectly affecting women which, Pokrovskaia believed, men would never undertake on their own initiative. Thus, despite her acute chagrin at the indifference of the new political parties to the 'woman question', and her appreciation of the inadequacies of the Duma as at present constituted, she welcomed it as the prerequisite for a peaceful solution to the social crisis. The Progressive Party should see itself in relation to the Duma as a loyal opposition to a parliamentary government.[12]

The Russian Women's Mutual Philanthropic Society was also anxious to make use of the changed political circumstances. Having failed to obtain any favourable response to the letters which it had addressed to Witte and the Council of Ministers the previous year, it decided to seek a wider audience and in February began to organise a petition which would be presented to the Duma soon after it met. The establishment of a legally elected national assembly was significant for the Mutual Philanthropic Society in opening the way for it to engage in public propaganda while remaining firmly within the bounds of the law. It established a rapport with moderate constitutionalists in the Kadet Party and prepared to exert a gentle pressure on the new parliament to extend the suffrage to women.[13]

But not all feminists gave the Duma an unequivocal welcome. Unlike the Women's Progressive Party and the Mutual Philanthropic Society, the Union of Equal Rights found that the summoning of Russia's first parliament presented something of a dilemma. The union was fully committed to the demand for a constituent assembly and had voted at its last congress to boycott the Bulygin Duma. The union's central bureau did not feel that the October Manifesto required a change of policy, and the boycott remained officially in force until jettisoned at the third congress in May.[14]

In practice, however, the Duma and the preceding election campaign presented too good an opportunity for union propaganda to be lightly neglected. Moreover, there were many in the union who shared the liberals' belief that the Duma laid the foundation stone of a constitutional order and that once a general male franchise were introduced, direct universal suffrage could not be far behind. As the election campaign progressed, reports began to come in from local sections that members were disregarding the boycott and becoming involved, as far as they could as voteless citizens, in the campaigning. The central bureau also adjusted to the new mood, even while maintaining the fiction of a total boycott.

This shift in attitude was partly the result of changes within the union itself and, in particular, the exodus early in 1906 of a large number of radicals, dissatisfied with the failure of the union either to support revolutionary activity or to attract large numbers of working women to membership. The schism affected mainly the St Petersburg section, which all but collapsed as a result.[15] Out of its ruins arose the Women's Political Club (*Zhenskii Politicheskii Klub*) dominated by social–democrats, both Bolshevik and Menshevik, but including many 'non-party' radicals. Their concerns were very similar to those of the Union of Equal Rights (universal suffrage, civil equality of the sexes and the overall liberation of society) but they aimed specifically at the 'female masses' working in St Petersburg factories.

The club survived only three months, from April up to the dissolution of the Duma, 'when the police systematically began to close all its meetings'; but in those months it gathered a membership of some 600, twice as many as the Union of Equal Rights had collected in the city the previous year.[16] How many of these members would have remained in the club had its activities not been prematurely terminated by the police is open to question: the coalition of social-democrats and 'non-party' socialists was as unstable as the union from which it sprang and there were violent disagreements between its members from the start. Kollontai, who remained implacably hostile to any feminist undertaking, accurately perceived the club's essential weakness:

> The women in this club . . . could not explain to themselves, let alone to others, what class they represented and what they conceived as their main objectives. They were unsure whether they should defend the interests of factory women, peasant women or working women in general, and whether they should pursue exclusively feminist aims or involve themselves in more general political questions; shuffling indecisively between these alternatives, the club was doomed to a short existence.[17]

None the less, during its short life the club's organisers could claim large audiences for its meetings, 'especially from working and semi-intelligentsia circles'. Without doubt, these included some of the women who had worked in Gapon's assembly eighteen months earlier and had formed women's 'circles' in Petersburg factories during 1905.

Meanwhile, a rump committee survived in the St Petersburg branch of the Union of Equal Rights. It was never able to muster enough new members to make the section viable once more, losing some of its potential supporters to both the Mutual Philanthropic Society and the Women's Progressive Party which were based in St Petersburg and which drew their support from politically moderate women of the intelligentsia. The section held out because of the dedication of a few individual women, notably Liubov' Gurevich, Ekaterina Shchepkina and Mariia Chekhova. Chekhova (who moved from Moscow to St Petersburg in 1906) remained the union's secretary throughout its existence and kept up the struggle for its survival until the very end. The St Petersburg section's location in the capital city, and home of the State Duma, aided its survival. Being at the centre of political developments in 1906, its members were invaluable when the union turned to fresh targets – the newly-elected members of the Duma.

The Duma elections were held in March and April, resulting in a victory for the opposition candidates, two-thirds of whom were either Kadets or Trudoviks. Both fractions were committed to a programme of sweeping social and political reforms in which they could not, and did not, expect much co-operation from the government. The Duma assembled on 27 April and was summoned to the Winter Palace to hear the tsar's Speech from the Throne. It immediately elected a commission to draft a Reply to the tsar, incorporating the demands of the elected representatives of the people, and this was presented to the Duma for debate on 2 May.

The feminists had been waiting anxiously for an indication that the Kadets and Trudoviks intended to introduce a women's suffrage bill at the earliest opportunity, but they were disappointed. The Reply was drafted to embrace as wide a cross-section of opinion as possible and committed the Duma only to an electoral law 'founded on the principles of universal suffrage, in accordance with the unanimous will of the people'. Just as distressing was its silence on women's civil equality: the Reply promised to abolish 'all restrictions and privileges dependent on rank, nationality and religion' – but not on sex.[18]

The draft Reply seemed to confirm the feminists' worst suspicions, and deputies belonging to the Trudovik and Kadet fractions were immediately inundated with telegrams from women's union sections all over Russia, demanding the inclusion of women's rights.[19] The Trudoviks were natural allies, since they objected for other reasons to the wording of the text and rejected Kadet claims that it expressed the will of the people. Vehement in their condemnation of the existing electoral law, they were enthusiastic supporters of female suffrage.

> When we say that the suffrage must be reformed on the basis of the four-part formula, we are forgetting, in this first Russian parliament, the Russian woman, who has joined as an equal in the struggle for freedom. [Prolonged applause] We forget that the son of a slave cannot be a citizen. [Thunderous applause][20]

The Kadet lawyer, Nabokov (who presented the draft) was not convinced that 'the unanimous will of the people' demanded female suffrage, but he did concede that women must have 'full rights before the law' (that is, equality in everything but the vote). He stated that their omission had been an 'oversight' which would be rectified in the final version. The Trudoviks, however, continued to press for the full seven-part suffrage formula, in company with a small number of Kadets, one of whom noted that if the Constitutional–Democratic Party meant to defend a programme containing the highly controversial proposal to expropriate landed estates, then it must also honour its pledge to support women's suffrage. 'I can only say that the Russian woman has bought that right, and at a high price.'

Despite the advocacy of some members, the majority voted against any change in the wording of this section of the Reply, either concurring with the Octobrist Count Geiden that it was possible to live without the seven-part formula in general, and women's suffrage in particular, or preferring to postpone the decision to a later debate. But the hostility masquerading as wit which regularly greeted women's suffrage bills in the British parliament made little appearance in the First State Duma, whose belief in the necessity for social change was as strong as its power to implement it was weak.[21]

For all practical purposes the debate on the Reply was a waste of time. The tsar punctured the Duma's self-esteem by refusing to receive the address personally and insisted that it be submitted to his ministers instead. They, predictably, rejected the Duma's propositions. Nevertheless the Duma went ahead with its legislative projects even while the tsar's ministers were contriving its dissolution. Among the proposed legislative reforms was a bill on civil equality.

Almost a fortnight after the debate on the Reply to the Speech from the Throne, a declaration signed by 111 members was read in the Duma. It proposed legislation on civil equality based on the principle that 'all citizens of both sexes are equal before the law'. It continued: 'Civil inequality has penetrated so deeply into all parts of our legislation and has so taken hold of every sphere of life, that its elimination by means of a single legislative act is impossible.' It outlined four separate categories of reforms, the last intended to give women equality in all aspects of the law 'insofar as the existence of responsibilities connected with these rights does not prevent it'.[22]

The declaration was greeted with enthusiasm in the Duma and another forty members hastened to sign it. The signatories were overwhelmingly Kadets, including staunch supporters of women's rights like Petrazhitskii, and, less predictably, Nabokov and Kokoshkin, neither of whom had been friends of women's rights in the past. Twenty-seven Trudoviks, thirteen autonomists and a number of non-party and social–democratic members also signed.[23]

On 5 June the Duma began to consider the establishment of a commission to draw up a bill. The Kadet Kokoshkin opened the debate by taking up the argument that Russia's system of law was infused with a spirit of inequality 'which like some malignant sore penetrates into every branch of legislation, into every part of our state organism'. He then enumerated the principal spheres of life where it was manifest: firstly, in the legal separation of social classes; secondly, in the legal subjection of the peasants; and thirdly, in sexual inequality.

In the first two categories, he said, Russia was unrivalled by any Western state. In the third, however, Russia could not claim to be unique, a fact which he predicted would be used by the opponents of women's rights as a pretext for inaction. Such objections, he stated, could only be expressions of 'age-old prejudice'. If France and Germany kept women in subjection, Russia's closest neighbour, Finland, was in the process of liberating them. 'We believe that Russia more than any other country is prepared for this reform.' Women already possessed the right to property and had proven themselves in the sphere of social activity. 'We know that women have served in the leading ranks of the liberation movement and have been unsurpassed by men. This is why we believe the time is ripe for reform'.[24]

Those who had read Kokoshkin's case against women's suffrage the previous year must have wondered at the change. Now he was the champion of equality, refuting opinions which he himself had used only twelve months before. Kokoshkin's conversion suggests that a year's active campaigning by the feminists had not been without effect, transforming an influential opponent into a useful ally. If one speech in the Duma was unlikely to alter the course of Russia's history, it did at least suggest that Kadets such as Kokoshkin were prepared to be more conciliatory towards women's rights. This perceptible shift of attitude began to break down feminists' suspicions of the liberals, drawing them further away from the left wing of politics towards the liberal centre, a trend that was very noticeable among women's union members in the latter part of 1906.

The debate on civil equality lasted four days, during which time deputies had ample opportunity to air their views on the female sex. None of the arguments employed would have been unfamiliar to a Western audience: for example, that women did not qualify for political rights because they did not serve the state in time of war; or, on the contrary, that women fulfilled their obligation to society in childbirth rather than on the battlefield.[25] But the question of women's rights could not be divorced from the particular political context in which the debate was held, as Kokoshkin's speech demonstrated.

This fact was made very clear by a peasant deputy, Kruglikov, one of the few speakers to make a strong case against female emancipation. Protesting that women's rights would destroy not only the peasants' way of life but the Orthodox faith as well, he quoted (to applause and laughter) the words of St Paul: 'Wives submit yourselves unto your own husbands'.[26] Kruglikov's was not the opposition of educated liberals but that of 'unenlightened' peasant men, whose hostility towards the emancipation of their wives was linked to a fear of fundamental social change in the village. Unlike the peasants who voted for the Trudoviks, Kruglikov's constituency was conservative and nationalist, opposed to autonomy for national minorities and to religious toleration. This association of female emancipation with the issue of minority rights was underlined by two Muslim Kadets from Ufa, who rejected the notion that Islam prohibited female equality, and argued that Muslim women had as great a claim to equal rights as Muslim men and Russian women.[27]

It was Lev Petrazhitskii, however, who made the most substantial contribution to the debate, in a speech which became one of the standard texts of the suffragists. The Russian Women's Mutual Philanthropic Society had managed to collect over 4,000 signatures for its equal rights petition. This had been handed to Petrazhitskii and a fellow Kadet for presentation to the Duma but, because the Duma had no right to receive public petitions, it remained unread. Petrazhitskii, a wholehearted supporter of women's emancipation, hoped to compensate for the petition's failure with his speech.[28]

He was not, he said, concerned to demonstrate the principle of equality: that was already self-evident. Instead he would restrict himself to pointing out the areas where reform was necessary, adding by way of warning that 'it would be naïve to think that on the basis of these laws women could obtain actual equality'. Quite the reverse. New laws would for a time benefit only the most determined women:

> Old prejudices, the egoistical interests of the representatives of the privileged sex and other obstacles will, with particular force at first, long prevent the achievement not only of full equality and justice, but even of some approximation to it.

He also warned that the peasants' customary law, which affected women variously in different parts of Russia, could not be swept away with one legislative act. In this sphere the Duma would have to proceed cautiously.

The laws which Petrazhitskii believed the Duma should undertake to reform before all else were inheritance law, access to education and government service, and suffrage. This last was 'the chief and, it might seem, the most radical point of our programme . . . It is this point to defend which . . . means to sacrifice one's reputation as a serious politician and even subject oneself to mockery.' Petrazhitskii believed that the involvement of women in politics was not only possible but necessary:

> I believe that it is desirable for women to enter politics, and the more they do so, the better it is for the state, society and progress. This thesis seems strange and paradoxical to you, I observe ironic smiles, but I hope that when you have listened to my explanation you will recognise that one ought at least to consider it.

'To engage in politics,' he argued, 'means to concern oneself with the common good,' to overcome a selfish preoccupation 'with one's small ego'. The old regime had depended on the encouragement of a narrow and apathetic attitude towards politics and on the persecution of political activity. The new order depended on the development of that sense of social responsibility (*obshchestvennost'*), which was so highly prized by the Russian intelligentsia. Petrazhitskii's unwavering support of women's suffrage was founded on his hope that women as mothers would inculcate this quality in their children and raise the nation's cultural level. 'The interest of the common good and of civilisation demands that we grant women political, that is, social rights and obligations.'[29]

The outcome of the debate was undramatic. The Duma voted to submit the Declaration of the 151 to its commission on civil equality which it then proceeded to elect. Of the thirty-three members chosen, half had signed the declaration, a guarantee that women's rights would get a hearing. Feminists had reason to feel satisfied that their demands were being considered but could feel only moderately hopeful that they would be accepted.[30]

Hitherto the Union of Equal Rights had responded ambivalently to the Duma's activities, maintaining a token boycott yet encouraging it to promote sexual equality. It attacked the Reply to the Speech from the Throne for leaving out the suffrage formula and criticised the Declaration of the 151 for its incomplete support of women's rights. The union kept up its pressure on the Duma during May and June, raising 4,500 signatures for a declaration demanding the vote and issuing each deputy with a copy of the text. In Moscow, union members were particularly successful in getting working-class women to sign. Regional branches as well as the central bureau sent letters and declarations, and published proclamations in local newspapers calling on women to petition the Duma. In St Petersburg women went in person to the Tauride Palace to lobby deputies, the Trudoviks in particular.[31]

The union's hand was also evident in a number of open letters from groups of peasant women in several provinces, complaining of the peasant woman's 'double burden' and asking for land and the vote. One had to be written for the women by a young girl in the village, another was clearly the work of a member of the union. Two of them remained unsigned for fear of retribution from the women's husbands and the authorities, but another (a vigorous protest against Kruglikov's speech) had fifty-five signatures. All these collective letters were good propaganda for the union and were issued as separate pamphlets.[32]

However, not all union members adopted such aggressive tactics. While some continued to see the Duma as an adversary to be conquered, the more diplomatic were cultivating relations with sympathetic deputies. In May it was suggested that the union prepare detailed proposals for reform of the legal code as it applied to women. Lacking the necessary expertise, the union decided to establish a small commission of members who would draw on the aid of trained lawyers. When the Duma's own commission on civil equality established a number of sub-committees, the chairman of the sub-committee on women's rights, Petrazhitskii, asked the union's commission to draw up a bill. If suitable, it would be presented to the Duma in the sub-committee's name.[33]

There followed a month of intense activity in the union's commission. The result was a draft law on women's equality (the first which had ever been drafted) with an accompanying table listing, article by article, the attendant changes in the legal code. The bill did not set out to solve the woman question. Except for the equalisation of inheritance rights it did not touch the economic aspects of the question and it left intact distinctions of class, nationality and religion as being outside its frame of reference. What it aimed to do was to establish the principle of sexual equality in civil and political rights, state service and education, and to give married women the same rights as those held by single women. Had it been enacted it would have given women greater legal equality than almost anywhere in the world at the time. As it was, the bill never saw the light of day. The Duma's fate was already sealed by the time the bill was sent to Petrazhitskii on 7 July. Two days later, troops occupied the Tauride Palace and the Duma was dissolved.[34]

The dissolution was a great blow, shattering liberal hopes that Russia had entered a new phase in its political life which would lead to the development of a constitutional monarchy. Although new elections were fixed for February 1907, there was no reason to suppose that the Second Duma would not be dissolved as prematurely as its predecessor. Perhaps the greatest disillusion came with the Vyborg Manifesto, a summons by Kadets and Trudoviks for a national embargo on the government. The silence which greeted it was the most telling indication possible that the revolution was over.

For the women's movement the consequences were severe. At no time before 1917 did another opportunity present itself for such a full public debate on women's rights. On those few occasions in the following eleven years when bills relating to women's rights were introduced into the Duma, the measures proposed either failed to attract sufficient support or were lacking in substance. With the dissolution and the banning from parliamentary candidacy of all those who had signed the Vyborg Manifesto, the suffragists lost many of their most enthusiastic advocates in the Duma, including Petrazhitskii.

The dissolution was, however, only one more turn of the screw. The women's movement had already been suffering from a loss of morale and a confusion of purpose which the Duma campaign had helped to mask. It had not recovered from the schisms of the early part of the year and factional squabbling seemed destined to become a permanent feature of women's politics. The failure of any single group to unite the nation's feminists could only debilitate the movement, a fact which was illustrated all too vividly at a mass meeting held in St Petersburg on 5 May.

Intended as a demonstration of unity by all the women's organisations in the city, it began on a celebratory note with speeches from

Finnish and Polish feminists. But it soon descended into bickering. Ol'ga Vol'kenshtein, a radical in the Union of Equal Rights, challenged women to shake off their indifference to emancipation and seize the moment to fight for their rights. Pokrovskaia voiced her suspicions of the Kadets as champions of women, prompting Liudmilla fon Ruttsen (a Kadet and a leader of the women's union) to come to the party's defence. At this point a group of social–democrats began to prevail on the meeting, accusing the Kadets of collusion with the Octobrists and asserting that the social democrats alone were friends of emancipation. The meeting broke up in disarray, after rejecting a proposal to send greetings to sympathetic deputies in the Duma, and throwing out a resolution on women's rights.[35]

Uncertainty about the future was also evident later in May, at the third and last national congress of the Union of Equal Rights, the minutes of which make rather dismal reading. Of the seventeen sections which submitted reports to the congress on their activities since October, almost all recorded a dramatic decline in membership during 1906. The flurry of activity of late 1905, when most sections had put women's rights to one side to concentrate on support for the political strike, famine relief and so on, was brought to a halt in many areas by the onset of reaction. The sections found themselves increasingly the victims of police harassment: meetings were banned or broken up and premises were searched. Members were rarely arrested, however, and when they were it was usually for their involvement in the local branches of the Union of Unions or other professional unions, as, for instance, in Smolensk where a women's union member was arrested for her association with the Peasants' Union. However, members of the Kharkov section were arrested for trying to organise domestic servants.[36]

In some areas sections flourished for only a couple of months. The Pskov branch, for example, which had been set up in October 1905, immediately recruited fifty members and became heavily involved in all the local political campaigns. It organised a number of meetings on the women's movement and on political questions in general, and seemed set to prosper. In December, however, it fell under suspicion for publicly congratulating the female assassin of General Sakharov; two members were arrested and the moderates hastily left. By May its meetings were being abandoned because of poor attendance. In Smolensk, a membership of 154 in November had fallen to forty by May, Tver could claim only thirty-eight members and Novgorod, twenty-three. Since the provinces were suffering so severely from the effects of martial law and the punitive expeditions (particularly in the Baltic and the Caucasus) it is hard to avoid the conclusion that the union, which to the casual observer seemed as active as during the previous year, was having to depend heavily on its Moscow section for morale and inspiration.[37]

In these circumstances there was little room for self-congratulation at the union's congress. Despite the central bureau's optimistic report recording the year's achievements, criticism of the section's shortcomings grew stronger as the three-day meeting proceeded. Of particular concern was the union's involvement in famine relief, canteens for the unemployed and aid to the persecuted and the poor. Vol'kenshtein, always one of the most uncompromising of the union's leaders, pointed out that such preoccupations had little to do with the campaign for women's rights and only frittered away the union's strength. Though Chekhova replied that 'such were the facts of life', other speakers agreed with Vol'kenshtein, and one complained that the union lacked a 'characteristic physiognomy' to distinguish it from other organisations in the liberation movement. At times Chekhova was the union's lone defender.[38]

The union's continuing commitment to campaigns not specifically related to equal rights led a number of delegates to raise once more the vexed question of the union's political programme. A delegate from Kiev, whose section had suffered disproportionately from the effects of reaction and party strife, stated that a political platform was divisive, and argued that each section should be given the autonomy to choose its own form of activity. Her proposal met considerable support from other delegates, not only from the provinces but also on the central bureau. Both Mirovich and Ol'ga Klirikova advocated an abbreviation of the union's political programme, with a correspondingly greater emphasis on women's rights, and Gurevich proposed that the union drop its demand for a constituent assembly.

Shchepkina was utterly opposed to any attempt to depoliticise the union:

> A union for the attainment of political equality is political to the core. Its activity is intimately linked to the general liberation movement, therefore it must have a concise political programme.

Chekhova too felt the proposal to be unwarranted. 'Up to this time our constitution has not prevented anyone from joining the union. SDs joined us and even set up special groups, the SRs have been very useful to us . . .' Moreover 'a political programme preserves us from undesirable elements on the right and unites everybody of progressive views'. Nikolai Chekhov, Chekhova's husband and the sole man in the union to achieve a position of any prominence, agreed. He stressed that a political platform did not place any obligation on local sections, since they were guaranteed freedom of action by the union's constitution, and he pointed out that to remove the political content from the programme would turn the union into a mere replica of the recently-formed League of Equal Rights for Women.[39]

The congress voted finally to maintain the union's political stance, but the debate underlined the acute differences which existed between its members. At the end of the debate, Gurevich proposed an amendment to the constitution permitting the formation of separate groups within a section, wherever that section's work was threatened by political disagreements. The amendment was accepted.

One of the strongest criticisms made at the congress was of the union's still limited appeal. Its leaders had always hoped to attract the 'broad masses', and many sections had worked hard to create links with the working-class and peasant populations. Some had approached local trade union organisations, while others had attempted to unionise domestic servants or establish women's circles in the villages. Their efforts were fraught with difficulty, too frequently diverted by factional squabbles with social–democrats or the attentions of the police. But despite all their work, the union remained obstinately rooted in the urban intelligentsia, and none of the remedies proposed at the congress to 'democratise' it seemed likely to yield great dividends. Several delegates proposed that the Duma (at this point in the fourth week of its short existence) be used as a propaganda medium, and advocated greater co-operation with the Trudovik group as a means of gaining access to the villages.

All the delegates agreed that more lectures and more pamphlets were required. For both they looked naturally to the capitals. One member had already drawn up proposals for an agitation commission, whose aim would be to concentrate the diffused propaganda activities of the sections and give them a greater sense of purpose. But her scheme, which involved the establishment of four sub-committees, was itself criticised for being too cumbersome. The proposal was submitted to the sections for consideration.[40]

Some time was also devoted to the problem of widening the union's publishing activities. In March, the union had set up a publications commission to produce literature on the woman question, both for an educated public and for popular consumption. But publishing was expensive and the union was running short of money. Moreover, the production of separate pamphlets and leaflets on an irregular basis did not compensate for the comparative neglect of the women's movement by the national press. The congress voted to accept an offer of collaboration from *Severnaia Rossiia* (*Northern Russia*) a newspaper of the peasant masses' and to canvass the possibility of co-operation with other sympathetic publications.[41]

Chekhova went further, and proposed that the union start its own journal; this was accepted in principle by the delegates despite the pertinent remarks of an objector that such a venture would not only have to contend with too many differing political views, but would also be preaching to the converted. The central bureau was instructed to draw up plans during the autumn, but the resulting journal, *Soiuz zhenshchin* (*Union of Women*) did not see the light of day until over a year later, in June 1907.[42]

If the Union of Equal Rights, the most active of all the women's organisations to emerge before 1917, encountered such difficulty in maintaining its dynamism during 1906, one is not surprised to discover that its rivals were faring no better. Little was heard of the Women's Progressive Party throughout the year despite its advertised intentions. The split in the party's ranks so soon after its formation hindered its development as a strongly feminist, but politically moderate, alternative to the Union of Equal Rights, and for the whole of 1906 at least it was outshone by the union. But members ensured the party's survival by deciding to seek legal authorisation for its activities, a move which alienated it still further from radical feminists. Legalisation was a lengthy process: the draft constitution for its club, submitted to the Petersburg chief of police in May, was not confirmed until December, and the club's first meeting was not held until March 1907.[43]

The Mutual Philanthropic Society also failed to make full use of its potential. After its admittedly impressive petition to the Duma in May, the society fell back on smaller-scale enterprises resembling those of the previous year, but fewer in number. It sent declarations to zemstvo and municipal assemblies in support of women's suffrage in local elections and the employment of women in local government, it called on the universities (which had recently been granted autonomy) to admit women, on the Ministry of Education to introduce coeducation in schools, and on the Ministry of Justice to change the laws of inheritance. It established canteens for the wives and children of the unemployed, collected money for famine relief and, perhaps surprisingly, gave aid where needed to recently-amnestied political prisoners. At the very end of 1906 it set up a 'women's rights section', whose main preoccupation for the following two years was to reset in motion the plans for a national congress of women which had been abandoned in 1905.[44]

All in all, leaders of the women's movement had little cause for optimism at the end of 1906. The Duma had been dissolved, the government remained deaf to the demand for female equality and, even among the opposition, few men were prepared to risk their reputations by campaigning for women's rights. But worse was the realisation that women's groups themselves had neither the power to mobilise large numbers of their sex for more than isolated demonstrations of solidarity, nor the ability to submerge their disagreements in the common cause. Feminist rhetoric boasted that women, lacking the egoistic ambitions of men, were naturally peace-loving and co-operative. The evidence of the past two years suggested the opposite.

Despite the organisational weakness of the Russian women's movement during 1906 and 1907 there were a number of hopeful signs that peasant and working-class women, who had participated somewhat hesitantly in the strikes and demonstrations of 1905, had not been frightened off by the political reaction.

Obtaining a clear picture of peasant women's involvement in the political events of 1905–6 is still virtually impossible; no systematic investigation was done at the time, and little research undertaken since then. Because contemporary observers often failed to isolate women in their reports of peasant riots, any attempt to subject the data to reliable statistical analysis is doomed from the start. Nevertheless, on some occasions women did initiate their own riots (*bab'i bunty*) – arming themselves with pitchforks, rakes and brooms to attack recruiting officers during the Russo–Japanese war, or to demand land from the local landowner. Sometimes women and children would be used as an 'advance guard' in pillaging raids on local estates. Women were probably less fully implicated than men in the peasant uprisings which seized the countryside during 1905 and 1906, though in southern Russia where women worked in large numbers as agricultural labourers, they participated in, and sometimes initiated, strikes on the plantations.[45]

Social and economic changes were also affecting the position of women in the villages. In some regions, women whose husbands were in the army or working in towns had acquired the right to act as the representative of the household in village meetings, and in some places they even took over positions of responsibility. But generally, peasant women remained the subordinate sex and they were perceived as such by all the political parties, reformist and revolutionary, which attempted to make contact with the peasant class during the revolutionary upheaval.

Much of the non-violent activity among peasant women was co-ordinated by individual members of the Union of Equal Rights who prompted many, if not all, of the peasant letters and petitions to the First Duma. One woman in Tula province, who collected signatures from women in her village for the union's declaration to the Duma, wrote: 'The idea of equal rights pleased them, to say the least; for them it constituted their long-awaited daily bread.'[46] Another woman sent the Trudoviks a long letter describing her work in several villages in Voronezh province, comparing the terrible backwardness of one village with another whose men no longer beat their wives and whose women were not afraid to talk about equal rights. Her letter is a fascinating insight into peasant women's attitudes (at least, as reported by an outsider). The women wished to know all about the Duma, which was then in session, and expressed forthright opinions on all the subjects raised. These included, naturally, women's rights, but also such issues as direct elections and property qualifications for the franchise. After a prolonged conversation with one group of women, the author distributed radical pamphlets to all the literate women and men in the village.[47]

Propaganda among peasants took more organised forms as well. In the autumn of 1906 a number of commissions to distribute literature on the woman question were set up by branches of the Union of Equal Rights. The St Petersburg branch alone sent out 10,000 books and pamphlets, some of which were sold to bookshops and interested individuals, the remainder being distributed free. The response from the villages was highly encouraging: a flood of letters came from local inhabitants, including peasant women themselves. But a hint of the enormous obstacles which any campaign would have to overcome was revealed by one sympathetic priest who wrote that he had been subjected to personal threats from his male parishioners after preaching a sermon on women's equality.[48]

In the towns women factory workers had been drawn into politics through the strikes of 1905, but apart from the recruitment of women into the Gapon assembly at the very beginning of the year, little effort was made to organise them. In the spring of 1906, the short-lived Women's Political Club in St Petersburg proved sufficiently attractive to working women to enable it to open four clubs in the city, the liveliest of which was in a heavily industrialised area of the Vasilevskii island. During the Duma election campaign, working women in a number of factories demanded to be included in the ballot, and in a Moscow perfume factory were so persistent that they forced the abandonment of the elections. Although they participated in strikes, few women had yet joined unions, sometimes because of their own timidity but as often as not because of men's antipathy. On occasion, women who had been welcomed as union members in the heyday of the revolution were shunned after the reaction, when the employers launched an assault on the gains of 1905 and unemployment soared.[49]

However, the few social–democrats who were alive to the revolutionary potential of working women had already begun to consider separate women's unions and clubs, despite the strong opposition of most party workers to such 'feminist deviation'. Women were already attending working-class clubs in St Petersburg, but they were always a small minority and were not generally made welcome by the men. In the spring of 1907 a group of female social–democrats in the capital, of whom Kollontai is the best remembered, began to organise public meetings specifically for working women, at which party propaganda was smuggled into an otherwise innocuous programme. In the autumn, when the party had been forced underground after the dissolution of the Second Duma, Kollontai and her colleagues set up a 'working women's mutual aid society' in St Petersburg, which sought and obtained legal authorisation and quickly attracted two to three hundred members. It flourished for some months before succumbing to internal squabbles, though it remained in existence until 1913. But even at the height of its popularity it was not immune to criticism from orthodox social–democrats, especially working-class men in the party. Even Vera Zasulich, whom Kollontai hoped to recruit, disapproved of this separatist venture.[50]

Both 'bourgeois' and revolutionary feminists tried hard to organise the huge numbers of domestic servants who were to be found in the cities and larger towns, but success was elusive. Servants were hard to contact, had no strike power as individuals and often lived in daily dread of being thrown on to the streets. A number of partially successful endeavours by social–democrats and women's union sections to unionise servants in 1905 were brought to a halt by the police, and only sporadic attempts were made thereafter. Feminist propaganda reached some servants through other channels: one leading Moscow member of the Union of Equal Rights reported that her cook, also a member, had been organising meetings in the kitchen (sometimes overflowing on to the backstairs) and that twenty-two signatures for the union's declaration to the First Duma had been collected from servants. That both mistress and servant could join the Union of Equal Rights while maintaining the conventions which kept servants 'below stairs', vividly illustrates the underlying conflict between sexual and class solidarity which the union was never able to resolve.[51]

Such signs that the mass of women were at last becoming interested in altering the course of their own lives could not but be encouraging to the feminists. The movement among working-class women in particular continued to grow after 1907, eventually surpassing the middle-class women's movement in the breadth of its activities. But its direction fell increasingly into the hands of the revolutionary parties. It was destined to become *the* women's movement of the Bolshevik Revolution, leaving the 'bourgeois' groups to disappear into emigration or prison, or simply into irrelevance. In 1906 and 1907 only the faintest glimmerings of this development were yet to be seen. At this point the gulf in aspirations and interests between the classes, though axiomatic to the social–democrats, was not evident to all, and organisations such as the Union of Equal Rights could still preach the 'all-class' nature of the women's campaign without appearing ridiculous.

Early in 1907, the Union of Equal Rights set out to mobilise these masses in a petition to the Second State Duma, whose elections were held in February. The text, recalling the declaration to the First Duma but less uncompromising in tone, reminded the deputies that the women of Russia looked to them for realisation of 'the great principles of freedom, justice and social equality', including women's suffrage. Several thousand petition forms were sent out all over the country and signatures collected in factories and workshops, remote villages and urban tenements. After three months of intensive campaigning, 19,984 women and men had signed or made their mark. The forms were triumphantly sent off to the Trudoviks with the request that the petition be presented during a debate on local self-government. But by then the Duma was in the throes of its last crisis and was dissolved on 3 June, bringing the union's efforts to naught.[52]

The petition was only one of several campaigns which had been designed to impress on the Duma the importance of women's rights. The Mutual Philanthropic Society, in collaboration with the tiny League of Equal Rights and eighteen other societies, collected over 7,000 signatures for a separate petition to the president of the Duma, while the Union of Equal Rights sent deputations to all those fractions whose programmes supported women's equality, urging them to fulfil their promises.[53] However, the circumstances in which the Second Duma found itself were very different from those of the previous year. The increased strength of extreme parties of both the right and the left and the consequent reduction of Kadet influence, introduced a state of tension and confrontation into its earliest debates which was most unfavourable to any discussion of justice and equality. In contrast to the eloquent speeches of its predecessor, the Second Duma found no time to debate women's rights, except for a brief dispute over the employment of women in the Duma chancellery. Even on this side issue the Kadets once again let down the feminists by refusing to vote for any change in the existing rules to give women wider opportunities in the Duma's own offices. As for the principal question of women's suffrage, it was barely raised. The Kadets honoured their programme by extending the vote to 'Russian citizens of both sexes' in a suffrage bill introduced on 17 April, but the Duma was dissolved before the opportunity was found to debate it.[54]

The women's movement had not lived up to its promise. In 1905, and even after the reaction had begun in early 1906, it seemed that Russian women might achieve what their Finnish neighbours, and fellow subjects of the tsar, were in the process of winning: a national assembly elected on the basis of universal suffrage, without distinction of sex. The Russians were disappointed first by the October Manifesto, then by the failure of the First Duma. Feminists had been fully aware that timing was critical: they were correct in their judgment that if women were not given equal rights in the first flush of parliamentary enthusiasm, they would remain disfranchised when enthusiasm gave way to expediency.

They could not, however, have anticipated the extent of the reaction. If they saw the mass petition to the Second Duma as a sign of renewed vigour in the equal rights movement, they were quickly disabused. Stolypin's coup against the Duma removed the last remaining hopes of radical change through constitutional channels until the overthrow of the tsar in February 1917. Instead, political activists in Russia were faced with the unenviable choice of pursuing their goals in defiance of the law or compromising their principles in order to continue working at all. Most feminists took the latter course, extracting from the regime such small concessions as were possible and resigning themselves to the 'grey humdrum days' which lay ahead.[55]

Notes

1 Regulations for elections to the Bulygin Duma excluded women except as proxy voters. The decree of 11 December 1905 made no change.
2 N. Mirovich, 'S″ezdy zemskikh i gorodskikh deiatelei' p. 171.
3 Mirovich, *Iz istorii* p. 3.
4 *Zhenskii vestnik* no. 1 (1906) p. 1.
5 Cited in N. Mirovich, 'Zhenskii vopros v soiuze 17 oktiabria' *Russkaia mysl'* no. 4 (1906) pt. 2 pp. 206–7.
6 Tyrkova-Williams, *Na putiakh* passim. For her earlier years see Tyrkova-Williams, *To, chego bol'she ne budet* (Paris: 1954).
7 Tyrkova-Williams, *Na putiakh* pp. 241–2; *Zhenskii vestnik* no. 5 (1906) p. 135. Akchurin (Iusuf Akchura) was co-founder of the moderate All-Russian Union of Muslims which allied with the Kadets in 1906.
8 *Sovremennik* no. 8 (1906).
9 *Zhenskii vestnik* no. 3 (1906) p. 93.
10 *Otchet tsentral'nago komiteta Konstitutsionno-Demokraticheskoi Partii* (Spb: 1907) p. 5; Tyrkova-Williams, *Na putiakh* pp. 292–3. Miliukov was barred from Duma candidacy as editor of two newspapers which fell foul of the law in 1905. Thomas Riha, *A Russian European. Paul Miliukov in Russian Politics* (Notre-Dame–London: 1969) p. 101.
11 V. Ivanovich (ed.) *Rossiiskiia partii, soiuzy i ligi* (Spb: 1906) pp. 22–3, 27, 106–7.
12 Speech at the general meeting of the party on 16 February 1906. *Zhenskii vestnik* no. 3 (1906) pp. 65–8.
13 *PZhK na 1907g.* pp. 370–71; *Zhenskii vestnik* no. 3 (1906) pp. 92–3; A.N. Shabanova, *Ocherk zhenskago dvizheniia v Rossii* (Spb: 1912) p. 16.
14 *Ravnopravie zhenshchin* p. 35; *Vserossiiskii soiuz ravnopravnosti zhenshchin*.
15 *Ravnopravie zhenshchin* pp. 13, 25, 26.
16 The Petersburg SRZh section had about 300 members at the end of 1905. *Vserossiiskii soiuz ravnopravnosti zhenshchin*. For the Women's Political Club see *PZhK na 1907g.* p. 373; *Ravnopravie zhenshchin* pp. 26, 52; Kollontai, 'Avtobiograficheskii ocherk' p. 271.
17 'Towards a History of the Working Women's Movement in Russia' in Alix

Holt (ed. and trans.) *Alexandra Kollontai. Selected Writings* (London: 1977) p. 50.

18 *Gosudarstvennaia Duma: stenograficheskie otchety 1906g. sessiia pervaia* (hereafter cited as *Gos. Duma I*) 2 May 1906, pp. 74, 75.

19 *Ravnopravie zhenshchin* p. 12; *PZhK na 1907g.* p. 359.

20 *Gos. Duma I* 2 May 1906, p. 84.

21 *Ibid.* 3 May 1906, pp. 120, 140.

22 *Ibid.* 15 May 1906, pp. 378–9. This last clause enraged members of the Union of Equal Rights. A motion to send greetings to the Duma was rejected at the union's May congress after delegates complained that the rider reduced the proposed equalisation to nothing. *Ravnopravie zhenshchin* p. 41.

23 *Gos. Duma I* 15 May 1906, pp. 378–9.

24 *Ibid.* 5 June 1906, pp. 1006–9.

25 *Ibid.* 6 June 1906, p. 1050; 8 June 1906, pp. 1097–8.

26 *Ibid.* 6 June 1906, pp. 1065–6.

27 The emancipation of women was part of a general awakening in Muslim society, though Muslim nationalists like Akchurin often remained hostile. For details of a tatar journal aimed specifically at women and sympathetic to their emancipation, see Alexandre Bennigsen, Chantal Lemercier-Quelquejay, *La Presse et le Mouvement National chez les Musulmans de Russie avant 1920* (Paris–The Hague: 1964) pp. 98–9.

28 L.I. Petrazhitskii, *O pol'ze politicheskikh prav zhenshchin* (Spb: 1907). Also in *Gos. Duma I* 6 June 1906, pp. 1058–62; Shabanova, *Ocherk* pp. 16–17; *PZhK na 1907 g.* p. 370.

29 *Gos. Duma I* 6 June 1906, pp. 1061–2.

30 *Ibid.* 12 June 1906 p. 1213.

31 Tyrkova-Williams, *Na putiakh* p. 287; Mirovich, *Iz istorii* p. 55; *Soiuz zhenshchin* no. 1 (1907) p. 6; *Ravnopravie zhenshchin* pp. 12, 25. A typed copy of one petition is in the London Library collection.

32 They came from Simbirsk, Samara, Tver, Iaroslav and Voronezh provinces. *PZhK na 1907 g.* pp. 363–4; Mirovich, *Iz istorii* pp. 47–9; *Ravnopravie zhenshchin* p. 53; F. Kalinychev (ed.) *Gosudarstvennaia Duma v Rossii v dokumentakh i materialakh* (M: 1957) pp. 180–81.

33 *Ravnopravie zhenshchin* pp. 37, 51.

34 The text of the bill and an account of the commission's work are in *PZhK na 1907 g.* pp. 374–421. See also *Soiuz zhenshchin* no. 1 (1907) pp. 3–5; *Ravnopravie zhenshchin* pp. 37, 51, 56.

35 *Zhenskii vestnik* no. 5 (1906) pp. 153–5.

36 *Ravnopravie zhenshchin* pp. 20, 23–4.

37 *Ibid.* pp. 14–16, 20, 27–28. It is unlikely that its membership was as high as the 8,000 estimated by the central bureau. This figure probably applies to late 1905.

38 *Ibid.* pp. 16–17.

39 *Ibid.* pp. 33–34, 39.

40 *Ibid.* pp. 38, 45–47.

41 *Severnaia Rossiia* was closed down in June. Another attempted collaboration was with a weekly journal aimed at a 'popular' readership, *Mir truda* (*World of Labour*), but the journal did not appear after a trial run. L.N. Beliaeva *et al.* (eds.) *Bibliografiia periodicheskikh izdanii Rossii 1901–16* (Leningrad: 1961) vol. ii, p. 328; vol. iii, p. 171.

42 *Ravnopravie zhenshchin* pp. 39–40.
43 *Zhenskii vestnik* no. 1 (1907) p. 30; no. 4 (1907) p. 123.
44 *PZhK na 1907 g.* pp. 370–71; Shabanova *Ocherk* p. 19.
45 Maureen Perrie, 'The Russian Peasant Movement of 1905–1907' *Past and Present* no. 57 (November 1972) pp. 144–5; Knight, *The Participation of Women in the Revolutionary Movement* pp. 185–90.
46 *Soiuz zhenshchin* no. 1 (1907) p. 10.
47 *Sbornik 'Izvestii krest'ianskikh deputatov' i 'Trudovoi Rossii'* (M: 1906) pp. 151–60.
48 *Soiuz zhenshchin* no. 4 (1907) p. 11.
49 *Ibid.* no. 1 (1907) p. 6; *Zhenskii vestnik* no. 4 (1906) p. 123; Aleksandra Kollontai, *Sotsial'nyia osnovy zhenskago voprosa* (Spb: 1909) p. 24; *Trudy vserossiiskago zhenskago s"ezda* pp. 314–17.
50 Kollontai, 'Avtobiograficheskii ocherk' pp. 272–5; S.N. Serditova *Bol'sheviki v bor'be za zhenskie proletarskie massy 1903 g.-fevral' 1917 g.* (M: 1959) pp. 59–60; Barbara Clements, *Bolshevik Feminist. The Life of Aleksandra Kollontai* (Bloomington, Indiana: 1979) p. 277.
51 *Ravnopravie zhenshchin* pp. 10, 23–5; Serditova, *Bol'sheviki v bor'be* pp. 56–7. One meeting of Petersburg servants in 1907 attracted 1,500 women. *Soiuz zhenshchin* no. 1 (1907), p. 19.
52 *Ibid.* pp. 5–7.
53 *Ibid.* pp. 8–9, 18–19; Shabanova, *Ocherk* p. 18.
54 *Gos. Duma II* vol. ii, 2 May 1907, p. 10; N.I. Astrov *et al.* (eds.) *Zakonodatel'nye proekty i predlozheniia Partii Narodnoi Svobody 1905–1907 gg.* (Spb: 1907) pp. 79–113.
55 N. Mirovich, *Vserossiikii zhenskii s"ezd* (M: 1909) p. 4.

4 The First All-Russian Congress of Women*

1908 found the women's movement in sombre mood:

> The dissolution of the Second Duma, the arrests and victimisation of deputies, the electoral law of 3 June, depriving a significant part of the population of the right to vote; the long list of tormenting repressions which have been dragged in its train – all this has told heavily on the energies of society.[1]

The prospects for social reform of any sort were bleak: the new electoral law favoured the conservative elements in society and the Third Duma was dominated by the Octobrists and the parties of the right, 'condemned to play a pitiful role as the ghosts of people's representatives.' Unless the government itself wished to sponsor legislation affecting women's rights, nothing could be expected from the Duma, as Pokrovskaia lamented:

> Women's optimistic expectations of equal rights which were aroused by the First State Duma had begun to fade by the time the second appeared. The Third Duma has totally destroyed them.[2]

Nor did women themselves seem likely to breathe new life into the campaign. Pokrovskaia's own Women's Progressive Party proved to be a very puny infant. Planned as a national women's party, it never became established outside St Petersburg and even in the capital existed only as a club. Attempts to open party branches in the provinces came to nothing. Her journal, *Zhenskii vestnik*, also continued to suffer from poor circulation, although she kept it alive (with some misgivings) until the Revolution.[3] The Union of Equal Rights, meanwhile, was in the final stages of disintegration. Its last congress, in May 1906, had already demonstrated the union's vulnerability in the face of political reaction, and the succeeding eighteen months had contributed still further to its decline. Of all the women's organisations it was the most susceptible to attack, with its radical connections and its lack of legal status. Like the liberation movement generally, the union's provincial branches suffered most severely, many being forced into liquidation months before the union finally ceased to function. The Taganrog

* A substantial portion of this chapter has been published as an article 'Russian Feminists and the First All-Russian Congress of Women', *Russian History* vol. iii, pt.2, (1976) pp. 123–49.

section was representative of many: it had apparently functioned without hindrance until its members protested against the imposition of 'enforced protection' in the town. From that moment, the group's meetings were banned and, after martial law was declared, it was closed down altogether.[4]

The information available is too limited to permit more than a general impression of the union's vicissitudes. But the union's journal, *Soiuz zhenshchin*, suggested at the end of 1908 that women's organisations (and therefore, one assumes, the union) had proved less robust in the provincial towns of Great Russia than in the west and south-west, where nationalism was a unifying force. In Kiev, for example, women's societies led an active, if unco-ordinated, existence, and in Vilna both Lithuanian and Polish societies continued to operate side by side. Orel, by contrast, had not one functioning women's group.

The poor response from provincial women to the initiatives of feminists in the capitals was the cause of some acrimonious exchanges in *Zhenskii vestnik*. In response to frequent assertions by Pokrovskaia and others that the provinces were showing a lamentable lack of drive, some correspondents replied that women in St Petersburg and Moscow possessed incalculable advantages, such as a lively press and a higher cultural level generally. They accused the 'metropolitans' of taking a condescending view of their provincial sisters, who had to bear the brunt of Russia's repressive regime from which the capitals were insulated.[5]

The weaknesses of the Union of Equal Rights had already become evident by the spring of 1907, when only thirty representatives attended a national conference in Moscow. Although they reported a 'lively interest' in the issue of women's emancipation (much of it stimulated by literature from the union) many delegates saw little hope for the union's future unless it adopted a more moderate constitution and applied for legal status. This proposal was quite unacceptable to the radicals and a decision was postponed to the autumn, when a second conference was again unable to reach agreement. The question was then put to the regional sections. Finally, in April 1908, at what was probably the union's last meeting, the proposal was rejected.[6]

But the picture is not entirely one of gloom. Despite the annihilation of the Union of Equal Rights and the decline generally in feminist activity, conditions had not prevented the survival of some groups and even the creation of others, for example in Rostov-on-Don. In Moscow, two 'women's clubs' were opened during the course of 1907, and two more in St Petersburg the following year. Although all had to accommodate themselves to the numerous petty restrictions governing social organisations in Russia at the time, it became clear that women's groups did not automatically come under suspicion in the way that they had ten or twenty years earlier, so long as they did not attack the government on sensitive issues or attract political extremists to their membership.[7]

It was to such groups throughout Russia that the Mutual Philanthropic Society hoped to appeal when it resurrected plans for the national women's congress, which had been jettisoned in 1905. The programme and regulations of that congress had been hedged in with restrictions. Only philanthropy and education were to be discussed, 'questions relating to politics, religion and nationality' being specifically ruled out.[8] As for attendance, only members of the Mutual Philanthropic Society and the governing bodies of other cultural and charitable organisations of women were to be eligible. In the conditions prevailing in 1904 (when the congress was approved) the RZhVBO counted it something of a triumph to have received permission at all, but others were less pleased. Pokrovskaia felt that a women's congress which considered social issues like children's education, the campaign against alcoholism or the movement for world peace without also tackling the question of equal rights, was fighting with tied hands: 'it's like tilting at windmills.' And Mirovich argued that, at the very least, the RZhVBO should attempt to ease the restrictions on admission, to admit men and those women unable to afford the enrolment fee.[9]

By the time the congress was due to meet, in June 1905, women's organisations had become fully involved in the struggle against autocracy, and even an apolitical body like the Mutual Philanthropic Society was suspect. At the last minute the St Petersburg governor-general, Trepov, demanded that all speeches be submitted in advance for censorship. The organisers replied that they had already received over one hundred speeches from delegates and declined to 'pass through a police filter of trustworthiness'. Instead, they cancelled the congress until a more favourable moment presented itself.[10]

Widespread interest in a national congress did not revive until the end of 1907. Opportunities for other forms of activity were now severely circumscribed; the State Duma offered little scope for propaganda and women's groups in Russia had begun to recognise that unless a concerted effort was made to achieve some sort of organisational unity, all their endeavours of the past three years would be dissipated.

This time, proposals for a national congress came from more than one quarter. The suffrage section of the Mutual Philanthropic Society had already been considering the idea for a number of months, when a conference of the Union of Equal Rights decided to call an All-Russian Congress on the Woman Question at Christmas or the New Year. Permission for the congress would be applied for through a legally-chartered women's organisation in Moscow, and a commission of union members from St Petersburg and Moscow was appointed to work out a programme. The congress was to appeal to a wide audience, male and female, and a special effort was to be made to attract peasant and working-class women. Every aspect of the 'woman question' would be discussed, including political and civil rights at home and abroad.[11]

No more was heard of this project, but only three weeks later the suffrage section of the RZhVBO held a meeting in St Petersburg to discuss proposals for a congress. Present at this meeting were at least three leading members of the Union of Equal Rights, including its secretary, Chekhova. Although nothing is known of the negotiations between the union and the Mutual Philanthropic Society in the preceding weeks, one may surmise that a good number of union members accepted the decision to collaborate, with reluctance, for fear that the RZhVBO would too readily submit to restraints imposed on it by the authorities. But the members of the dying union were in no position to oppose the collaboration, and the Mutual Philanthropic Society quickly assumed responsibility for the proposed venture.[12]

In the event, the prestige and persistence of the society were much needed. Although the organisers had no difficulty in obtaining preliminary authorisation for the congress (which was planned for June 1908), getting the programme approved was more troublesome. Submitted to the Ministry of the Interior early in 1908, it was passed after a delay of several months and with a number of amendments, none of which was acceptable to the organisers.

The content of the programme had already been the subject of some debate in the RZhVBO. While some members felt that it should follow the lines of the 1905 project and concentrate on ethical and cultural questions, the majority found this far too narrow and insisted on the inclusion of civil and political rights. The draft programme which was sent to the ministry was thus considerably more radical than the one authorised three years earlier, and had clearly been influenced by the scheme proposed by the Union of Equal Rights in October.[13] But the ministry's amendments excised its most controversial paragraph, 'the struggle for political and civil rights at home and abroad', along with the draft constitution for a Russian National Council of Women. Both were later reinstated, but in substantially altered form and only after the persistent entreaties of the organisers.

The ministry also put restrictions on attendance, limiting it to representatives of women's associations whose aims accorded with those of the programme and to individuals specifically invited. It stipulated that no men were to attend, and no foreigners of either sex. The Organising Commission had unanimously agreed that men should be admitted on equal terms with women and protested against their exclusion. Further petitioning finally yielded the concession that men could be invited as speakers, without voting rights. The prohibition on foreigners remained, though Russians resident abroad were admitted.[14]

Even without the ministry's interference, however, attendance was proving to be a problem. The initial response to the congress from women's societies throughout the country was poor: five weeks before the congress was due to open only forty speeches had been received and few people had bothered to register. At the end of April the organisers decided to cut their losses and postpone the congress until December, hoping that in the interim they could muster a respectable audience. But the continued slow registration prompted Shabanova to complain in October that Russian women were displaying a lamentable indifference to an occasion of such significance to themselves and society, and as late as November feared that no more than 200 would be present. Finally, with premises booked for an audience of two hundred, there came a sudden rush to register, which threw the promoters into a state of panic. When the congress opened on 10 December, enrolment stood at 1,053.[15]

Of this number, almost three-quarters came from the capital itself, about fifty from Moscow and a few from abroad. The rest came from all four corners of the Empire, but especially from the south and west, confirming the impression that activity in central Russia had been badly hit by the reaction. Even so, the vast majority were Russians, though national minorities were well enough represented for xenophobic observers to make adverse comment.[16] National animosities were almost absent from the proceedings themselves, and the congress was quick to react to hints of racial prejudice. After a stirring speech on the hardships faced by Jewish women, one speaker rashly complained that the Jews lived very well in her home town (Ekaterinoslav) and were overcrowding the schools. She was verbally assaulted from all sides for her unworthy sentiments, and a resolution was passed demanding the complete removal of legal restrictions on the Jews, 'the most oppressed nationality in Russia'.[17]

In social composition, the congress was overwhelmingly middle class. Among the organisers were a good number of well-born ladies, 'typical St Petersburg *dames-patronesses*' (in the hostile epithet of one commentator), but the mass of members were of lower social status, many engaged in the professions or in public and private institutions, or married to men in such occupations. A questionnaire, completed by about 250 of the delegates, found that over half earned their own living, over half had a secondary education, and a third had graduated from women's higher courses.[18] Other social classes were poorly represented. The organisers had not deliberately excluded them and had, indeed, issued appeals for all women to unite in the common cause, but it was not to be expected that a formal occasion, arranged by a conventional philanthropic society with all the pomp and circumstance appropriate to the City Duma (and taking place in working hours), would make a dramatic impact on women in factory and village. Besides, the only women eligible to seek attendance were those already in clubs and unions, and such women formed a minute percentage of Russia's female population. Even students were debarred.

There was, however, a small contingent of working women, almost all from St Petersburg, who made an impression on the proceedings quite disproportionate to their numbers. There were no more than thirty-five, but they had been carefully prepared by a band of radical women from the intelligentsia (mainly social–democrats) as the Workers' Group, committed to opposing the feminist slogans of the congress, and stressing class war as the dynamic of capitalist society. They were conspicuous, from the very opening of the proceedings, by their physical appearance: under-nourished and cheaply clothed, they presented a stark contrast to the well-covered women of the upper ranks. They accentuated their distinctiveness by keeping together in one corner of the hall, well away from the congress promoters.[19]

However, it would be a mistake to see the Workers' Group as united by a common goal. In fact, the composition of the group reflected all the conflicting tendencies in the Russian labour movement, above all the intensifying feud between Bolsheviks and Mensheviks. Even before the congress opened, the principle of participating in a bourgeois event was hotly disputed, and during the congress the group often failed to establish an agreed line. The Bolshevik party organisation was particularly hostile, at first refusing to recognise the Union Bureau which had been set up to co-ordinate the group, then belatedly trying to take it over. The feuding within the group mostly took place behind closed doors, but splits were revealed from time to time, and the prevailing disunity made the group's contribution to the congress less effective than it might otherwise have been.[20]

The Worker's Group was composed almost entirely of women working in factories and workshops, and active in trade unions. Domestic servants were largely absent from the congress. The radicals made the most of this fact. Middle- and upper-class women's dependence on the inferior status of their servants was a valuable weapon with which to expose 'bourgeois' slogans of equal rights as a hypocritical sham.[21]

As for peasant women, only one (from Lithuania) mustered the necessary self-confidence and money to make the journey. This was a serious deficiency, in view of the sheer size of the peasant class in Russia and the critical situation facing Russian agriculture. Moreover, peasant women suffered particularly badly, both in relation to society and in relation to peasant men: their oppressed status is, of course, one reason why they failed to appear at the congress. But it is not a complete explanation. After all, women from the peasantry had been mobilised, only two or three years before by the Union of Equal Rights, to send letters and petitions and even to attend union conferences; news of the 1908 congress itself reached the villages. Trudovik members of the Duma sympathetic to the women's movement reported that by no means all were sunk in inertia and deaf to the message of the congress.[22] Their absence was seized upon as evidence of the organisers' unwillingness to grapple with the fundamental problems of society, an accusation which is partially justified.

The members of the Mutual Philanthropic Society had never addressed themselves to the 'dark masses', or given serious consideration to the 'peasant question'. Their sympathies extended to peasant women as individual victims of hunger, disease and men's sexuality and violence. But they were defeated in advance by the difficulties involved in finding representatives from the village to speak for their estate. Whereas working women's clubs and industrial unions provided a ready-made source of working-class delegates, peasant women could only have been invited individually, and travelling expenses paid. In its earlier days, the Union of Equal Rights might well have made these arrangements, but in its moribund condition it had neither the resources nor the impetus to do so. Moreover, official blessing for the congress was conditional on the organisers' good behaviour. As events were to show, the authorities interpreted the programme strictly; discussion of fundamental problems (and notably the question of agriculture) was stopped more than once as being 'out of order'.

Besides the delegates, two outside elements attended this first 'women's parliament'; the press and the police. The congress that Shabanova had earlier feared would be such a failure attracted the correspondents of most newspapers in the capital and provinces, and coverage was generous. Foreigners, barred as delegates, were admitted as reporters, and came from at least eight countries, including Britain.[23] The representatives of the city's police force were less welcome. They kept a very close eye, naturally, on the Workers' Group. After a noisy session on 12 December, the hall was dramatically evacuated, and all tickets checked in the hope of finding interlopers, while towards the end of the congress Aleksandra Kollontai (a leader of the group) was obliged to disappear abroad to avoid arrest.[24] The presence of the police was obviously intended to intimidate, and although it failed to prevent a remarkably free (and passionate) exchange of opinions, the praesidium was on tenterhooks during many of the sessions, for fear that the congress would be prematurely closed.

* * *

On the evening of 10 December, in the Aleksandrovskii Hall of the City Duma, Shabanova opened the congress with the customary rituals. There was a celebratory air about the proceedings, which was given verbal expression in Filosofova's welcoming speech. This, she said, was one of the happiest days of her life.

> Fate was kind to me in my youth and gave me the joy of witnessing the liberation of the serfs. Now, in my declining years I am witnessing the liberation of women.

She recalled the 'glorious years of the 1860s', and paid tribute to her companions of those times, who had fought so hard for the right of women to be educated and to work. She trusted that in the not too distant future, women would have taken their place not only in this St Petersburg Duma, but in the State Duma itself, alongside their male comrades.[25]

Shabanova then laid out the aims of the congress: it was to inform, it was to awaken women to consciousness of their inferior status, and it was to promote united action. She had no illusions about the possibility of creating one united women's party. Instead, she advised, the women's movement should resemble the human body: just as the separate functions of a body contributed to the continuation of one life, so should the separate activities of women serve one common aim. She refuted those who criticised the movement for isolating one sex from the other. This was a temporary necessity. Without organisation, no victory could be achieved. If the congress produced any response to the call for unity, it would have served its purpose.[26]

The first response, however, was a forewarning of that disunity which, in the less polite atmosphere of the regular sessions, was to accompany every major debate. V.I. Volkova, appearing last on behalf of the Workers' Group, dispelled the euphoria generated by preceding speakers, and claimed that it was the achievement of working women to have made the congress possible in the 'lifeless existence of contemporary Russia'. Working women, she warned, were there to represent their own class, and would not be separated from the organised proletariat. With these words, the first session came to a close, the lines already drawn up for the contest.[27]

The programme, as finally approved by the Ministry of the Interior, comprised four main sections: women's role in philanthropy and 'cultural activity' (*prosvetitel'naia deiatel'nost'*); women in the economy, family and society; the political and civil position of women in Russia and abroad; and women's education. As one would expect, the adversaries converged on the two central sections dealing with economic and political problems. The other sections were somewhat quieter. The first, relating principally to voluntary work – the Society for the Protection of Women, children's summer colonies, work in prisons, the

Salvation Army, and many similar – attracted small audiences and little controversy, as its content was unlikely to draw the interest of radicals. The fourth section, devoted to education, was livelier. The problem of education was not only integral to the women's movement. It was also one of the most contentious issues in the conflict between the government and its opponents (and within the government itself), and nowhere more so than in the sphere of higher education. The extremely delicate state of relations between the autocracy and the universities helps to explain why the admission of women remained such a prickly topic, even after it was accepted in other countries.

At the time of the congress, women aspiring to university education still faced numerous obstacles. In the spring of 1908 the new and reactionary Minister of Education, Shvarts, had banned women as 'auditors' in the universities, less than two years after they had first been admitted. Although attendance at the university had given women no qualifications, they were able to study subjects not provided in the women's higher courses, while some university administrations had allowed them to take examinations. The issue of women auditors was thus a highly sensitive one at the congress and a critical speech on the subject was soon brought to a halt by the steward.[28] The higher courses themselves were not secure against attack. Not until 1910 (and then as a result of concerted efforts) were they recognised as institutions of higher education, and only the following year were women permitted to take the state examinations. But despite their perennial difficulties and the threat of dissolution in times of student upheaval, the higher courses had already achieved an unofficial status as women's universities and provided an education virtually identical to that received by men. The congress, therefore, had as much reason to celebrate women's achievements as to deplore their reverses.[29]

The fourth section did not wholly neglect those millions of illiterate women for whom higher education was irrelevant, and several speeches were devoted to the problem. But the most popular items on the section's agenda related not to the educational needs of adults, but to the upbringing of children, the generation of the future. The goals of education were seen not as examination qualifications or personal advancement, but as the encouragement of a spirit of co-operation in children. The section was particularly interested in current experiments in education for the very young, such as Froebel kindergartens. Nursery schools (and crèches) had an immediate practical value as well, especially for working-class women unable to look after their children, or pay others to do so. But such matter-of-fact considerations were only part of their attraction. It was hoped that early schooling, on progressive principles, would contribute to a healthier moral climate.[30]

Similarly, hopes were pinned on coeducation. This was considered sufficiently important to merit a whole session's debate. Bringing children up together, it was argued, would remove the strain and artificiality which normally accompanied communication between the two sexes in adolescence. In particular, it would teach boys to respect members of the opposite sex as equals. One of the most passionate defenders of the theory, Nikolai Chekhov, maintained that society needed to rear one generation, not two opposing sexes, and that scientific knowledge did not support separate education. Another speaker added, in support, that in commercial schools (run by the Ministry of Finance) where coeducation existed, 'flirting is completely absent'.[31] Sex education, too, was greatly favoured. Its proponents believed that it would remove secrecy and guilt amongst adolescents and combat the corrupting influences prevalent in society.

* * *

The principal issues to incite discord were all matters of pressing concern: the peasant crisis, women in industry, problems of marriage, maternity and morals, women's suffrage, and the 'organisational tasks' of the women's movement.

Discussion of the peasant question was hindered by the authorities' sensitivity to criticism on this issue, and by the absence of a peasant 'lobby'. The latter was the more significant. Out of a total of 160 speeches, no more than half a dozen pertained to peasant women (compared with at least twelve on working-class women and matters relating to industry). Of these six, only two attempted to draw a picture of Russian women's life in the fields, and one of these was propaganda for the government's agrarian reform and the break-up of the traditional peasant commune. A third speaker described the life of Ukrainian peasant women, another spoke of Cossack women on the Don. This was virtually all the delegates learnt of the vast population that lived by cultivation of the soil. Even the debates lacked a certain passion, although controversy was not absent. The speaker from the Ukraine was severely criticised for appearing to suggest that peasant women could not benefit from political rights when their cultural level was so low, while Kuskova attacked the principle behind the agrarian reform, and had her first brush with the police officer on duty for disparaging the financial system of the state.[32]

The first sparks flew when one E.N. Polovtseva moved a resolution on the need for state aid to craft industries, in order to combat 'one of the greatest evils in our countryside', namely the 'idleness of the female population'. Delegates, who had had the unceasing toil of peasant women described to them only minutes earlier, found this statement hard to swallow. The Workers' Group upbraided Polovtseva for her bourgeois condescension, and moved their own resolution deploring the exploitation endemic in craft work, which they described as a 'relic' of an outmoded economic system. They also demanded legislative protection for all those working in this sphere. The resolution was carried by an overwhelming majority.[33]

For all its lowly status on the agenda, it was the peasant issue which was instrumental in the premature closing of the second section, on the last day of the section's deliberations. The incident demonstrated just how little leeway the authorities were prepared to grant on this issue. A general debate on the agrarian question had not been permitted and resolutions were postponed. Finally Kuskova attempted to present a compromise resolution, bridging the gap between the Workers' Group (which could not agree on its own version) and the feminists:

> Only the radical solution of the agrarian question, the raising of the cultural level of the population and the intensification of agriculture, which is at present under-productive, can emancipate the peasantry, including the peasant-woman . . .

She got no further. The police steward intervened and she stepped down, protesting that the absence of a resolution was preferable to an emasculated one. It was not Kuskova however, but the propagandist of the government's agrarian reform who caused the session to be closed. She, too, attempted to read a resolution, but was interrupted almost immediately and warned that the agrarian question was not on the agenda. After continuing to a statement of 'general rights', she was stopped again and the session was declared closed. The incident naturally produced great consternation, and reinforced the ever-present fear that the congress would be prohibited from concluding its business.[34]

The authorities were clearly far less tolerant of free debate on the peasant question than they were of debate on industrial issues. The social–democrats of the Workers' Group spoke almost unhindered about the iniquities of contemporary capitalism and the need for working-class organisation. The group had come fully armed to destroy the fond illusion that working women were the 'younger sisters' of the feminists, and in need of their protection. They were determined to demonstrate the impossibility of co-operation across class barriers. Their weapons were twofold: an exposure of the life of factory women, and an analysis (though generally crude) of the theoretical foundations of the exploitation that they endured at the hands of the very women who claimed to desire their liberation. Delegates heard about unsafe machinery, dangerous chemicals, excessively long working days, low pay and the almost total absence of insurance for sickness, unemployment or maternity.

The question of pay was topical. It had become apparent that since 1905 employers had been replacing male workers with female in many industries, thus annulling the gains made during the revolutionary year. Women were paid very much lower wages (sometimes only half the men's rate) and were poorly unionised, partly because of apathy and police persecution, but also partly because of the hostility of the male workers whom they were undercutting. In a period of high unemployment, there was no provision for loss of work. Several speakers painted a grim picture of the hazards facing pregnant women. Maternity insurance and leave were almost unknown, and consequently women sometimes gave birth on the factory floor. Infant mortality was appallingly high, allegedly reaching 64 per cent in the first year of life. In workshops, women did not enjoy even the minimal protection granted to factory workers, and there was no inspection.[35]

Faced with such information, no one could disagree that the plight of working women was unenviable; there was a remarkable unanimity on the need to protect female labour, through restrictions on working hours, the safeguarding of machinery, the prohibition of women's work in certain industries, medical facilities and factory inspection. State insurance was regarded as essential, along with special provisions for pregnancy and maternity. Moreover, the section also approved a general resolution proposed by the Workers' Group, which stated that the prerequisite for improvement in workers' conditions was the recognition of the rights of assembly and 'agitation' and the freedom of the press, all of which were possible 'under the full democratisation of the state system'. This, however, was buried by the Editing Commission and did not appear in the congress resolutions.[36]

None of these resolutions touched on the basic issues, and when these were broached, consensus turned to dissension. The Workers' Group put its case forcefully: working women's demands were dictated primarily by immediate economic necessity – the earning of a 'crust of bread', in Kollontai's words. Women of the middle classes, she argued, possessed economic security and pursued other goals, especially equality with the men of their own class. When they espoused democratic principles such as universal suffrage or freedom of speech and conscience, they fought for them as abstract rights, unconnected with the harsh struggle for survival, and readily compromised or abandoned. Even when they professed concern about the evils of industrialisation or the peasants' land hunger, their class loyalties prevented them from offering radical solutions. In vain did 'equal-righters' (*ravnopravki*) like Miliukova and Mirovich protest that women had specific interests in common. On the contrary, said Kuskova. There could be no united action, even on such day-to-day issues as maternity benefits. The desperate needs of a proletarian woman were not felt by a bourgeois.[37]

The fundamental disagreement over unity was nowhere demonstrated more clearly than in the sessions devoted to marriage and the family, the 'traditional sphere' of women. For most feminists, the family was the nucleus of society, the source of social morality, and the ideal environment for the upbringing of children. However, women knew from their own experience that the ideal was frequently violated, and was exploited by opponents of emancipation to keep women tied to the home and deprived of citizenship. Some of the more radical feminists saw bourgeois marriage as the villain of the piece. One such was Anastasiia Chebotarevskaia, a writer and the wife of the symbolist poet Fedor Sologub, who cited Bebel's dictum that middle-class marriage in its present form was institutionalised prostitution, in which a woman sold her body to her husband in return for maintenence, but was denied an equal status in the rearing of their children or in relations with the outside world. Chebotarevskaia linked women's emancipation to the dissolution of the traditional monogamous marriage and its replacement by some form of 'free union', a theme which was developed by M.L. Vakhtina in another session.[38]

Other speakers were disturbed by the impact of economic development on the family, some feminists agreeing with their Marxist adversaries that 'the conditions of contemporary life' were destroying the working-class family, tearing women from the home and forcing them into the factory. But social–democrats drew conclusions which feminists could not accept. 'Working women are fighting for their *full rights (polnopravie)* for their full liberation as workers and as women,' said one, 'in contrast to bourgeois equal rights (*ravnopravie*).' Bourgeois women were to throw off the legal shackles which disabled them inside and outside the home, while continuing to exploit the working class (particularly their servants). Marxists sought to destroy the 'single master of contemporary life – capital'.[39]

Kuskova, with somewhat different emphasis, which reflected her positive evaluation of the working intelligentsia (and her ambiguous position between feminists and social–democrats), declared that the women's movement itself was divided into two incompatible elements: those who worked and those who were dependent on men. The progressive aspect of the movement was a result of the economic changes of the nineteenth century, which had made women into breadwinners. Those who were not economically independent were 'kept women', preservers of the hearth through force of circumstance, not through free choice.[40]

Feminists countered by arguing that women were united by their lack of rights (and quoted Bebel to prove it!). Women's inferior status was enshrined in legal codes and customary law. I.V. Gessen, one of a group of male Kadet speakers, described the law of the Russian state as being 'saturated with a prohibitive spirit' in regard to women, which was rivalled only by the laws relating to the nationalities. Moreover, as other speakers pointed out, a woman's labour did not determine her status in the family: peasant women worked at least as hard as their husbands, but were the most oppressed class of all, hardly conscious that their oppression was insupportable. Whatever the divisions between women of differing economic status, there were problems which all women faced. Besides the disabilities that they encountered at work, their inheritance rights were inequitable, their rights of guardianship were circumscribed, the divorce laws punitive, while the odious passport law made separation difficult. Women, being physically weaker, needed special legislative protection. As an illustration of what could be achieved when women agitated on their own behalf, several speakers referred to the work of the newly-elected women deputies in Finland, who were campaigning for a revision of the marriage laws.[41]

Perhaps the greatest problems facing women who wished, or were obliged, to emancipate themselves from a domestic existence, were related to their children. Maternity insurance and paid leave would help to solve the difficulties confronting pregnant women, but what was one to do with children as they grew up? Among the well-to-do, the question hardly arose. Mothers were used to handing over most of the tasks of child-rearing to servants (often former serfs of the family). But among the growing ranks of the female intelligentsia, and, of course, the proletariat, the problem was immediate. Middle-class women, in particular, found their loyalties badly divided. Schools could not take over all the functions of child-rearing. 'The mother is the natural educator of her children,' proclaimed one speaker, but what sort of education, she asked, could peasant or working women give? What, moreover, could the upper-class lady, whose only function was to be decorative, offer her children?[42]

Some found the answer in the full recognition by society of maternity as equal to men's work, a solution which would encourage women to bring up their children themselves. This was not a revolutionary conclusion, and failed to consider that such recognition would have to be accompanied by heavy financial compensations for loss of essential earnings. But its advocates differed from the conservative adversaries of the women's movement, in their concern that the much-desecrated 'sanctity of motherhood' should be honoured and not used to justify women's exclusion from other provinces, and from political and civil rights. Rights and legislative protection were indispensable, to enable women to fulfil their biological role and to preserve the integrity of the family. To a greater or lesser extent, these views expressed the feelings of the majority at the congress.

When feminists talked about preserving the family, they were thinking also of sexual morality. The 'dual moral standard', which assumed the chastity of respectable women and the sexual indulgence of men, was a pet theme of the period, in Russia no less than elsewhere. To say that European society was obsessed with the 'social evil' of prostitution (and its attendant, venereal disease) would be no exaggeration. A steady stream of books and articles flowed from the publishing houses each year, and patent cures for syphilis and gonorrhoea were advertised in all the newspapers. It was no trivial preoccupation. Migration to the cities, very low wages and insecurity of employment in industry and domestic service, plus grossly inadequate medical facilities, had undoubtedly converted an age-old institution into a major social problem. In turn, the growth of social welfare and philanthropic organisations had transformed a campaign against prostitution, which had begun with the demand for the abolition of state inspection and state control of prostitutes in the 1860s and 1870s, into a thriving international 'cause'.[43] Though the 'abolitionist' campaign involved reformers who often had little or nothing to do with the women's movement itself, there were some notable exceptions, such as Pokrovskaia, a seasoned crusader against the dual standard.

To feminists, the 'gangrene of contemporary civilisation' was a symptom of the inequality of the sexes, which left a woman's husband (and her sons) free to indulge in debauchery, while she languished at home. The more conservative saw the answer exclusively in moral terms. Society must create an 'equal moral standard'. Through women's example of self-restraint, men could be taught to control their over-developed sexual appetites. This solution was assailed by more progressive women for ignoring not only human psychology but also the social and economic aspects of the question. Improvements in the economic position of women (particularly peasants, factory workers and servants), plus the recognition of civil and political equality, would provide the practical and psychological weapons to stamp out the evil. An equal standard was essential, but this could not be cultivated by moral pressures alone.[44]

None of this satisfied the Workers' Group. The crisis in the family and the growth of prostitution were both symptoms of the gathering crisis of capitalism. Capitalism had broken up the family. The marriage rate was falling because of men's inability to support a family. Prostitution was growing partly as a result of this, and partly as a result of women's impossibly low wages. One speaker actually stated that prostitution was caused by capitalism, an assertion which did not go unchallenged.[45] The Workers' Group objected to the 'palliatives' proposed by bourgeois women. They argued that no solution was possible until a socialist society was created, although some conceded that legislative protection for mothers and their children would cushion them against the worst excesses of the system. In the society of the future, women would be valued as a productive force equal to men, while their children would become the responsibility of the community.

* * *

Having failed to establish unanimity on the social and economic aspects of woman's subjugation, the congress could not be expected to reach agreement on the political issues. The congress had been intended to establish the foundations for future joint action. But it was clear from the beginning that too many diverse elements were present. Most obvious was the irreconcilable and virulent dispute between feminists and social–democrats as to the proper place for women in the political struggle.

The Worker's Group accused the feminists of using the women's movement to divert women from the general struggle against capitalism and divide the working class. To illustrate this, they quoted the example of women's suffrage. The 'first party in the world' to put female suffrage on its banner, said Kollontai, had been that of the social–democrats. The attainment of universal suffrage, as in Finland, could not have been achieved without them. Bourgeois women, she went on, always limited their demands to a franchise based on property. Not only would this exclude working women, it would also be used to uphold the class interests of the bourgeoisie against the 'democratic demands' of the proletariat.[46]

The feminists would not accept this. The women's movement, as an integral part of the general social movement, was fighting for the rights of *all* women, facing the hostility and indifference of men from all sections of society, not excluding the working class. A qualified franchise was sometimes necessary as the first step towards complete suffrage. Men, they pointed out, had also been obliged to receive enfranchisement in stages. At one session devoted to the issue, the atmosphere had already become explosive when Mirovich 'poured oil on the flames' by referring to an incident at the last congress of the Socialist International in Stuttgart. She claimed that a number of men had walked out when the issue of women's suffrage had been put to the vote. Her words produced uproar. Kollontai attempted to refute the 'slanderous attacks' of her opponent, but was shouted down and the session brought to a temporary standstill.[47]

Later in the same session, Mirovich set off another storm when she expressed surprise that those who found it impossible to participate in joint work should be present at the congress. At another session, an equally ardent feminist, Anna Kal'manovich, made a speech which was highly critical of all the political parties, particularly the social–democrats for their ambivalent attitude to the women's movement. Ignoring frequent interruptions, she quoted the views of three Western social–democratic women on their own male comrades, and their reasons for establishing working women's organisations. She argued that underprivileged groups, including women, had to fight for their rights. Defending herself against the charge of man-hatred, she stated that just as there were 'patriots of the fatherland', so she was a 'patriot of women'.[48]

All the storms which blew up over the issue of suffrage and politics involved the development of the women's movement abroad. Universal suffrage in Finland, qualified franchise in Norway, the SPD at Stuttgart, the British Labour Party and suffragettes: all provided an occasion for fresh outbursts of acrimony. Conversely, there was a dearth of material on the state of the movement in Russia, apart from a short speech on the tasks of organisation, another on women's journals and a few brief descriptions of women's clubs. Kuskova saw this as a fatal flaw in the congress:

> The woman of Russia takes a vital interest in the question of how English suffragists 'break windows' and is probably quite ignorant of the legislative projects which Russian ministers present to the Duma on her behalf.

She conceded that government censorship had severely restricted the scope of debate, but maintained that the outlook of Russian feminists themselves was equally to blame.[49] There was much truth in this verdict. Censorship of the programme had, after all, been directed as much at the international links of the women's movement as at its domestic concerns, though with little effect. Undoubtedly the uncongenial conditions prevailing at home encouraged feminists to pay closer attention instead to the activities of women's organisations in other countries.

It would be a mistake, when depicting the noisy scenes between feminists and social–democrats, to imply that the 'bourgeois' side was wholly united. Feminists were themselves divided by the same disagreements which pitted them against the revolutionaries, namely, the degree to which collaboration was actually possible across class barriers, and the extent to which the organisation of women detracted from the broader struggle for social liberation.

Mirovich and Kal'manovich, militant survivors of the Union of Equal Rights, were convinced that a women's organisation, representing all classes, was both possible and necessary. Men, even Liberationist men, they said, were unreliable allies. The Kadets, complained Kal'manovich, threw women's rights overboard like 'unnecessary ballast'. But other speakers, while recognising that rights would not be won unless women worked for them, rejected her conclusions. The view that women must work within their own social milieu was heard more and more frequently during the week, as class antagonisms proved to be more than just a figment of the Workers' Group's collective imagination. Ol'ga Shapir, a member of the Organisation Commission, put it bluntly:

> As for unity . . . I regard it as impossible in a class society. I regard the constant appeals of the workers' party for disunity as useful, in forcing us to renounce a vain hope.

Her lack of faith in joint political activity led her to suggest that the movement should concentrate on the inner emancipation of women, through the 'raising of consciousness' (a phrase frequently used at the time) to free them from the shackles of a slave mentality.[50] Tyrkova's objections to Mirovich and Kal'manovich were somewhat different. She did not oppose the organisation of women. Indeed, it was essential for the achievement of practical goals, and as a means of developing women's political maturity. But she was unhappy about exclusively female parties. Women must work within the existing parties for their own, and society's, liberation.[51]

Such divisions reduced still further the admittedly remote possibility (given the political climate) of women creating an effective lobby for social and legal reform. Ultimately, the quarrels amongst reformists had a more profound significance for the future of the women's movement than had the noisier conflicts between them and the social–democrats. Besides, their confrontations with the Workers' Group had, to some extent, been artificially incited. Mirovich brought the opprobrium of more moderate feminists down upon her head for suggesting that if the group thought collaboration impossible, it was welcome to leave the congress; but she was actually announcing (whether she knew it or not) the social–democrats' pre-arranged tactics.

Between 1907 and 1914 the social–democrats made repeated use of legally-chartered congresses to agitate 'for the democratic and socialist demands of the proletariat', sending 'workers' groups' and individual delegates to heckle and disrupt the proceedings.[52] However, the tactics of these groups were often the subject of acrimonious factional disputes, as had rapidly become clear at the women's congress. Officially, the group had been instructed by the Union Bureau to express the 'minority view' forcefully and to leave the congress if free discussion and 'agitation' were restricted. But the group was split: the Bolshevik representative insisted that it should leave at the earliest opportunity, the Mensheviks preferred to wait, and other members preferred not to leave at all. The organisers of the congress, pressed as they were for time, and anxious not to incur the displeasure of the police, gave the group repeated opportunities to depart, by omitting speeches and curtailing debate. But it was not until the last session of the whole proceedings, on 16 December, that the group staged its exit.[53]

Appropriately, the cause was a resolution voicing the political demands of the congress. In an early session of the third section, Mirovich and Kollontai had each proposed a resolution, stating political principles on behalf of their respective factions. The first proclaimed the necessity for active and passive suffrage, on the same terms as men, in elections to the State Duma and the organs of local self-government. The second insisted on nothing less than the 'seven-tailed' formula. Both were placed before the Editing Commission, which appears to have bowed to the threat of police intervention, and decided to propose its own 'general political' resolution, 'expressing the sentiments of the congress majority'. This stated that the 'principal goal' of women must be the 'establishment of a democratic system, on the basis of universal suffrage without distinction of sex, religion or nationality', as the 'chief instrument' for their full emancipation and liberation. To further this goal, women were to 'devote their energies both to existing general organisations and to the creation of separate women's unions, which will unite and attract women in general to conscious political and social life'.[54]

The Workers' Group naturally objected to the content of the resolution and, above all, to the absence of the full 'seven tails' of the suffrage formula. But it objected even more to the way in which the new resolution had been agreed upon. Kuskova, who had been on the Editing Commission, pointed out that only resolutions voted by the sections themselves could be put to the congress. A heated debate ensued as to whether the third section had voted on the two earlier resolutions, Miliukova stating that it had not done so simply because of an oversight. The Workers' Group refused to vote on the new draft, but the congress at last approved a ballot. The members of the group made this their pretext to withdraw. A special declaration, maintaining the impossibility of co-operation between hostile classes, was read, after which the delegates walked out. This dramatic gesture was, however, ruined by the lack of clear leadership within the group, which had affected its behaviour throughout the week. The intransigents in the group made their exit first, leaving the more conciliatory members to follow only after renewed debate. The disputed resolution, meanwhile, was passed 'amidst tumultuous applause' and the congress proceeded to the remaining ballots.[55]

The intended impact of the Workers' Group's walk-out was diminished further by the incident which occurred at the closing assembly that same evening. With all the business of the congress completed, Sof'ia Dekhtereva, a woman active in the movement, rose to speak on a theme which was grimly relevant: the executions being performed almost daily throughout Russia.

In bidding farewell to the congress I should like to remind you of a dreadful event which is taking place every day before our eyes and which carries off, or rather, tears from our midst hundreds of lives. I am speaking of the death penalty. We all know about it; knowing about it we cannot remain indifferent spectators. We wives and mothers must be the first to speak out for all to hear and publicly oppose the death penalty.[56]

The audience's response was overwhelming. Capital punishment had become one of the principal targets of the opposition since 1905, when the government first began to use it on a wide scale. But few opportunities for mass protest existed in the repressive environment of those years, and to stage-manage a public demonstration at a general session of a major congress was quite a coup. The police officer present evidently thought so and ordered Dekhtereva off the platform. To forestall further police action Shabanova hastily closed the congress, but her voice was lost in the commotion. In vain, the officer tried to get the hall cleared, and went off in defeat to the telephone, leaving the audience free to congratulate the initiator of the uproar before dispersing slowly.[57]

* * *

Thus the First All-Russian Congress of Women came to an end, its members unsure if it had closed formally, or if it had been closed by the police. The question was immaterial. The congress had been held, its transactions were recorded. Now all that remained was to evaluate its achievements and await the repercussions in society.

Reactions in the press during the week had followed predictable political lines. The principal liberal newspapers, *Rech'* and *Russkiia vedomosti*, supported the liberationist elements, and stressed the significance of the event for the general struggle against autocracy; the conservative *Novoe vremia*, meanwhile, gave a cautious welcome to the meeting, before throwing up its hands in horror at the extreme behaviour of some feminists and those 'who call themselves the representatives of the workers, the proletariat.' The paper's correspondent, M. Men'shikov, added his own contribution, a sarcastic review of feminist pretensions and vanities.[58]

But the most outrageous public response came shortly afterwards, from the extreme right-wing deputy for Bessarabia, V.M. Purishkevich, a man notorious for his provocative behaviour and language. In letters to Filosofova, Shabanova and Pokrovskaia, he expressed his satisfaction at the closing of the congress, which he compared to a brothel. Filosofova took him to court and, after a colourful trial, he was sentenced to one month's imprisonment (later commuted by the tsar).[59]

Meanwhile, the dissatisfactions of the Workers' Group with the Organising Commission's behaviour, were being aired in the newspapers. The group found an unexpected ally in Pokrovskaia, who was equally indignant at the 'illegality' of the controversial ballot, and at the watering down of many other resolutions by the Editing Commission. Also, at greater length, she complained that the principal organisers had displayed a 'noticeable indifference' towards her particular hobby-horse, the shameful issue of prostitution. Pokrovskaia's complaints were exaggerated. Though a speech of hers had been omitted from one of the joint assemblies, almost a whole session had been devoted to the issue, and the final congress resolution had incorporated the main points of Pokrovskaia's own proposal.[60] Others were more generally dissatisfied with the congress. Kuskova, in particular, was critical of the level of debate and deplored the frequent descent into bickering which, she said, was reminiscent of a public meeting. She accused women of being like children when it came to politics and felt that the best-informed speeches had been given by men.[61]

Disappointingly, however, the congress did little to stimulate discussion in society at large. It provoked nothing like the ferment of ideas which marked the emergence of the 'woman question' as a major social issue in the 1860s, nor anything like the upsurge of organisational activity of 1905 and 1906. The vital spark of optimism was lacking. This was lamented in an editorial in *Soiuz zhenshchin*, soon after the congress. It suggested that factionalism was destroying the possibilities for enthusiastic 'agitational work' and instead was producing a restrained 'objective tone'. The author regretted that the congress had not halted the decline into factionalism or promoted the 'concrete tasks' of the women's movement.[62]

However, the congress had made some impression on the population. The response of working-class women to the Union Bureau's preparatory work had been most encouraging and the social-democratic party organisations henceforth found it expedient to pay more attention to 'this rather inert and barely organised mass', particularly by creating working women's clubs.[63] Despite many recriminations over the Workers' Group's performance, commentators recognised that the very appearance of the group at the congress had been invaluable for working women's self-confidence, and trusted that the gains would not be dissipated.

In the 'bourgeois' camp, *Soiuz zhenshchin* seemed to be recovering from its dejection and, by the spring of 1909, its perennial financial difficulties had been eased, for a while at least, by new readers attracted by the congress. A number of the journal's contributors, including its editor, Chekhova, found a new organisational base in the Russian

League of Equal Rights for Women which at last took on an active existence, two years after its formal registration. Most encouraging of all, there were indications that women in the provinces, so often criticised for their lack of initiative, were also interested in joining the league.[64]

Though it failed to live up to the more exaggerated expectations of its participants, the 1908 congress undoubtedly helped to keep alive a demoralised movement, and make possible the 'small deeds' which formed the bulk of its achievement after the delegates had dispersed. Above all, it was valuable in demonstrating to an often sceptical public that women were perfectly capable of organising a major event without disaster. 'Just think!' the sceptics were heard to declare, 'women have organised everything and are running the whole congress themselves. Astonishing!'[65] Despite the storms and schisms, the congress had established that women could discuss matters close to their heart in an informed manner and with a remarkable respect for the opinions of others. Even critics like Pokrovskaia had every expectation that the event would not be the last of its kind and they looked forward to a second as 'a step forward on the path to equal rights.'[66]

Notes

1 *Soiuz zhenshchin* no. 1 (1908) p. 1.
2 *Zhenskii vestnik* no. 1 (1908) p. 1.
3 *Ibid.* no. 7–8 (1907) p. 190; *Soiuz zhenshchin* no. 2 (1908) p. 17.
4 *Ibid.* no. 2 (1907) p. 16.
5 *Ibid.* no. 11 (1908) pp. 15–16; *Zhenskii vestnik* no. 12 (1908) p. 298.
6 *Soiuz zhenshchin* no. 2 (1907) p. 16; no. 3 (1907) p. 12; *Women's Franchise* 4 June 1908 (no pagination). There is no detailed information available on these conferences. Mirovich suggested that the balance of opinion swung sharply in favour of the intransigents after the government's 'coup' in June 1907, when it became clear that legalisation was impossible unless the union abandoned all its most cherished principles. *Jus Suffragii*, 15 August 1908 (no pagination). The exact date of the union's demise is unknown; it apparently faded away during 1908.
7 *Soiuz zhenshchin* no. 1 (1907) p. 19; no. 2 (1907) p. 18; no. 4 (1907) p. 20; no. 5 (1907) p. 16; *Zhenskii vestnik* no. 6 (1908) p. 166.
8 *Ibid.* no. 1 (1905) p. 19; *Trudy 1-go vserossiiskago s"ezda* p. i (hereafter cited as *Trudy*); Mirovich, 'O pervom s"ezde russkikh deiatel'nits', pp. 132–3.
9 *Ibid.* pp. 133–4; *Zhenskii vestnik* no. 1 (1905) pp. 1–2.
10 Shabanova cited in *Rech'* 11 December 1908, p. 6; *International Council of Women: Report for 1904–1905* (Aberdeen: 1905) pp. 67–9.
11 *Soiuz zhenshchin* no. 3 (1907) p. 12.
12 Though several former members of the union, plus Pokrovskaia from the Women's Progressive Party, were on the Organising Commission, all the principal offices were taken by RZhVBO leaders. *Trudy* p.ii.
13 *Soiuz zhenshchin* no. 5 (1907) p. 18.

14 *Zhenskii vestnik* no. 3 (1908) pp. 89–90; *International Woman Suffrage Alliance: Report on the Fifth Conference and First Quinquennial* (London: 1909) p. 64; Mirovich, *Vserossiiskii zhenskii s″ezd* p. 5.
15 *Soiuz zhenshchin* no. 10 (1908) p. 2; *Trudy* p. v, viii.
16 *Novoe vremia* 14 December 1908, p. 3. After the congress the extreme right-wing Union of Russian Women petitioned the authorities for permission to hold a congress of their own, for 'truly Russian women'. *Soiuz zhenshchin* no. 3 (1909) p. 17.
17 *Trudy* pp. 523–4.
18 A. Ermanskii, 'Vserossiiskii zhenskii s″ezd' in *Sovremennyi mir* no. 1 (1909) pp. 103–4.
19 *Novaia Rus'* 11 December 1908, p. 4.
20 *Sotsial'demokrat* no. 4 (1909) pp. 2–5; *Golos sotsial'demokrata* no. 10–11 (1908) pp. 9–13, 25–26; no. 12 (1909) pp. 6–9. For more detail on the Workers' Group see Knight, *The Participation of Women in the Revolutionary Movement* pp. 151–4; Goldberg, *The Russian Women's Movement* pp. 187–99.
21 Two speeches on the hardships faced by servants were delivered to the congress, but neither was published.
22 *Sbornik pamiati A.P. Filosofovoi* vol. i, p. 437.
23 *Trudy* p. viii.
24 Z. Mirovich, 'Pervyi vserossiiskii zhenskii s″ezd' *Vestnik Evropy* no. 1 (1909) p. 413; *Novaia Rus'* 13 December 1908, p. 4; Kollontai, 'Avtobiograficheskii ocherk' p. 279.
25 *Trudy* pp. 1–2.
26 *Ibid*. pp. 9–13.
27 *Ibid*. p. 19.
28 *Trudy* p. 620. See *Zhenskii vestnik* no. 10 (1908) pp. 217–19 for Shvarts's circular. It caused such an outcry that the tsar permitted women who had already enrolled at university courses to complete them. No further enrolments were allowed. *Soiuz zhenshchin* no. 5–6 (1909) p. 2.
29 S.N. Valk (ed.) *Sankt-Peterburgskie vysshie zhenskie (Bestuzhevskie) kursy 1878–1918* 2nd. ed. (Leningrad: 1973) pp. 19–20, 61–3; *Trudy* pp. 530–35, 837–48.
30 *Ibid*. pp. 598ff.
31 *Ibid*. p. 657.
32 *Ibid*. pp. 199, 202–11.
33 *Ibid*. pp. 198, 200.
34 *Ibid*. p. 390; *Novaia Rus'* 16 December 1908, p. 2.
35 *Trudy* pp. 298, 306; *Novaia Rus'* 5 December 1908, p. 5; 14 December, p. 3. See Glickman 'The Russian Factory Woman' pp. 69–71.
36 *Trudy* pp. 310, 821–3.
37 *Ibid*. pp. 743, 792.
38 Chebotarevskaia's statement apparently 'shocked the old ladies' in the audience, including the chairwoman. *Novaia Rus'* 15 December 1908, p. 3; Ermanskii, 'Vserossiiskii zhenskii s″ezd' p. 107; *Trudy* pp. 549–57, 372–8.
39 *Ibid*. pp. 318, 340.
40 *Ibid*. pp. 767–8.
41 *Ibid*. pp. 356, 456, 494, 756.
42 *Ibid*. p. 380.

43 State regulation was introduced into France by Napoleon and adopted by a number of European nations during the nineteenth century. Regulation was imposed in St Petersburg in 1843 and other cities followed suit. *Ents. slovar' Brokgauz-Efron* vol. xxv, p. 482.

44 *Trudy* pp. 272, 283, 367–74.

45 *Ibid.* p. 274.

46 *Ibid.* p. 456.

47 *Ibid.* pp. 494, 523; Tyrkova, 'Pervyi zhenskii s″ezd' p. 202.

48 *Ibid.* pp. 496, 769, 779–91.

49 E. Kuskova, 'Zhenskii vopros i zhenskii s″ezd' pt. 2, *Obrazovanie* no. 2 (1909) p. 37. For her observations on the censorship of the agenda see 'Zhenskii vopros' pt. 1, *Obrazovanie* no. 1 (1909) p. 97.

50 *Ibid.* pp. 496, 769.

51 *Rech'* 14 December 1908, p. 4.

52 *Proletarii* no. 50 (1908) cited in Ralph Carter Elwood, *Russian Social–Democracy in the Underground* (Assen: 1974) p. 204; Kollontai, 'Avtobiograficheskii ocherk' pp. 275–6.

53 *Novaia Rus'* 25 November 1908, p. 5. See also *Sotsial'demokrat* and *Golos sotsial 'demokrata* cited above.

54 *Trudy* pp. 495, 819–20; *Novaia Rus'* 14 December 1908, p. 3.

55 *Trudy* pp. 819–20; Serditova, *Bol'sheviki v bor'be za zhenskie proletarskie massy* p. 69.

56 *Novaia Rus'* 17 December 1908, p. 2. At least 952 executions took place in 1908 (632 in 1907). No week had passed without an execution, and the weekly maximum was thirty-six. Mikhail Mogilianskii, 'Smertnaia kazn' v 1908g.' *Pravo* no. 52 (1908) cols. 2926–7.

57 *Rech'* 17 December 1908, p. 3. Immediately after the congress, a protest signed by several thousand women was sent to the Duma, where a bill to abolish the death penalty was debated in January. The bill was 'buried' in committee. *Soiuz zhenshchin* no. 1. (1909) p. 8.

58 *Novoe vremia* 11 December 1908, p. 4; 13 December, p. 13; 14 December, p. 3.

59 *Sbornik pamiati A.P. Filosofovoi* vol. i, p. 436; *Soiuz zhenshchin* no. 2 (1909) pp. 13–17; no. 3 (1909) pp. 15–17.

60 *Novaia Rus'* 18 December 1908, p. 5; Kuskova, 'Zhenskii vopros' pt. 2, pp. 36–7; *Trudy* pp. 272–86, 823.

61 Kuskova, 'Zhenskii vopros' pt. 2, pp. 36, 38, 43. For a rebuttal of this charge see A.A. Kal'manovich, *Pretenzii k zhenskomu dvizheniiu voobshche i k 1-mu vserossiiskomu zhenskomu s″ezdu v chastnosti* (Spb: 1910) p. 9. See Goldberg, *The Russian Women's Movement* pp. 252–8 for discussion of the Workers' Group.

62 *Soiuz zhenshchin* no. 1 (1909) pp. 1–2.

63 *Sotsial'demokrat* no. 4 (1909) p. 2.

64 *Soiuz zhenshchin* no. 2 (1909) pp. 17–18, 20.

65 A. Tyrkova, 'Pervye shagi. Pervyi zhenskii vserossiiskii s″ezd' *Novyi zhurnal dlia vsekh* no. 1 (1909) col. 116.

66 *Zhenskii vestnik* no. 1 (1909) p. 3.

5 The World Outside

In her criticisms of the 1908 congress, Kuskova had accused Russian feminists of being excessively preoccupied with the minutiae of suffrage campaigns abroad and neglecting the practical details of social liberation at home. But the internationalism which she saw as a seductive diversion from serious work was regarded by feminists as the essence of the women's movement, and never more so than in the decade following the 1905 Revolution. With the growth of a native campaign for political rights, the ideas of suffrage movements in other countries had become relevant to Russia for the first time, while the temporary breakdown of government control over organisations, and the easing of restrictions on travel and communication, made affiliation to an international women's association possible where it had not been before.

Feminists in Russia had always shared a cosmopolitan outlook. They were educated members of the middle and upper classes, many of whom were able to travel outside Russia and observe the laws and customs of other countries. Some went abroad for pleasure, others to study, some for political reasons. Even those without the financial resources or the need to leave Russia were often well read in the standard works of foreign literature, and a considerable number earned their living by teaching or translating from the major European languages.

With few exceptions, Russian feminists were 'westernisers', sharing the intelligentsia's acute awareness of Russia's cultural and economic backwardness. From the movement's earliest days they had acknowledged their debt to foreign ideas and influences and trusted that the establishment of links with women abroad would help to consolidate their own efforts at home. As Filosofova's biographer commented, such contacts as they made reassured the embattled Russians that their work 'brought Russia closer to Europe and separated it from Asia.'

These early contacts had little practical significance. In 1873, an unsuccessful attempt was made to establish an International Women's League in New York. Three of its founding members were Russians living abroad, who hoped to create an affiliated branch in Russia itself. The move was premature. Neither at home, where political conditions were hardly propitious, nor in Europe or North America, were women's organisations sufficiently developed to allow expansion overseas, and the project lapsed. Not for another decade was any further effort made to bring together women from different countries into an international union.[1]

In 1882 Elizabeth Cady Stanton, a pioneer of the American women's movement who had been one of the initiators of the celebrated Seneca Falls Convention thirty-four years earlier, visited England and France. During her stay she 'conceived the idea of an International Council of Women interested in the movement for suffrage, and pressed its consideration on the leading reformers in those countries.' A committee of correspondence was established to further the project, and Mrs Stanton returned home with her suffragist colleague, Susan B. Anthony. The idea was slow to mature, but in 1887, the National Women's Suffrage Association in Washington issued an invitation to women throughout the world to attend the inaugural congress of the council the following year:

> However the governments, religions, laws, and customs of nations may differ, all are agreed on one point, namely man's sovereignty in the State, in the Church, and in the Home. In an International Council women may hope to devise new and more effective methods for securing the equality and justice which they have so long and so earnestly sought. Such a Council will impress the important lesson that the position of women anywhere affects their position everywhere. Much is said of universal brotherhood, but, for weal or for woe, more subtle and more binding is universal sisterhood.[2]

The founders of the new sisterhood stressed the importance of political rights:

> Women, recognising the disparity between their labors and their achievements, will no doubt agree that they have been trammeled by their political subordination. Those active in great philanthropic enterprises sooner or later realise that, so long as women are not acknowledged to be the political equals of men, their judgment on public questions will have but little weight.

At the same time, the council was to aspire to wider goals and invitations to join it were sent to 'representative organisations in every department of women's work'. These included the Women's Christian Temperance Union, the National Vigilance Association and assorted religious sects in America and Europe.[3] The involvement of organisations whose principal purpose was moral reform rather than women's rights had a decisive effect in determining the character of the council. By the time its first quinquennial meeting was held in 1893 (arranged to coincide with the grandiose World Columbian Exposition in Chicago), Stanton's project for a body of women 'interested in the movement for suffrage' had been transmuted into a council which not only put philanthropy before politics but which even shied away from a campaign for the vote. While few ICW members were opposed to women's suffrage, many regarded it as a contentious issue, conflicting with the council's stated desire for unity. An organisation embracing such a diversity of cultures and political systems, it was felt, should avoid controversy, and the suffrage campaign was quietly left to the discretion of separate national organisations.[4]

The council's avoidance of day-to-day political issues was not simply a reluctance to get embroiled in disputes. It was equally a reflection of the strong evangelical spirit in which it was created. The council had a mission to perform:

> In every country we see the wisest statesmen at their wits' end vainly trying to meet the puzzling questions of the hour: in Russia it is Nihilism; in Germany, Socialism; in France, Communism; in England, Home Rule for Ireland and the Disestablishment of the Church, and in America, Land, Labor, Taxes, Tariffs, Temperance, and Woman Suffrage. Where shall we look for the new power by which the race can be lifted up and the human mind made capable of coping with the daily-increasing complications of this new civilisation?[5]

Where else, but to women? Spiritual force, rather than numerical equality, was to be women's great contribution, and this was to be harnessed by the International Council of Women.

The 'Council idea' proved attractive. Initially slow to expand, the council grew rapidly after 1897, and by 1910 represented women in most of western and central Europe, Scandinavia, Canada, Australasia and the Argentine. Though intended to appeal to women of all classes, its composition was overwhelmingly middle-class, leavened by a sprinkling of titled ladies and patronised by royalty on occasion.

An organisation which concentrated on 'questions relating to the commonwealth and the family', should have been ideally suited to the circumscribed Russian women's movement of that period. Feminism in Russia had long since lost the association with radical politics so characteristic of its development in the 1860s. Obliged to eschew any form of political involvement, its leaders saw no option but to restrict their activities to the educational and 'cultural' fields, and even so encountered many obstacles.

Certainly, the formation of the ICW aroused interest in St Petersburg and Moscow, bringing with it the promise of new inspiration from outside. The women's movement in Russia was already beginning to recover from the setbacks which it had suffered for a decade after the assassination of Alexander II, sharing the new mood of activism which seized the educated public generally in the early 1890s. Women in St Petersburg collaborated in preparing an exhibit for the women's section of the World Columbian Exposition in Chicago, while the example of women's organisations abroad prompted the establishment of the Russian Women's Mutual Philanthropic Society, the first general association of its kind to be permitted in Russia.[6] The founders of the new society were fully conscious of the need to exploit the spirit of internationalism, and set about making it the nucleus of a projected Russian National Council of Women. Anna Filosofova, the society's honorary president, was soon invited to become one of the International Council's honorary vice-presidents, and a delegation from St Petersburg was sent to the council's London congress in 1899.[7]

The band of Russian women which went to London was able to observe at first hand an international movement gaining each year in self-confidence and respectability. 'The general appearance of the assembly,' reported Lidiia Davydova soon after the event, 'testified more eloquently than any words to the fact that the women's movement has outlived its original, revolutionary stage and that "bluestockings" and emancipated women of the old type have passed on into the realm of legend.'[8]

The congress was presided over by Lady Aberdeen, 'the embodiment of a *dame patronesse* in the best sense of the word'. True to its origins, the congress avoided politics and concentrated on the other aspects of contemporary life to which women felt they could make a particular contribution. The Russians' own share in the proceedings was limited: they gave half a dozen speeches, including one on higher education and two on women doctors. But they were there more as observers than as active participants, a small group numerically swamped by 'Anglo–Saxons' and Germans.

Hopes of greater involvement in the women's movement abroad through the ICW soon ran up against the Russian government's constant suspicion of even the smallest manifestation of initiative within society in general, and of foreign influences in particular. Over the next fifteen years, the government steadfastly refused all applications for permission to form a Russian National Council of Women, a rebuff which naturally weakened links between Russia and the ICW. But Filosofova took her duties as honorary vice-president very seriously. She quickly established a cordial relationship with the Countess of Aberdeen and devoted the remaining decade of her life to the promotion of the council.[9]

Prospects for Russian affiliation seemed momentarily brighter in 1905. During the spring the Mutual Philanthropic Society circulated draft proposals for a National Council to the leaders of women's groups throughout the country and announced its intention of using the national congress which it planned to hold in St Petersburg to discuss the project. When the congress was indefinitely postponed the Council project lapsed too and was not taken up again for two more years.[10]

The resurrection of plans for a national women's congress in 1908 raised the question once again. On this occasion the task of renewing the battle with the Ministry of the Interior for approval of the council statute was assumed almost singlehandedly by Filosofova, to whom alone it remained of paramount importance. To little avail. Although the congress (after some dispute) approved the statute, the Ministry of the Interior refused to confirm it. Sporadic efforts were made thereafter to win government approval, but even Filosofova began to lose heart, and she died in 1912 without seeing the realisation of her dream. Not until after the overthrow of the tsar was permission forthcoming for a Russian National Council.[11]

The attraction of the ICW had, in any case, been much reduced by the creation of another international women's organisation, the International Woman Suffrage Alliance (IWSA). The formation of the alliance, which broke away from the ICW in 1904, brought the suffrage issue to the fore internationally in the feminist movement. Eleven years earlier, when the founder members of the ICW had chosen to set aside women's suffrage in the interests of a non-partisan organisation, they were reflecting a domestic disenchantment with the suffrage campaign, which had hitherto yielded such meagre results and which seemed too narrow to encompass all the aspirations of the women's movement. By the turn of the century, suffragism had become a live issue once more. In the United States, the National American Woman Suffrage Association, with only 13,150 members in 1893, began to expand after 1900 and by 1907 numbered over 45,000.[12] In Britain, a prolonged split in suffragist ranks had been healed by the formation of the National Union of Women's Suffrage Societies in 1897, while a new militant wing, the Women's Social and Political Union, was founded in 1903. In Germany, the very first national suffrage association was launched in 1902, and elsewhere in Europe, particularly in the Netherlands and Scandinavia, women were joining suffrage societies in increasing numbers.

The IWSA, like the ICW, was dreamt up in the United States. Its initiators were leading members of the American suffrage movement, notably Susan B. Anthony, now over eighty but still a dedicated campaigner, and the younger Carrie Chapman Catt, a formidable organiser who became the heart and soul of the international suffrage alliance. On their prompting, the National American Woman Suffrage Association invited delegates from suffrage societies in nine countries to its annual convention in 1902.[13] A committee was elected, and two years later the IWSA held its first congress in Berlin, to coincide with the ICW's quinquennial which many suffragists were expected to attend.

The specific object of the IWSA was to 'secure the enfranchisement of the women of all nations, and to unite the friends of woman suffrage throughout the world in organised cooperation and fraternal helpfulness'.[14] Despite some hostility among ICW members to the prospect of a rival, the founding of the IWSA did not represent a schism in the international movement. Mrs Catt delivered a rousing speech to the ICW congress and national councils of women soon began to send delegates to IWSA meetings. The ICW itself, adapting to the shift of interest within the women's movement, set up its own standing committee for Suffrage and the Rights of Citizenship in 1904, although this did not lead to a substantially greater political involvement on the part of the council.[15]

Russia's role in these developments was, as one might expect, modest. In 1902, when the IWSA was first mooted, interest in women's suffrage in Russia was, to all intents and purposes, non-existent, and even two years later there was no sign of a suffrage campaign.[16] The formation of the Union of Equal Rights in the spring of 1905, made the IWSA appropriate to Russian conditions for the first time. While for the early months of the union's career its members were too caught up in the domestic drama to spare more than a fleeting glance at events abroad, the defeat of the revolution gave them cause to look outside Russia once more for moral support. The union decided to join the IWSA and sent six delegates to the next conference of the alliance, which was held in Copenhagen in August 1906.

Here they met an enthusiastic and effusive welcome from the president, Mrs Catt:

> The world has long prophesied that, sooner or later, an uprising must come in Russia, and the system which has so long denied the right of free speech and personal liberty to the people would be overthrown. Now that that time has come, it is a great satisfaction to know that the women of that country are neither forgetting their own future nor permitting others to forget it . . . We welcome the Union of Russian Women as a family might welcome daughters who had long been shut away in prison. We have not been permitted to know our Russian sisters, but we love them, we are unacquainted with their program, yet we understand it. We recognise them as comrades in our common cause. All hail to these heroines of Russia, for such they are, and may the dove of liberty soon perch upon their banners![17]

Mirovich was the principal spokesman of the union. Her speech was a short history of the Union of Equal Rights and the suffrage movement in Russia between February 1905 and the dissolution of the First Duma. While making due reference to the common motivations of women's movements all over the world, she also drew out the particular features which, she felt, set Russia apart from its neighbours.

> In Russia woman was always virtually man's equal: equal in lack of rights. And in Russia women endured the long, tormenting years alongside men, fought in their ranks against the monstrous tyranny of the government: for enlightenment, for freedom . . . often sacrificing everything in life that was dear and of value: their personal interests, their family ties, their freedom . . .

As a result of their sacrifices, she continued, women in Russia occupied a 'unique position compared with that of women in other countries: the position of sister and comrade in life.' Granted, prejudice against female emancipation was still strong. Nevertheless, in recent months, all the progressive elements in society had supported women's rights; this was a 'moral victory', attributed not only to 'history' but also to the 'active propaganda' of the Union of Equal Rights.

Whether or not, in her first appearance before the IWSA, Mirovich was indulging somewhat in the rhetoric demanded by such occasions, her words expressed a genuine faith in the goodwill of male colleagues in the liberation movement which was not altogether consonant with the experiences of the Union of Equal Rights during the past year. But her speech ended less optimistically, with an account of the Duma's dissolution and the temporary halting of the union's activities. 'The progress is now stopped in Russia. We are again face to face with our worst enemies.'[18]

Besides using the conference to advertise the Union of Equal Rights, the Russian delegation also took the opportunity to make a public protest against the vast Anglo–French loan to the Russian government, which had recently been concluded. Mirovich appealed to members of the IWSA 'to use their utmost exertions to influence public opinion in their respective countries to condemn those capitalists who assist in the floating of new loans for the existing government of Russia, by thus giving the Russian government the means to renew this strife with new force.' Although the IWSA itself had no authority to undertake such protest, there is no doubt that the Russian speakers, and Mirovich in particular, had made a strong impression on their audience. The day's sessions closed with a declaration by the German feminist, Lida Gustava Heymann, that members should 'help the struggling Russians' and 'show the utmost disapprobation of those who are not ashamed to give Russian autocracy their financial support'.[19]

The Russians were given a further opportunity to inform their sympathisers abroad when the IWSA launched a monthly journal *Jus Suffragii* a month later. Although its readership was, by the nature of the journal, limited, and offered no substitute for the mass home audience which the Union of Equal Rights had hoped in vain to create, *Jus Suffragii* did provide the Russians with an outlet for their despair at the course which political life (and the women's campaign) was taking. Profiting from the absence of censorship, the correspondents did not mince their words. They reported the harassment of candidates and supporters during the election campaign for the Second State Duma, the growing conviction that the Duma would share the fate of its predecessor, and fears that such an eventuality would lead to a 'great uprising' in the country. 'Considering all the suffering endured by those who stand for liberty and justice and also the great danger which menaces Russia, our woman's question is in the background at present,' wrote Mirovich, the journal's most regular correspondent, who contributed bulletins on the women's movement in Russia for several years until her death in 1913.[20]

Naturally, readers were kept well informed of the problems of low morale and police harassment which plagued the Union of Equal Rights and which finally extinguished it. Particularly interesting was a letter from Eliza Goncharova, from her home in Riazan, written in the weeks when the union was collecting signatures for its monster petition to the Second Duma.

> I have very little to say, living in a small, provincial town. We can scarcely assemble and work, very often we even don't know whom we are helping with money, books or work. Those women we do help are afraid of showing themselves for the moment, and so we find a terror-stricken mass of women, to whom you must first suggest that they have a right to demand justice and to sign their names under petitions to express their needs . . .

The Second Duma was dissolved like the First, but no 'great uprising' followed. Instead, the Russian correspondents could only record a further tightening of police control over the opposition. 'There is not much to say on the woman's movement in Russia during the end of 1907,' Mirovich lamented:

> It is quite evident that the revolution is put down. The movement for liberty has been checked; while reaction stands triumphant and mighty . . .[21]

Hardly surprisingly, the decline of the women's movement in Russia was accompanied by some evaporation of interest on the part of suffragists abroad. While Russia captured the headlines of the foreign press and women's suffrage was debated in the Duma, the possibility of the Empire becoming the first major state to establish full equality of the sexes could not be dismissed. But when hopes for political reform of any kind proved to be illusory, the attention of foreign suffragists was directed elsewhere. Though Russian delegates attended all four IWSA congresses held between 1908 and 1913, they never again elicited an enthusiastic response from their audience such as they had produced at Copenhagen in 1906.

It might have been expected that, with the disintegration of the Union of Equal Rights, the IWSA's Russian link would be broken. But the union's successor, the Russian League of Equal Rights for Women, assumed the role as advocate for Russia and remained affiliated until after 1917. The presence of many former members of the Union of Equal Rights in the new league (including the most dedicated 'internationalists', like Mirovich and Kal'manovich) helped to maintain continuity and ensured a sympathetic response from the IWSA to the problems besetting its Russian section.[22]

Ultimately, however, the IWSA was unable to rescue the Russian women's movement. Though it provided a much-needed forum for the feminists in the early months of reaction, it had no power to restore to vigour a movement already debilitated by internal factors. Indeed, it may be questioned whether the alliance (or the International Council of Women) affected the activities of any national women's movement very profoundly. While suffragists found it desirable to establish formal links between their national societies, none of them seems to have felt that an international organisation had much relevance for the determination of policy and tactics in individual countries. The two international organisations, whatever the hopes of their founders, never assumed a role in relation to national women's movements comparable, for example, to the close relationship of the Second International to socialist parties before 1914. Polemics over principle and strategy of the sort which characterised the Socialist International's career (and that of its affiliate, the Socialist Women's International), hardly touched the feminists' organisations.

The IWSA and ICW may claim to have been successful in their more restricted roles. Both gave an opportunity to women to meet foreign colleagues, exchange information and celebrate the ritual of sisterly solidarity. By their mere existence they provided ample testimony to the transformation, over a period of less than fifty years, of women's status and expectations in widely differing societies.

In any case, the significance of a phenomenon is to be measured not merely by its deeds, but equally by the importance which was assigned to it at the time. For feminists generally, the two organisations represented the spirit of co-operation between women of all nations, which they saw as intrinsic to the movement: a force for peace and harmony in a world increasingly threatened by war and moral decay. 'We have been baptised in that spirit of the twentieth century which the world calls Internationalism,' declared the president of the IWSA. 'It is a sentiment like love, or religion, or patriotism, which is to be experienced rather than defined in words.' Nowhere was it more prized than by feminists in Russia, so receptive to external stimuli and so immediately aware of the destructive power of nationalism and arbitrary rule. 'In these days when the negative aspects of life hold sway and darkness prevails over light,' Mirovich wrote not long after her return from Copenhagen, a congress such as the one she had just attended 'flashed like a ray of light in the general gloom', as a reminder that people could cultivate in themselves, and in their society, a respect for the customs and opinions of others and learn 'to regard themselves more modestly'.[23]

If proof were needed of the importance which feminists in Russia attached to foreign examples, it was provided by the literature of the women's movement, abounding as it did in translations from all the major European languages. In this, the movement had changed very little since its inception fifty years earlier. Russian feminists' reverence for the imported word was matched by a shortage of home-produced works. 'The literature in Russian on the woman question is not distinguished by its particular wealth,' the editors of *Soiuz zhenshchin* noted in its very first issue, whilst proposing to remedy the defect. In the same issue, they announced the publication of three new pamphlets, all of which were translations from German.[24]

Nor was the attention paid to the women's movement abroad confined to separate pamphlets and books. All three journals of the Russian movement in this period, reserved space each month for a chronicle of the victories and vicissitudes of women in other countries. Often, an item would entail no more than a brief note, but sometimes reports would be more detailed in their coverage of, for example, the second reading of a bill in the House of Commons, or the extension of girls' education in Germany. The subjects chosen for lectures also testified to a continuing interest in international developments. Lectures and seminars had always enjoyed great popularity in Russia, where access to books and newspapers was limited. Lectures were an important means of propaganda, despite the obstacles put in their way by the authorities intent on preventing the dissemination of dangerous knowledge. In 1905 and 1906, government restrictions proved less effective and women's groups took advantage of the situation to hold public lectures on controversial themes.

In 1906, much of this work was co-ordinated by the Union of Equal Rights. In the autumn, spurred on by its recent success at Copenhagen, the central bureau set out to create a programme of lectures to be given in towns throughout the Empire during the winter and following spring. Of the half-dozen subjects prepared, three were exclusively devoted to women's movements outside Russia, and two more interpretations of the Russian movement in a wider context. Some were given to small cultural circles, but others were given at public meetings and drew audiences of several hundred.[25]

They were not, however, invariably well received by the local administration. Often, debates were curtailed or forbidden, and on some occasions a lecture was banned altogether. Although this was just one instance of the offensive which the government was waging on the intelligentsia and which affected all aspects of cultural life in 1906 and later, it seems clear that the authorities in some towns were particularly sensitive to foreign themes. A lecture on 'the women's movement in contemporary England', which Mirovich had been permitted to read in Moscow and Smolensk, was banned in Ivanovo-Voznesensk on the grounds that it might 'stir up the local textile workers'. In Riazan, the same lecture was prohibited when the chief of police learnt that it was to discuss the Women's Social and Political Union, which had recently begun to use militant (though not yet violent) tactics.[26]

This was not a mere whim on the part of a local bureaucrat. It was in keeping with the policy of the Ministry of the Interior in its refusal to sanction a National Council of Women and with its ban on foreigners at the 1908 congress. The authorities had undoubtedly learnt from experience that ideas from abroad exercised a potent influence on the social and political thought of the Russian intelligentsia, but they had not learnt that it was all the more potent for being forbidden fruit.

Interest in the women's movement abroad was almost certainly at its most intense in these few years. But the weakening of international links which occurred during the reaction was more a reflection of the progressive enfeeblement of the Russian movement, than a sign of a fundamental shift in focus. Even then, women's journals continued to report international news and women's groups attempted to maintain their life-line to the outside world.

Naturally enough, suffragists the world over found great comfort in the example of those few nations where women's suffrage had already been won. The list had grown since the beginning of the century, but even in 1910 women had been enfranchised in no more than four countries, only one of which (Norway) was a fully self-governing state. Among the four was Finland, a small country of three million people and the first in Europe to grant full universal suffrage.

Finland, for long under Swedish rule, had been annexed by Alexander I in 1808. Unlike other nations ruled by the tsars, it had been allowed to retain its former constitution, but the autonomy which had been fully respected by Nicholas I and Alexander II came under increasing attack by their successors. It was removed altogether by the government manifesto of February 1899, elevating Russian over Finnish law. This attack on the Finns' constitutional rights was accompanied by a policy of russification, in the administration as well as in education and religion, whose aim seemed to be to eradicate not simply the Finnish constitution, but its culture as well. The Finns responded with a determined show of opposition and non-co-operation, involving sectors of the population which had hitherto played little or no role in the political life of the country. A significant proportion of them were women.

The Finnish women's movement had developed along similar lines to those of other countries, bringing some reform of women's legal rights, increased educational opportunities and greater access to employment.[27] It was represented by two national organisations, the conservative Finnish Women's Association (founded in 1884) and the more radical Union of Women's Rights (established eight years later). Both were cultural rather than political associations. Although the latter advocated female suffrage, neither made much effort before 1904 to change the antiquated electoral system in favour of women. Like their counterparts abroad, both were organisations of the upper and middle classes and did not claim to represent the mass of Finnish women.

As in Russia, the women's movement was transformed under the impact of political crisis, with the difference that in Finland the opposition was pitted against an external aggressor. 'Our language, our religion, our customs, everything that was sacred to us was threatened by our foes,' recalled Annie Furuhjelm, leader of the Union of Women's Rights. 'Hundreds, even thousands of women of all classes, who perhaps up to this time had never given a thought to their rights, or rather their want of rights, enrolled in the ranks of the opposition . . .'[28] Women joined the clandestine political organisations which sprang up after the government's coup d'état. They collected signatures for protest petitions, printed and distributed leaflets and raised money. Russian observers of the women's campaign commented enviously on the degree of unity achieved, which was indeed remarkable in a country where class conflict was accompanied by an underlying tension between the Finns and an influential Swedish minority. But profound differences did exist, which surfaced at the end of 1904.[29]

The assassination of the much-hated governor-general Bobrikov, in June 1904, had been followed by an intensification of political opposition, in which women continued to play an active part. The idea of women's suffrage became more relevant the more they became involved in political campaigning, and in November 1904, a mass meeting of over 1,000 women was organised in Helsingfors (Helsinki) by the Union of Women's Rights, with the purpose of raising a suffrage petition. Represented there were all but the most conservative of women's groups, including the social–democratic associations which had been formed simultaneously with the establishment of the Social–Democratic Party. Finnish social–democracy in this period was less antagonistic towards non-revolutionary parties than its counterpart in Russia, and opportunities for co-operation and compromise between them existed. Nonetheless, the November women's meeting was far from united. The moderate Union of Women's Rights had close ties with the constitutionalist party and took a cautious stand on the reform of the electoral laws. The social–democrats demanded unconditional universal suffrage. That their influence in Finland was strong was demonstrated at the women's meeting, where an overwhelming majority rejected any compromise on the suffrage formula. From that moment, the social–democrats and their supporters became the dominant voice in the women's suffrage campaign.

Although the spring of 1905 brought some concessions from the Russian government, the opposition did not abate. Acts of revolutionary violence increased. Finally, a general strike in the autumn, coordinated with the strike in Russia and organised by both constitutionalists and social–democrats, extracted a manifesto from the tsar on 4 November, in which he conceded Finland's right to its own constitution.

The opposition, which had been temporarily united during the strike, split up once more. Women, meanwhile were now able to concentrate their attentions on the campaign for the vote. Although public opinion strongly favoured universal male suffrage, its extension to women was not a foregone conclusion. Six months of campaigning showed the extent of popular support. When the Finnish parliament met in May 1906 to consider reform of the electoral law, it voted overwhelmingly for universal suffrage, without distinction of sex. In July, the tsar signed the new statute giving Finland a unicameral parliament of 200 deputies, elected by all citizens over the age of twenty-four.

This outcome caused a great stir internationally. It seemed to be a tremendous moral victory by a tiny nation over a large imperial power, given extra piquancy by the granting of female suffrage. Among suffragists themselves, the result was hailed as 'one of the greatest reforms of our time'.[30] A month after the tsar put his signature to the new law, the leader of the Finnish Union of Women's Rights, Furuhjelm, was given an ovation at the Copenhagen congress of the International Woman Suffrage Alliance. 'We have been like an army climbing slowly and laboriously up a steep, difficult and rocky mountain,' declaimed Carrie Chapman Catt:

> We have looked upward, and have found uncertain stretches of time and effort between us and the longed for summit . . . yet suddenly, almost without warning, we see upon that summit another army. How came it there? It has neither descended from heaven, nor climbed the long, hard journey. Yet there above us, all the women of Finland stand today. Each wears the royal crown of the sovereignty of the self-governing citizen.[31]

To Russian women, of course, the victory had a special significance. Both Finns and Russians had been waging a battle against a common enemy. The success of the one could only serve as a reminder to the other of how little had been gained in Russia from eighteen months' intense activity. It also emphasised the profound differences in social structure and psychological makeup which distinguished the two cultures. Mirovich, for example, argued that the Finnish character was marked by a strong democratic spirit and love of freedom, which gave women the opportunity to participate fully in the affairs of the nation. Whereas the Russians had to grapple with a corrupting legacy of serfdom, the Finns could dispense with an outmoded political system without major social upheaval. Moreover, she pointed out, the Russian liberation movement had to contend with conflicting forces within its own society, while the liberation struggle of the Finns was directed at an external enemy. This view was echoed by Vera Figner, who saw in Finland, not only the victory of a small nation over an empire, but also the triumph of the working masses, male and female, over privilege and exploitation.

The contribution of Finnish social–democrats to the women's victory naturally gave rise to many a dispute within Russia between feminists and Marxists. To the latter, it was evident that universal suffrage was the achievement of a united class-conscious proletariat and owed nothing to bourgeois separatist feminism. Kollontai (the social–democrats' expert on Finland) was particularly scathing in her attacks on the feminists, and, even two years later, was using the Finnish victory as a stick with which to beat them. But the feminists fought back. Pokrovskaia, far from accepting that social–democratic participation in the Finnish suffrage struggle was a defeat for feminist separatism, saw the whole campaign as an example of united action between the classes which Russian women would do well to follow.[32]

Having congratulated the Finns, a little enviously, on their success, the Russian feminists waited to see 'how they would fulfil their new mission', hoping that the example of the Finns would have favourable consequences for themselves. The initial results were impressive. Confounding the prediction of anti-suffragists that women, once enfranchised, would not bother to vote, 60 per cent of the female electorate went to the polls in 1907, the first elections under the new system. More remarkably, nineteen women were elected, including nine social–democrats and six Old Finns.[33] Their worthiness as legislators was hardly put to the test. As soon as it met, parliament found itself in a state of conflict with the Russian government. It suffered a series of dissolutions up to 1910, when its constitutional powers were decimated and Bobrikov's russification campaign resurrected in full force. However, even in these unhappy circumstances, the women deputies became involved in a wide range of legislative projects affecting social welfare, which might suggest that, under normal conditions, their contribution would have been distinguished by an emphasis on health, welfare, moral reform and the protection of women and children.[34]

Finland's experience of women's suffrage clearly disappointed the most optimistic expectations of feminists around the world. The emancipation of women did not bring with it that moral transformation of Finnish society predicted by the more utopian feminists. Even without the state of permanent political crisis, the situation would probably have been little different, as the example of New Zealand showed well.[35] On the other hand, the country had not suffered as a result of women's suffrage, nor was the family undermined, as opponents had declared it would be. However small its direct impact on the country's destiny, Finland's experience could do the suffrage cause no harm.

The progress of women's emancipation in Finland was a matter of close concern to Russian feminists, because of their geographical proximity and their common interest in the liberalisation of the tsarist regime. But whatever the strength of their sympathy for the Finns (and for the women of the other subject nations in the Empire) they never paid as much attention to the women's movements near to hand as they did to the suffrage campaign in Britain, a country with which, to all appearances, they had little in common culturally or politically. But Britain exercised a special fascination on feminists abroad during the last decade before the First World War, because it was the only country in the world where the suffrage campaign seemed to be assuming the proportions of a revolutionary upheaval:

> Picture to yourself a conflagration gradually taking hold of a whole country. For a long time the fire smoulders. Now and then small sparks shoot out, flicker and die. Then suddenly the fire flares up, seizes the ground and spreads rapidly, impetuously, sweeping the obstacles from its path . . . Such is the scene of the women's movement which has seized England over the past three years, dividing the country into two camps.[36]

The immediate cause of this unexpected eruption was the Women's Social and Political Union (or WSPU). Founded by Emmeline Pankhurst in 1903, it began life as an informal organisation of women in Manchester, many of them members or sympathisers of the local Independent Labour Party and including a considerable number of working-class women. Its initial aim was principally to pressurise the ILP into a whole-hearted acceptance of women's suffrage, and at first it made little impression on society at large. By 1905, however, Mrs Pankhurst's eldest daughter, Christabel, decided that the WSPU was 'making no headway' and that bolder tactics, more eye-catching than pamphleting and public speaking, were needed. The new policy was inaugurated in October 1905, when she and Annie Kenney engineered their own arrest at a large Liberal election meeting in Manchester. The WSPU became news and its membership grew. Within six months it had established an office in London and had begun to develop from an amateur provincial suffrage society, into a well-run national organisation. With the Liberals in power, it launched an increasingly violent campaign to force the government into conceding women's suffrage, in the process antagonising not only its anti-suffragist opponents but also the moderate wing of the suffrage movement whose members were to be found in the National Union of Women's Suffrage Societies.[37]

The transformation of the suffrage movement into a live issue in Britain produced much comment abroad. The course of women's emancipation in Britain over the past forty years had been steady, but slow. The progressive extension of male suffrage had not apparently improved the chances of women (despite their partial admission to municipal franchise), and for several years during the 1890s their campaign seemed to have lost all dynamism. Russian delegates to the London congress of the International Council of Women in 1899, had noted the profound conservatism of the 'typical Englishman', which permeated all levels of British society and which was expressed in a self-satisfaction with the country's achievements and a hostility to any sudden change. Suffragists in these years sought encouragement not in England, but in the colonies of New Zealand and Australia, and in the United States. Even seven or eight years later, observers felt that the 'traditions of old England' remained a barrier to progress not encountered in the younger civilisations of America ('the cradle of the women's political movement') or in Britain's colonies.[38]

Hence the interest aroused by the suffragettes:

> For forty years English women, by nature and tradition self-possessed, composed, carefully avoiding anything in the slightest bit 'shoking' [sic], waged a struggle for their political and civil rights within strictly constitutional bounds, by meetings and petitions. And moved not one step nearer their goal . . . At last frustrated with beating the air, women went on to the offensive, unafraid of the worst thing in the world – appearing ridiculous.

Like most Russian feminists who commented on developments in Britain, this correspondent noted the dedication and self-confidence which had been injected into the suffrage campaign by the new organisation. Although she might quarrel with the tactics of the WSPU in attacking the Liberal Party when it was already in difficulties, 'one cannot deny that women in England have succeeded in displaying themselves as a force to be seriously reckoned with.'[39]

The Russian response to the suffragettes' exploits was remarkable in its intense involvement, not just in the campaign itself, but also in the intricacies of British party politics as they affected women's suffrage. The feminist press carried regular articles on Britain in this period and a reader of *Soiuz zhenshchin*, in particular, would have gained a detailed impression of political life there, of the government's Budget crisis and its constitutional clash with the House of Lords. Of the handful of feminists who took a specialist interest in Britain and reported on it for the journals, Mirovich was certainly the most prolific and, it would seem, the most widely read. She was a devoted, though at times critical, anglophile who spent much time in England from the 1890s until her death in 1913 (even speaking at suffrage meetings in Hyde Park) and became well acquainted with its institutions, customs and inhabitants.[40]

She was a passionate feminist and a leading member of the Union of Equal Rights in Moscow, but also a Kadet who was not afraid of making enemies among the social–democrats, as her performance at the 1908 congress showed. Indeed, her antagonism towards the social–democrats was unusually fierce and spilled over into her commentary on feminism abroad. In other respects, however, her observations on the movement in Britain were representative of feminist opinion in Russia, especially the change in her attitude towards the contending suffragist factions, as the militant campaign became more violent.

Before the emergence of the WSPU as a national organisation, her English contacts were members of the National Union of Women's Suffrage Societies, led by Millicent Fawcett. Mirovich was instrumental in organising the telegram of sympathy which the Union of Equal Rights sent to the NUWSS in May 1905, and early the following year arranged for NUWSS pamphlets and leaflets to be sent to Russia to boost the women's union's meagre propaganda material.[41] In later years, however, she became very impatient with the Fawcett organisation, criticising it for being too ladylike and for failing to attract 'the populace': 'it lacks the ability to draw a crowd'. She was also upset by its relationship with the militants, which was one of mutual irritation sometimes erupting into open hostility.[42]

However, neither she nor most feminists in Russia were unequivocal supporters of the militants. Long before the WSPU campaign had resorted to the unrestrained violence of its last phase (from 1912), feminists in Russia had begun to take exception to the Pankhurst organisation's high-handed behaviour towards those in the suffrage movement who disagreed with its tactics. In 1907, the Pankhursts had precipitated a split in the WSPU, forcing out a significant proportion of its members and abandoning any pretence of democracy within the leadership. The dissidents, led by Charlotte Despard and Teresa Billington-Greig, established the Women's Freedom League (or WFL) which pursued the militancy of the WSPU (though rejecting its escalating violence) while maintaining a commitment to working women, which the WSPU was in the process of shedding. The breakaway organisation quickly drew the sympathy of Russian observers, particularly Mirovich and Figner, who were attracted most of all by its rejection of 'autocratic' methods and by Charlotte Despard's wider political sympathies. While WSPU leaders behaved as if nothing outside the suffrage campaign possessed any significance for women, Mrs Despard was a keen supporter of the Russian revolutionary movement and, on one occasion, invited Figner to speak about Russia to a group of workers at her home in Battersea.[43]

The Russians were, in general, only observers of the conflicts between suffragists and suffragettes, but at the London congress of the IWSA in 1909 they became personally involved in a quarrel between the official British delegation (NUWSS) and a 'fraternal delegation' from the Women's Freedom League. The WFL representatives wished to have their contribution to the suffrage campaign officially noted and since they could not, as guests, propose any amendment to a resolution themselves, the Russian delegates undertook to do so. The British delegation objected strongly to the amendment, and was even more indignant when Mirovich and Goncharova then proposed, to a roar of applause, that the congress express its sympathy for the 387 militant suffragettes imprisoned so far by the British government. To save the congress from further embarrassment, the chairman ruled the amendment out of order.[44]

The Women's Freedom League never assumed a dominant role in the British suffrage campaign and its Russian friends consistently over-rated its significance. Meanwhile they continued to regard the WSPU with a mixture of admiration and disapproval. What they admired most was the union's ability to hold the headlines, recruit members and raise money. The latter, particularly, was reported with envy. 'The practical English are well aware that sympathy for any cause is valuable inasmuch as it takes some kind of real form,' as Liudmilla fon Ruttsen noted meaningfully.[45] But, in her speech on England to the 1908 congress, she reflected the divided feelings of many feminists towards the 'extraordinarily aggressive character' of WSPU tactics. Only three weeks earlier, suffragette hecklers had totally disrupted a suffrage meeting at the Albert Hall, organised by the Women's Liberal Federation and addressed by Lloyd George. Their action had naturally enraged not only members of the Cabinet but the constitutional suffragists as well. Ruttsen was inclined to agree with them, arguing that the tactics of confrontation were wrong 'in this case'. But her condemnation of this incident was more than matched by her praise for their dedication to the cause and their willingness to risk imprisonment, a fate which, she said, had become quite familiar to Russians but was new to English women.[46]

The use of violence to obtain political ends was a highly-charged issue in Russia during these years. The dilemma facing Russian liberals, who found it impossible to condemn the revolutionary terror of which they disapproved whilst the government employed coercive measures in retaliation, was reflected in their evaluation of suffragette violence in Britain. Certainly, the extent and nature of the militant tactics employed by the WSPU before the end of 1912 were but pale echoes of SR terrorism in Russia, and were more than equalled by the rough treatment meted out by the government. Nonetheless, the rules of admissible behaviour were being broken, though in a cause which Russian feminists held to be just, and their response to WSPU militancy in Britain was as ambivalent as that of the Kadets to the SRs' policy of assassination at home.[47]

Some expressed their unease by minimising the extent of the violence. 'During the whole period of the struggle,' Mirovich commented in the early stages of militancy, 'there have been no acts of violence, if you disregard a few broken panes in Asquith's windows.' Even Kal'manovich, who was throughout a more ardent supporter of the WSPU than most of her colleagues, denied that stone-throwing was official WSPU policy. 'If a number of [militants] sometimes threw stones at windows or permitted themselves some other form of action, this was more often a case of individual temperament than the tactics of an organisation.'[48] But, although eventually obliged to concede that the violence was instigated, or at least encouraged, by the suffragette leadership, the Russians could find good reasons for not opposing it; they argued (as did many English sympathisers) that no social movement had achieved its ends without resorting to force, and cited the riots which had ushered in the Reform Act of 1832.[49]

There was never any question, however, that they would copy suffragette tactics. What seemed 'heroic' when viewed from a distance would have seemed immoral in Russia itself, where the level of violence in political life was already too high. Moreover, their acceptance of violence in England had its limits. As attacks on property became more frequent and less discriminating, sympathy for the suffragettes' cause was tempered by disapproval of their 'excesses', which were seen as jeopardising the chances of any future parliamentary bill.[50] Even so, waning sympathy for the suffragettes did not lead Russian observers towards a more lenient view of the British government's response; if anything, their indignation grew more intense. *Zhenskii vestnik*, in particular, kept up a barrage of criticism, attacking Asquith and his cabinet in terms which it would hardly have risked using about its own government. The more draconian the measures employed by the British authorities in their attempts to put down the militancy, the more heroic the suffragettes appeared in Pokrovskaia's eyes. About Emily Davison's suicide on Derby Day she wrote:

> Miss Davison was a passionate advocate of women's equality . . . There are many such passionate, daring and selfless advocates of women's rights in England. They use the most diverse means to protest against women's lack of equality. But instead of giving way to the natural course of history the English government carries on the struggle against the suffragettes with staggering stupidity, as if they were common criminals, imprisoning them, sentencing

them to hard labour, occupying their premises like some den of thieves, forbidding their meetings, etc. Asquith, apparently, is unaware that he is waging a struggle not against the militants, but against progress. All the worse for him.[51]

Pokrovskaia was undoubtedly more forgiving of the suffragettes' excesses than many of her fellow feminists. But even the far more moderate journal, *Zhenskoe delo*, (which dismissed Davison's suicide as a mad gesture) was perturbed by the British government's behaviour, arguing that its infringement of civil liberties was 'quite unheard of in this country of political freedom.'[52]

It was not the issue of violence alone which made the British suffragettes controversial in Russian eyes. As much a matter of debate was their demand for equal rather than universal suffrage. Since 1832, electoral reform in Britain had been achieved by periodic extensions of the franchise, the last major reform being in 1884. The result was far from universal manhood suffrage. Even in 1911 about 40 per cent of adult men were not on the electoral register.[53] There was, therefore, no reason to expect the women's suffrage campaign to make universal female suffrage its immediate goal. Instead, the bills and amendments which were introduced with monotonous regularity between 1867 and 1914, aimed at no more than a limited enfranchisement of women. None of these bills would have given the vote to more than one and a half or two million women (out of an adult female population of 13 million) and some were still more restrictive.

On this point, the leaders of the Women's Social and Political Union were no more radical than the constitutional suffragists; if anything, they were even more willing to sacrifice the votes of working-class women to the demands of political strategy. In doing so, they clashed with the advocates of universal suffrage, many of whom had joined the newly-established Labour Party. Although a minority of the party's members favoured a limited enfranchisement of women as a first step, the majority of socialists baulked at any proposal which would enfranchise propertied women alone and thus strengthen the position of the property-owning classes in general. The WSPU, for its part, was more than a little suspicious of socialist objections to the 'ladies' vote', detecting (in many cases correctly) a disguised opposition to women's suffrage *per se*.

At the height of the 1905 Revolution, British demands for a qualified franchise were something of an embarrassment to feminists in Russia, especially to the Union of Equal Rights, whose campaign for political rights was based on universal suffrage without regard for class or social standing. But when the prospects for universal suffrage faded, Russian suffragists began to appreciate the wisdom of moderation. For this, they naturally came under fire from social–democrats like Kollontai, who charged feminists in Russia and abroad with using women's suffrage as an 'antidote against the democratic demands of the working class'.[54] They were particularly virulent in their criticism of the English suffragettes. Kollontai, for one, devoted several pages of her monumental polemic against the feminists, *The Social Foundations of the Woman Question*, to an assault on the suffragettes' exploitation of mass militancy for undemocratic ends. But her real targets were nearer home:

Our Russian *ravnopravki* regard the struggle of Englishwomen for a limited franchise with complete sympathy . . . Those very women, who even now are themselves carrying the heavy burden of being denied political rights, those very women who, it would seem, know from their own experience what it means to have no opportunity to defend their closest interests, lightheartedly rush to the defence of an electoral system which leaves the most exploited and downtrodden section of the female population without rights as before.[55]

The feminists were unshaken. They continued to defend the political wisdom of gradual reform, and rebutted left-wing objections that the suffrage movement was a middle-class concern, by listing the working-class women's organisations which had joined the campaign. They seized at every opportunity to illustrate the indifference or hostility of many working-class men towards women's suffrage (universal or otherwise) and counterposed Keir Hardie's principled stand against Labour Party colleagues in advocating equal political rights for both sexes as an immediate goal. Even Vera Figner, with her revolutionary past, could see the merit of partial enfranchisement, 'given the well-known conservatism of English society'.[56]

The point at issue between feminists and social–democrats in Russia was not, in reality, the future of the British political system or the effectiveness of the suffragettes. Both factions were continuing a tradition, well-established among the Russian intelligentsia, of importing foreign weapons to supply a war of words at home. This war was at its most intense when opportunities for action in Russia were limited, as the repeated confrontations at the 1908 congress so vividly demonstrated. But the desire to score points against the opposition was not the only reason for the feminists' interest in events abroad. Underlying all the debates over the aims and tactics of women's organisations in other countries, was their concern to measure the progress of the women's movement in Russia itself. Cut off by their geographical and political isolation from the mainstream of Western feminism and hampered in their activities at home by government interference, Russian feminists had looked to Europe and America, both for inspiration and for a standard of comparison.

In the early days of the women's movement, before the establishment of large-scale feminist organisations in the West, the Russians had some reason to feel pleased with their achievements, particularly in the realm of education. Indeed, it was even possible to boast that Russian women had greater access to secondary and higher education than anywhere else in Europe.[57] But after 1881, when all avenues for further development were closed off, activists in the movement had to fight hard, even to keep the gains they had made. In the twenty years which followed, they had ample opportunity to reflect on Russia's backwardness. Although an occasional voice could be heard to maintain that Russian women possessed an 'inner freedom' often lacking in their apparently emancipated sisters in the West, supporters of women's equality more frequently complained that women in Russia were indifferent to their rights and even unaware of their inequality. Until women were able to organise, wrote one sympathetic but critical observer in 1905, 'one may speak of the woman question in Russia, but hardly of the women's movement in the generally accepted meaning of that expression.'[58] True, feminists such as Mirovich believed that men and women in Russia shared an 'equality in their lack of rights', or at least did so until the granting of voting rights to men in 1905. But Mirovich was the first to argue that the West had much to give Russia, and was one of the most persistent in her attempts to forge closer ties with women abroad.

1905 gave Russian feminists their first chance to participate fully in the international movement. But their involvement brought no lasting benefit to their own work. Instead it simply reinforced their consciousness that the movement for women's rights in Russia (and particularly the suffrage campaign) lacked the self-confidence so noticeable elsewhere, and that their achievements were negligible when compared with other countries. The point was put with some considerable bitterness by Tyrkova at the end of 1913:

> We may without exaggeration speak of a women's army of millions united in an unarmed struggle for a better life, for a more fitting and responsible position in the family, in society, in the state . . . Only here in Russia is nothing, or practically nothing happening. Once Russian women were in the vanguard . . . Now the situation has changed . . . In Russia there is no women's movement, no strong women's organisations, no literature . . . Backward and indifferent to their own fate [women] listen to the swelling chorus of international women's organisations from a distance, and themselves sit with folded hands. Do Russian women hope that rights will be given to them without those efforts and strivings to which Englishwomen, Frenchwomen, Americans, Germans and even Chinese devote their energies?[59]

Perhaps Tyrkova was over-dramatising the achievements of feminism abroad, but her reaction was not untypical. She was simply expressing the disenchantment and frustration felt by feminists in Russia, as they observed the progress of women in other countries and the state of their own movement in the declining years of the old regime.

Notes

1 *Sbornik pamiati A.P. Filosofovoi* vol. i, pp. 188, 239–40. A similar organisation initiated by the Swiss feminist, Maria Goegg, in 1868, lasted only three years. Evans, *The Feminists* pp. 247–8.

2 *Report of the International Council of Women* (Washington: 1888) pp. 9–10. The council was commonly known by its initials, ICW.

3 *Ibid.* pp. 11, 44.

4 Flexner, *Century of Struggle* pp. 181–6.

5 Stanton in *Report of the ICW . . . 1888* p. 438.

6 Stasov, *Stasova* pp. 411–12.

7 It represented fifteen societies in Russia. *The International Congress of Women, London 1899* (London: 1900) p. 130.

8 L. Davydova, 'Na zhenskom mezhdunarodnom kongresse' *Mir bozhii* no. 8 (1899) pt. 2, p. 42. She excepted from this judgement the French delegate 'from whose speeches came a whiff of something antique, full of long-forgotten phrases about the tyranny of men and women's revenge.' See also N. Mirovich, 'Dva kongressa zhenskoi frondy' *Sbornik na pomoshch'* p. 243–55.

9 Unpublished correspondence between Filosofova and Lady Aberdeen is in the ICW archive, Public Archives of Canada, Ottawa.

10 *ICW Report for 1904–1905* pp. 67–69.

11 *International Council of Women Report for 1907–1908* (Aberdeen: 1908) p. 177. A copy of its statute dated 15 March 1917 and a letter from its president, Shabanova, are in the ICW archive. Before 1917, radical feminists criticised the Mutual Philanthropic Society for submitting to the obstructionism of the Ministry. Even Lady Aberdeen suggested that an informal committee be set up in Russia, instead of a Ministry-approved council. Letter to Filosofova, 7 February 1910. ICW archive.

12 Aileen S. Kraditor, *The Ideas of the Woman Suffrage Movement 1890–1920* (New York: 1971) p. 5.

13 *Report of the First International Woman Suffrage Conference* (New York: 1902).

14 Constitution of the IWSA, art. 2.

15 *Der Internationale Frauen-kongress in Berlin 1904* (Berlin: n.d.) p. 550.

16 There were no Russian delegates to the 1904 Berlin meetings, though Filosofova and a colleague were billed to speak at the ICW congress. Germany's sympathy towards Japan in the war with Russia made Filosofova cancel her visit. *Sbornik pamiati A.P. Filosofovoi* vol. i, p. 409; G. Grossman, 'Mezhdunarodnyi zhenskii kongress v Berline' *Pravda* no. 7–8 (1904) p. 180.

17 *Report Second and Third Conferences of the International Woman Suffrage Alliance* (Copenhagen: 1906) pp. 48–49.

18 Mirovich, *Iz istorii* pp. 3–4. The abbreviated English text is in *Second and Third Conferences of the IWSA* pp. 97–102.

19 *Ibid.* pp. 27, 34.

20 *Jus Suffragii* 15 March 1907 (no pagination).

21 *Ibid.* 15 April 1907; 15 January 1908.

22 See Mrs Catt's sympathetic speech to the London congress in 1909. *IWSA Report of the Fifth Conference* pp. 64–5; N. Mirovich, ' "Zhenskii parlament" v Londone' *Russkaia mysl'* no. 7 (1909) pt. 2, pp. 124–37.

23 *IWSA Report of the Fifth Conference* p. 63; N. Mirovich, *Zhenskoe dvizhenie v Evrope i Amerike* (M: 1907) pp. 8–9.

24 *Soiuz zhenshchin* no. 1 (1907) pp. 22–3. They were all works by social–democrats. See also the list of books recommended by the Union of Equal Rights, two-thirds of which were of foreign origin. *PZhK na 1907g*. pp. 365–9; also the union's pamphlet *Ukazatel' vazhneishikh sochinenii po zhenskomu voprosu* (M: 1907).

25 *Soiuz zhenshchin* no. 1 (1907) pp. 21–2.

26 *Ibid*. no. 2 (1907) p. 16.

27 Helsingfors university admitted women in 1870. By 1905, 564 of the 2,640 students were women.

28 *Second and Third Conference of the IWSA* p. 77.

29 N. Mirovich, 'Pobeda zhenskago dvizheniia v Finliandii' *Russkaia mysl'* no. 7 (1907) pt. 2, pp. 118–36; V. Figner, 'Zhenskoe dvizhenie v Finliandii' *PZhK na 1908g*. pt. 5, pp. 9–17.

30 Mirovich, 'Pobeda zhenskago dvizheniia' p. 133.

31 *Second and Third Conferences of the IWSA* p. 49.

32 *Trudy 1-go vserossiiskago zhenskago s"ezda* pp. 456, 766. For the feminists' stand see *Zhenskii vestnik* no. 1 (1907) p. 25, no. 3 (1908) p. 65.

33 Mirovich, 'Pobeda zhenskago dvizheniia' pp. 135–6; *PZhK na 1911g*. p. 82; *ICW Report on the Quinquennial Meetings Rome 1914* (Karlsruhe: n.d.) p. 385. Women continued to be comparatively well represented in the Seim: 25 in 1908, 14 in 1912 and 21 in 1913. The majority were social–democrats.

34 Of twenty-nine bills introduced by women up to 1911, the Seim passed six. *PZhK na 1911 g*. p. 82.

35 However, women in New Zealand were not given passive suffrage until 1919. Patricia Grimshaw, *Women's Suffrage in New Zealand* (Auckland: 1972) p. 111.

36 N. Mirovich, 'Novyi fazis zhenskago dvizheniia v sovremennoi Anglii' *Vestnik Evropy* no. 8 (1909) pp. 810–11.

37 The story of the WSPU is well documented. The fullest account is in Andrew Rosen, *Rise Up Women! The Militant Campaign of the Women's Social and Political Union 1903–1914* (London: 1974).

38 Mirovich, 'Dva kongressa' pp. 243–4; Davydova, 'Na zhenskom mezhdunarodnom kongresse' pp. 49–50; I.D. Novik, *Bor'ba za politicheskie prava zhenshchin* (M: 1906) pp. 3, 19.

39 *Soiuz zhenshchin* no. 4 (1908) pp. 15–16.

40 It was probably Mirovich who sent type-written minutes of the Union of Equal Rights proceedings (and Union of Unions congresses) to Charles Hagberg Wright, the librarian of the London Library. Hagberg Wright, a russophile who took a close interest in the liberation movement, received a number of books and pamphlets from Mirovich, including her own biography of Madame Roland.

41 Letter to Edith Palliser, 28 March (10 April) 1906, Fawcett Library autograph letters.

42 Mirovich, ' "Zhenskii parlament" v Londone' p. 126.

43 See Figner's interesting observations on the suffragettes in *PZhK na 1910 g*. pt. 3 p. 13. See Mirovich, 'Novyi fazis zhenskago dvizheniia' for a WFL meeting which Mirovich attended in 1908.

44 *IWSA: Report of the Fifth Conference* pp. 46–7; Mirovich, ' "Zhenskii

parlament" v Londone' p. 131; *Soiuz zhenshchin* no. 5–6 (1909) p. 11.

45 *Ibid.* no. 3 (1909) p. 4. See also no. 4 (1908) p. 16.

46 *Trudy 1-go vserossiiskago zhenskago s"ezda* p. 472.

47 The parallel between the repressive measures used in Russia and the British government's policy of forcibly feeding suffragettes on hunger strike was not lost on the suffragettes' supporters in Britain. 'We cannot denounce torture in Russia and support it in England,' wrote two liberal journalists. E. Sylvia Pankhurst, *The Suffragette Movement* (London: 1931) p. 318. Suffragette literature is full of references to 'Russian barbarism' and 'Cossack atrocities'.

48 A.A. Kal'manovich, *Suffrazhistki i suffrazhetki* (Spb: 1911) p. 2; Mirovich, 'Novy fazis zhenskago dvizheniia' p. 816. Kal'manovich later translated Christabel Pankhurst's histrionic assault on the immorality of men, 'The Great Scourge and How To End It' [*Strashnyi bich* (Spb: 1914)].

49 Mirovich in *Zhenskoe delo* no. 3 (1910) pp. 6–8. Figner, a former terrorist, was less squeamish than others on the question of violence and was apparently undismayed by the outburst of one stone-thrower that 'it will be a bomb next time'. *PZhK na 1909 g.* pt. 6, p. 111.

50 *Zhenskoe delo* no. 4 (1913) pp. 16–7; *Zhenskii vestnik* no. 1 (1913) p. 23.

51 *Ibid.* no. 7–8 (1913) p. 172.

52 *Zhenskoe delo* no. 10 (1913) p. 21.

53 Neal Blewett, 'The Franchise in the United Kingdom 1885–1918' *Past and Present* no. 32 (1965) p. 56.

54 *Trudy 1-go vserossiiskago zhenskago s"ezda* pp. 456–7.

55 Kollontai, *Sotsial'nyia osnovy* p. 270.

56 *PZhK na 1909g.* pt. 6, p. 103. All the arguments used by the suffragists in Britain are found in *Soiuz zhenshchin* passim. See Liddington and Norris, *One Hand Tied Behind Us* for a convincing argument that working-class participation was much higher than previously supposed.

57 Likhacheva, *Materialy dlia istorii zhenskago obrazovaniia* vol. ii, pp. 646–7.

58 V.M. Khvostov, *Zhenshchina nakanune novoi epokhi* (M: 1905) p. 90. This was a constant theme of Pokrovskaia's. For Russian women's 'inner freedom' see Zinaida Vengerova, 'Feminizm i zhenskaia svoboda' *Obrazovanie* no. 5–6 (1898) pt. 1, pp. 73–90; P.I. Maslova, *Zhenshchina o zhenshchine* (Spb: 1907).

59 *PZhK na 1914 g.* pp. 343–7.

6 Rapid Retreat and Gradual Recovery

By the time Tyrkova uttered her indictment of Russian women at the end of 1913, the movement which she had effectively written off was beginning to show signs of a sense of purpose noticeably lacking in the years following the 1908 Congress. Although her unfavourable comparison of Russian feminism with the women's movement abroad was quite justified, she had overlooked, in her pessimism, developments which seemed to promise a new upsurge of feminist initiative in Russia. Whether the revival would have proved short-lived one cannot say: it was cut off abruptly by the outbreak of the First World War. But while it lasted it was a welcome release from the caution and disenchantment of the previous five years.

Those years were marked by a severe decline in the energies of the opposition. The reaction had deprived revolutionary and constitutional parties alike of much of the following which they had attracted in 1905. Arrests, harassment of members, shortage of funds and intra-party disputes made political activity hazardous and unrewarding: by October 1907, the Kadets had lost 75,000 of their 100,000 membership and the continued deterioration thereafter was 'nothing less than disastrous'.[1] The revolutionary parties fared no better in these years; membership dropped and party activists went underground or emigrated once more. In the Duma, the Octobrists, ever mindful of the strong and vociferous minority to their right, enjoyed a shaky preeminence, but they formed what was more a coalition than a party, and one whose cohesion became increasingly susceptible to attack during the life of the Third Duma.

The stifling of open political activity in this period and the resurgence of conservative opinion (particularly in the provinces) could not but be reflected in the women's movement. Not only had its active supporters dwindled in number, but those who remained took a noticeably more compromising stand on current political issues than they had done in 1905 and 1906. No longer did women's groups demand from the Duma universal suffrage regardless of sex, religion and nationality, as the Union of Equal Rights had done in 1906. Instead, they advocated equal suffrage for both sexes based on the existing electoral law. Demands (like the abolition of capital punishment) which were unrelated to women's issues also disappeared from petitions and manifestos, so that as the movement became more politically moderate, it also became more specifically feminist.

This trend was most graphically illustrated by the career of the Russian League of Equal Rights for Women, the successor of the Union of Equal Rights. Registered in St Petersburg in March 1907, the league had led such a shadowy existence in its first eighteen months, that by the end of 1908 it was believed to have died 'a natural death'. The 1908 Congress brought a timely reprieve. Immediately afterwards, a number of leading feminists decided to pursue the idea, so hotly disputed at the congress itself, of a new national organisation. The League of Equal Rights presented itself as the ideal base, since it was a society which already had official sanction and whose members were apparently more than willing to co-operate. Within a month of the congress, the League had been reconstituted, its original leaders all but disappearing from the scene. They were replaced by familiar faces from the women's rights campaign: Chekhova as president, Shchepkina as head of its lecturing commission, Kal'manovich, Tyrkova, Ruttsen and other well known campaigners from the Union of Equal Rights. In later years, they too sank into the background. After Chekhova returned to Moscow in 1910, the presidency went to Poliksena Shishkina-Iavein (like Shabanova and Pokrovskaia, a doctor practising in St Petersburg) and new names began to appear in the league's records.[2]

The league, like the Union of Equal Rights before it, aimed to recruit members from as wide a circle as possible but, unlike the union, did not tie itself to a detailed platform. Chekhova's hope was that women all over Russia who sympathised with the principle of equal rights would enrol as members, even if they contributed little to the organisation besides their membership fee:

> If only one woman in a thousand joins the league, it will then have 75,000 members, which means that it will be strong and wealthy both in numbers and resources.[3]

Her goal proved to be vastly over-ambitious. At no time did its membership exceed 2,000 and generally it hovered around 1,500. Only three sections (in Moscow, Kharkov and Tomsk) were opened outside St Petersburg and membership was concentrated heavily in the capital.[4] Though the league proved to be more stable than its predecessor, functioning right up to the Revolution, it was by no means free from internal feuds and disputes, apparently of a more personal nature than the polemics which had forced the Union of Equal Rights into dissolution. Most damaging was a row which split the Moscow section only eighteen months after its formation. In itself, the dispute was extremely petty, but it aroused such passions among its participants that for a while the very future of the Moscow organisation was put in jeopardy.

The section had been founded early in 1910, largely on the initiative of former members of the Union of Equal Rights. Two of these, Mirovich and Mariia Blandova, were chosen the following year to represent the Moscow section at the Stockholm congress of the IWSA, fixed for June. The third member of the Moscow delegation was Mariia Raikh, doctor of philosophy and correspondent on the women's movement in Germany for the feminist press. At the Stockholm congress, a dispute blew up between Mirovich and Raikh over the latter's request for the Moscow delegation to be given more time on the agenda. This she had apparently been authorised to do by the Moscow section, much to the indignation of Mirovich and of the St Petersburg leadership. On their return to Russia, Raikh formally complained to the Moscow section that Mirovich had tried to block the request, on the pretext that she, Raikh, lacked the authority to make it. Even worse, she accused Mirovich of having insinuated that she had no right to speak for Russian women, because she was Jewish. Mirovich vehemently rebutted both accusations, dismissing the charge of anti-semitism as slander.[5]

At a section meeting in October, the Moscow council upheld Raikh's complaint, interpreting Mirovich's stand as an attack on its own authority. The quarrel now turned into a test of strength, not simply between the Moscow council and its dissident members, but between Moscow and the St Petersburg leadership, which supported Mirovich throughout. It culminated in a turbulent general assembly of the Moscow section, which voted (after more than a third of the members had left) to uphold the council's decision. Mirovich, accusing the council of 'usurping power', resigned from the section and was followed by a number of her colleagues. The whole affair, which had been well aired in the Moscow press, did not enhance the league's reputation and left a legacy of distrust between its Moscow and St Petersburg members, which had not completely dissipated by 1914.[6]

The St Petersburg section, however, had its own problems, which stemmed from a long-standing rivalry between the original founders of the league and the new membership which had joined in 1909. After a few years, the dispute came into the open at a general meeting in 1913, when a letter signed by 105 members criticised the founders for introducing party quarrels into the section and 'compromising our women's organisation in the eyes of society'. In what amounted to the final overthrow of the old guard, the meeting voted to remove the statutory four seats on the executive council which founder members had occupied since 1909 and, with a parting shot, threatened court proceedings against one of them for non-payment of an electricity bill incurred on the league's premises.[7]

Despite these upsets, the league could with some justice claim to be 'the most popular women's organisation in Russia' during these years. The competition was not very intense. Pokrovskaia's Women's Progressive Party had not proved viable outside the capital, while the Mutual Philanthropic Society never regained the popularity of its earliest years: membership in 1913 stood at 600, just over a third of its 1899 peak.[8] Even the initiatives of those social-democrats who had begun to see the value of separate women's clubs for building a 'proletarian consciousness' among working-class women, had not achieved any lasting success by 1913. The Working Women's Mutual Aid Society, which Kollontai had helped to establish in 1907, went through several crises before being closed down by the police six years later. The same fate befell the Third Women's Club (which, despite its name, was open to both sexes). Founded in 1912, it attracted a membership of some 800 men and women, organised social evenings, lectures and political discussions and finally fell victim to the police at the end of 1913.[9]

The organisational difficulties which plagued the women's movement in this period were matched by the anaemic quality of much of its campaigning. The situation was scarcely improved by the appearance of a new women's journal, which replaced *Soiuz zhenshchin* as the only alternative to the humourless *Zhenskii vestnik*. The new journal, *Zhenskoe delo* (*Women's Cause*) was quite a departure from the serious-minded feminism of its forerunners. Its founding editor (a man) was at pains to dissociate it from the radicalism of 1905, as well as from the latter-day militancy of the English suffragettes. Concerned to give the journal a more popular image reminiscent of a standard women's magazine, he offered readers a bland mixture, in which reports on the activities of the women's movement were interspersed with the latest fashions, theatre reviews and entertaining trivia. *Zhenskoe delo* also displayed a rather sanctimonious religiosity quite foreign to the rationalist traditions of the Russian intelligentsia, though characteristic of the more conservative wing of the women's movement abroad. In this, it was undoubtedly reflecting the marked revival of interest among the Russian educated public in religious questions and in its search for spiritual as well as political solutions to society's ills.

Insofar as it took a stand on feminist issues, *Zhenskoe delo* supported the initiatives of the League of Equal Rights and the Mutual Philanthropic Society, which were generally of a rather cautious nature. Most striking in these organisations' campaigns between 1908 and 1911, was the virtual submergence of political rights. This was due almost entirely to the prevailing political conditions: with the Kadets and Trudoviks occupying a weak position in the Third Duma, there was little possibility of challenging the restrictive electoral law imposed in June 1907, or of resurrecting the radical schemes of 1906. Only one legislative proposal affecting women's rights in state elections (a universal suffrage bill introduced by the Trudoviks) was put to the Third Duma before the end of 1911, and that failed without ever being debated.[10] More revealing, propaganda among women's groups themselves, for the extension of political rights, was negligible. It was not until political opposition to autocracy was revived in 1912, that the feminists took up the question with some vestige of their earlier vigour.

Women's franchise did remain something of a live issue in the 'non-political' sphere of local self-government, whose reform was a central preoccupation of both government and Duma during the five years of Stolypin's premiership. Here it seemed that feminists had won converts to their cause and from an unexpected quarter. During 1907 (when detailed proposals for zemstvo reform were being debated), the question of women's franchise in local elections was raised once again in the zemstvo assemblies, as it had been during the liberation period. The zemstvos of 1907 were no longer the progressive institutions of two or three years earlier; nevertheless, despite their increased conservatism and the outright hostility of right-wing members to any measure of female enfranchisement, the prevailing opinion within them was quite favourable. At a zemstvo congress in Moscow in the summer of 1907, a resolution was passed calling for limited active voting rights for women in local government.[11]

Some months later, thirty members of the Duma introduced a proposal (based on the zemstvo congress resolution) to give suitably qualified women the right to vote in local elections. The signatories were all moderate conservatives, including leading Octobrists like Guchkov and Rodzianko. Taken together, the zemstvo resolution and the Duma proposal seemed to usher in a more accommodating attitude on the part of the conservatives towards women's rights. But on closer examination the proposal proved to be less impressive, principally because it gave women only active voting rights and explicitly denied them access to elected office.[12]

The denial of passive voting rights was unacceptable to all but a handful of feminists, and even those who did not object in principle to a franchise based on property were suspicious of the motivation for such a reform. The Octobrists had not favoured women's suffrage in the past and had made few concessions in recent months. Their apparent conversion now to a limited measure of enfranchisement in local government was interpreted as an opportunist tactic to use women's votes to bolster their own position. It did not escape the feminists' notice that the parties of the centre and right would almost certainly be the principal beneficiaries of a reform which enfranchised only female property-owners, while women's exclusion from elected office would remove any threat to the male monopoly of authority.

In the event, the opportunity to strengthen the conservative, property-owning electorate did not prove to be an overwhelming argument in favour of women's suffrage, now or later. By no means all Octobrists supported the proposal of the thirty deputies and when the measure failed, along with the whole zemstvo reform, little regret was expressed at its loss.[13] The fact is that the subject was only of fleeting interest to conservatives in Russia. Opposed in principle to women's suffrage in state elections, they did not put much store by it in local elections either – even for vulgar political motives. Had they seriously envisaged women as a bulwark against radical change, conservatives would undoubtedly have supported far more vigorously than they did any attempt to enfranchise the considerable number of property-owning women in local government and possibly in the State Duma as well. (In some districts, women formed 51 per cent of the landowning population, while on average they formed 39 per cent.)[14] Granted, the disagreements which split the Octobrists in these years militated against any successful legislation. But generally, conservatives tended to regard the obstacles to enfranchisement as overriding the possible advantages to themselves. Women's suffrage was inopportune if not undesirable, an issue which needlessly complicated political life.[15]

If anything, conservative opinion in Russia was even less favourably disposed towards women's enfranchisement than it was abroad. In several Western countries, women were acquiring the local government franchise during the very period when their political rights in state elections were being most vehemently contested. In Britain, for example, there had been a steady increase in women's municipal franchise between 1869 and 1907, while the parliamentary franchise remained beyond their grasp. Often it was the greatest opponents of the parliamentary franchise who most fervently believed that women had an important role to play in local government, bringing their experience as managers of the domestic household to the affairs of the community. There, it was held, women could exercise their own peculiar capacities, far removed from the imperial concerns which were the preserve of parliament.[16]

The same attitude existed in Russia, but it was less persuasive. Because local self-government was a sensitive political issue, the right of women to participate in it was not so readily conceded by moderates and conservatives, or else it was limited to the lowest levels of involvement. Perhaps more important, moderate conservative opinion in Russia was weak when compared with Britain or the United States, while the strength of the extreme right wing was correspondingly greater. This was of no help to the cause of women's suffrage, which suffered during the reaction from its open association with the most radical demands of 1905. Despite the greater moderation of women's rights groups after 1907, the radical link remained a potent one and was reinforced by the opposition parties themselves, all of which continued to defend women's enfranchisement in the context of a broad programme of democratic reform.[17]

Conservative views on women's suffrage in local government were put to the test on several more occasions during the life of the Third Duma. On only one issue was there any promise of success: the government's attempted reorganisation of peasant administration. The volost zemstvo bill, introduced in October 1908, was intended to replace the segregated peasant institution of the volost (an area covering several villages) with a small zemstvo unit representing all the inhabitants in the area, responsible for taxation and administration of local affairs. It spent over two years in committee before being debated in the Duma, during which time it underwent substantial revisions, one giving passive, as well as active, voting rights to qualified women.[18]

These new proposals, though an improvement on the government's bill, did not satisfy women's groups. Not only were women specifically denied the right to hold office; in addition, the curial voting system and the property franchise deprived the majority of the female population, and notably peasant women, of any role in it at all. Women's organisations lobbied the Duma to amend the bill and found ready support in the opposition parties, all of which had other reasons for dissatisfaction, notably with its narrow property franchise. The Kadet deputy, Shingarev, was eloquent on this point: the zemstvos were 'a concern of the whole people', not least of those who owned no property. The reform, he said, was as important to Jews and peasants as it was to landowners. But, whether the franchise were to be based on property or not, women should still have equal rights with men. This was particularly necessary in a 'country lacking culture, poor in cultivated resources, like Russia'.

> If a woman can be a teacher or a doctor, if a woman can be elected by nature to the sacred duty of motherhood, if the education of the nation's citizens lies on her shoulders, please tell me just who can infringe her rights in the organs of self-government?[19]

The Kadets moved that women be made eligible for elected office, but the amendment was overwhelmingly rejected.

It was not, however, until Duma bills were sent to the upper house, the State Council, that the full extent of conservative opposition to women's suffrage (indeed to any broadening of the franchise) was revealed. The State Council, set up as a counterweight to the Duma (half its members were nominated by the tsar) successfully impeded many a legislative venture put before the Duma. Such a fate befell the volost zemstvo proposal. Women's franchise did not survive scrutiny by the Council's committee and was excised from the bill even before the whole house had been given a chance to air its views on the subject.[20]

* * *

The whole question of female franchise in local government, as considered by the Third Duma, was not one to arouse great passions in the breasts of even the most ardent suffragists, and their response to the zemstvo reform proposals was notable for its half-heartedness. It was as if they were already fully aware that the bills had little chance of being enacted and that demands for equal suffrage were more a matter of form than substance. Nonetheless, the Duma debates themselves had indicated a greater public acceptance of sexual equality than was the case before 1905, an impression which is confirmed when one looks at other areas of feminist activity in these years. It was in such areas as inheritance law, personal rights and access to education, rather than political rights, that a number of small but significant advances were made in the years before 1914.

Reform of women's inheritance rights had been extensively advocated during the past fifty years, as much by opponents of the existing system of patrimonial property law as by feminists themselves. Under a system which strictly curtailed the freedom of testamentary disposition, female inheritance rights were fixed by law. A woman received one-seventh of the immoveable and one-quarter of the moveable property of her deceased husband; a daughter (with surviving brothers), one-fourteenth and one-eighth respectively. In the absence of direct male heirs, daughters inherited equally.[21] Despite the criticisms to which the rules were subjected, no sustained effort was made to change them until 1909, when the Russian Women's Mutual Philanthropic Society promoted a bill establishing equal inheritance for both sexes. This was presented to the Duma by a group of Octobrist deputies and approved by the Ministry of Justice, which resubmitted it in revised form the following year. The bill met no substantial opposition in the Duma but was less well treated by the State Council where the original goal of the bill disappeared in a debate over the fragmentation of landed estates and the extension of the rights of testamentary disposition. The resultant legislation gave women equal rights in moveable and urban property, but restricted their share of rural landed property to no more than one-seventh, in an attempt to inhibit the further fragmentation of landed estates. This compromise was accepted by the Duma and became law on 3 June 1912.[22]

Of greater significance to the mass of the female population was the passage of a bill that widened the personal rights of married women, and which became law in March 1914. Its most notable feature was to grant a married woman the right to obtain her own internal passport without her husband's consent, thus effectively permitting spouses to live apart. The bill was a compromise between the requirements of the civil law code, which stated that a married couple must live together in a place of the husband's choosing, and a growing body of opinion which favoured wider grounds for divorce and legal separation in the case of an unsuccessful marriage. Until the new law was passed, a married woman could acquire a separate residence permit if her husband agreed, but only for a fixed period of time. After its expiry she had either to return home or obtain her husband's consent to a new permit. Divorce was heavily discouraged. Not only were grounds for dissolution restricted (adultery, prolonged sexual incapacity, five years' continuous absence and deprivation of civil rights), it was also a cumbersome and expensive procedure.[23]

The 1914 legislation had a complicated history. Reform of the burdensome laws relating to married women's personal rights had long been a goal of feminists, and there was plenty of material to illustrate the hardships and tragedies arising from women's inability to extricate themselves from an intolerable home life. The question had been considered on more than one occasion in the past thirty years, but without any significant change in the regulations, principally because of opposition from the Holy Synod. Certainly, it had been made easier for a woman to obtain a legal separation from a violent husband, and sometimes local administrators used their own discretion to give a wife her own passport. But still, women had little room for manoeuvre.[24]

Given the near-impossibility of a woman without substantial means obtaining a divorce under Russian law – and the extremely poor prospects for reform of that law – women's groups now decided to concentrate on recognition of the right to legal separation. Thus, in the spring of 1910, the Mutual Philanthropic Society presented the Duma with its own draft bill. This was introduced by seventy-three delegates from the Octobrists and opposition benches on 10 May. In addition to establishing legal separation through a civil court, the bill gave the court jurisdiction over the personal and property relations between the separated couple, and between them and their children, and entitled a woman to obtain her own internal passport without her husband's consent.[25]

The bill was a sufficiently moderate proposal to win the support of the majority in the Duma. Not only did it avoid the question of divorce, it also side-stepped the controversial issue of the internal passport, an institution which opposition parties believed should be abolished in its entirety. Feminists, and by no means only the most radical, shared this view of the 'archaic passport system', which they condemned as 'one of the relics of slavery' and an infringement of personal freedom. But in the hostile political climate after 1906, they preferred to seek the system's reform rather than expend all their energies on a fruitless campaign for its abolition.[26]

However, despite the bill's moderation, it did not escape drastic pruning during its lengthy progress through the legislative chambers. Like the bill on inheritance, it was taken up by the Ministry of Justice for reworking and re-emerged in April 1912 with its central pillar, the establishment of legal separation, completely removed. The new bill retained the old requirement that a married couple must live together, and simply widened the grounds for separation under existing law to include cruelty or grossly insulting behaviour, violation of the obligations and rights of marriage and dangerous physical or mental illness. The bill's scope was further reduced by the State Council, which rejected a proposal to make a woman's inclusion on her husband's passport subject to her own consent. The Council also limited the rights of a married woman to enter employment or education, or to negotiate a loan without her husband's approval, to those women already separated from their spouses. As several opposition speakers noted in the Duma, the latter restriction would encourage marital instability rather than the reverse, since a woman intent on acquiring an education, or taking up employment against her husband's wishes, would be obliged to abandon her family to do so.[27]

Opposition parties on the left deplored the limitations of the bill in its final version. The Right, however, saw it as an assault on the way of life of the 'modest Russian people'. The peasant economy, heavily dependent on family labour, would be ruined by the new law because 'any forward young woman whose husband had called her a fool one evening could obtain a passport next morning and go off to town'. But the hostility of the Right (and the abstention of the social-democrats) was not sufficient to deprive the bill of a majority and it passed through its last stage in the Duma on 4 February 1914.[28]

The reform, though it bore little resemblance to the original proposal, was a significant piece of legislation. It was a recognition in law of a fact which was slowly being established, namely that a woman did not lose her identity as an individual once she was married. In practical terms, it had considerable potential, not only enabling a woman to achieve a *de facto* separation in an unsuccessful marriage, but also contributing to the access of married women (albeit estranged from their husbands) to employment and education. To what extent it would have been an adequate substitute for a reformed divorce law is impossible to estimate, since normal civilian life was disrupted by the outbreak of war only a few months after the law was enacted. Certainly, contemporaries were under no illusion that it was a satisfactory compromise and continued to press for a more substantial reform. But the major provisions, establishing a married woman's right to mobility and a choice of occupation, could not but undermine the tsarist marriage code, a fact which was recognised by Soviet legislators. The law was incorporated, substantially intact, in the first Soviet decree on marriage in December 1917.[29]

The extension of inheritance rights and the married woman's passport (plus a number of other minor reforms and adjustments) were further evidence of growing public acceptance of women's greater independence and equality. The continued denial of the suffrage may have seemed to suggest that little had changed in society's attitudes, but this was not in fact the case: despite the marked decline in feminist activity and organisation, sexual equality was more widely accepted in the years after 1905, and non-political issues affecting women were discussed in the press with greater frankness. Such freedom was particularly noticeable in the discussion of sexual ethics and personal relations between men and women.

In the 1860s the 'woman question' revolved around education, employment and the establishment of a women's autonomy in her relations with her father and husband. Fifty years later the debates had become rather more complex (perhaps because women themselves were now the major participants). Personal independence was no longer the exclusive goal; now emancipated women were also looking for fulfilment in sexual relations (usually, but not necessarily, within marriage) and in motherhood. Some feminists, it is true, continued to regard marriage as a poor alternative to a career. Pokrovskaia's short stories featured heroines who resisted the blandishments of matrimony for the sake of their independence. But the image of the man-hating amazon, fostered by anti-feminists everywhere, was far from reality for most feminists, either in Russia or in the West.[30]

Discussion of motherhood and the family brought with it an unprecedented surge of interest in a host of related questions, including birth-control (or 'neo-malthusianism') and abortion. Neither topic became a campaigning issue in the women's movement in Russia (nor elsewhere before the First World War), but both were now debated in public with a remarkable lack of inhibition.[31] Of particular concern, above all to the medical profession, were the criminal penalties attached to abortion. With the number of abortions apparently rising at an alarming rate, it was evident that legal sanctions were ineffective, if not positively harmful. Several doctors at a congress of gynaecologists in December 1911 argued that, for both medical and social reasons, abortion should be legalised, a view which was repeated eighteen months later at a meeting of the principal medical association in Russia, the Pirogov Society of Doctors. On this occasion a feminist doctor, L. Gorovits, assailed the existing laws as an infringement of women's individual responsibility and stated that no woman wished to be simply an 'apparatus for child production'.[32]

As one might expect, the issue aroused strong feelings in society at large. Some objected to abortion on principle, as devaluing human life, others because it would allegedly encourage immorality. Even feminists like Pokrovskaia, who saw abortion as inevitable under existing social conditions and supported its legalisation, classed it with prostitution and infanticide as an 'abnormal and brutal' way of limiting the birth rate. But overall opinion in professional circles seemed to be moving in favour of legalisation: whereas the Pirogov congress had refused to adopt a radical resolution (passed in one of its sections), a congress of criminologists early in 1914 voted by a majority of thirty-nine to nineteen, for abortion to be made lawful in certain instances. Their view was not, however, shared in government circles. Only a few weeks later a government commission recommended a punishment of four to five years' imprisonment plus loss of civil rights for a woman procuring her own abortion, and four to six years' hard labour for the doctor performing it (eight to ten years if the woman died).[33]

If abortion was not a major campaigning issue in this period, prostitution most certainly was. The strength of public concern was well demonstrated by the mass of literature which appeared annually, both in Russia and abroad, in the form of moralising tracts, learned treatises and statistical enquiries. Feminists, of course, had a particular interest in the matter, as was shown at the 1908 Congress. Eighteen months later they were given another opportunity to demolish the 'dual moral standard', at the First All-Russian Congress on the Struggle Against the Trade in Women and its Causes.

The event was promoted by the Russian Society for the Protection of Women (*Rossiiskoe Obshchestvo Zashchity Zhenshchin*), a body with impeccable credentials, which had been campaigning against the social evil since the turn of the century. The origins of this society illustrate perfectly the international dimensions of the campaign against vice. In 1899, the secretary of the National Vigilance Association in Britain had come to St Petersburg in the course of a European tour, with the intention of recruiting support for an international congress on the white slave trade, to be held in London the same year. As a result of his visit, a St Petersburg committee was formed and a delegation despatched to London. Encouraged by its initial contacts with moral reformers abroad, the committee decided to extend its activities, and within a few months had received official permission to establish a national Society for the Protection of Women. From the start, it maintained good foreign connections and was closely involved in a series of congresses to which official delegations from the major European states were invited. At the first such event, sponsored by the French government in 1902, a convention was signed by sixteen nations to standardise the laws of those countries relating to the white slave trade.[34]

At home, the society set itself the dual task of rescuing women who had already fallen into the clutches of vice, and of preventing young girls (in particular those arriving in towns from the countryside) from doing likewise. Its methods were those employed by philanthropic organisations all over the world: it established hostels and clubs for working women, found employment for girls in safe occupations, published improving literature and sponsored legislation to outlaw procurers.[35]

The congress organised by the society in 1910 turned out to be a far more disputatious event then anticipated, at times reminiscent of the stormier sessions of the 1908 Congress. This was due in part to the emotive nature of the subject discussed, but also to the heterogeneous attendance, which ranged from half a dozen invited representatives of government ministries, to a radical delegation from Moscow whose influence on the proceedings was comparable to that exerted by the Worker's Group at the earlier congress. The Moscow delegation's presence was not by itself responsible for the oppositional tone of many of the speeches. All the leading feminists in St Petersburg (and not a few from the provinces) had turned up for the congress and were as keen as the radicals to discuss the issue in its widest social context. Not surprisingly, their behaviour provoked the intervention of one of the representatives from the Ministry of the Interior, who on several occasions rose to object that the discussion was assuming a political character at odds with the aims of the congress and used his authority to get debates and resolutions curtailed.[36]

Notwithstanding his interference, and the routine censorship imposed by the police stewards, all the sessions proved remarkably outspoken. Two themes, both politically loaded, dominated the first two sections: women's economic inequality and their lack of political rights. A survey made just before the congress opened had shown that 32 per cent of the prostitutes questioned had been drawn into the profession after losing a job or because their wages were low. Most speakers (both from the workers' delegation and from among the feminists) saw no reason to dispute the link between poverty and prostitution and had little difficulty in persuading their audience that higher wages and improved working conditions would go a long way towards combatting the social evil.[37]

They were no less insistent on the need for civil and political equality. From a strictly practical point of view, they saw equal rights as being essential in giving women an opportunity to work for those economic improvements without which there could be no end to prostitution. This was an argument employed most directly by Tyrkova, who, at the end of a long speech on pay and working conditions, proposed a resolution advocating 'the participation of women in both the organs of local and municipal self-government and in the central legislative institutions'. But feminists also saw political equality as essential for a psychological transformation of sexual morality: when women's social status was raised, the dual moral standard would disappear. Not only feminists took this line. The respected psychiatrist, V.M. Behkterev, a conservative in the matter of sexual ethics, advocated the full equality of the sexes to guarantee 'the health and morality of the mother and educator of the future generation'.[38]

Not all the participants put social and economic considerations uppermost. Several speakers laid the blame for increased prostitution on the decadence of contemporary culture, which accorded the status of literature to such 'pornographic' works as *Sanin* by Mikhail Artsybashev. *Sanin* had been enjoying a *succès de scandale* ever since its publication in 1907: its amorality, hedonism (and poor literary style) had been condemned at length by conservatives and progressives alike. But Artsybashev was not the only sinner: one speaker, from the St Petersburg House of Mercy, placed *Sanin* with the works of Baudelaire, Verlaine, Wilde and Sologub as sources of the 'moral insanity' of western civilisation, 'the most widespread disease of our century'. He was referring to more than sexual morality alone. Like so many contemporary commentators, he was linking the relaxation of sexual morals, the proliferation of pornography and the decadent movement in art with what he perceived to be the progressive collapse of society's values. Thus, the salvation of the country's youth from debauchery was a matter of national significance. However, the means with which he proposed to tackle the problem seemed quite inadequate for the task. Apart from a general appeal to moral rectitude, all he could offer was censorship of libraries and a minimum age limit on admission to brothels and places of entertainment.[39]

However controversial, the themes of artistic decadence, economic hardship and lack of legal rights were overshadowed at the congress by the issue of police regulation, which occupied a full third of the programme. The system whereby prostitutes were officially registered with the police in certified brothels and obliged to undergo regular medical inspection for venereal disease, had long fallen into disrepute throughout Europe. It was attacked as an infringement of personal liberty, an official sanction of vice and, moreover, a violation of the law code which made prostitution a crime. In addition, it apparently failed in its ostensible purpose, which was to contain the spread of disease. This last argument, being a purely practical one, was the most effective weapon in the abolitionists' hands and one which they did not fail to use. If regulation could not be adequately defended on the grounds of expediency, then it was difficult to defend it at all.

Several speakers at the congress attempted to do so, none the less, claiming that even in its imperfect form regulation was some insurance against disease and that without it syphilis would run riot throughout the country. Abolitionists refuted this contention by citing statistics for those countries, notably Britain and Scandinavia, which had already done away with the system. In both, the incidence of venereal disease had actually fallen since abolition. Improved medical facilities, they argued, not police regulation, were the means to eradicate the scourge of syphilis. Other speakers cited less practical reasons for condemning the system. 'Regulation is a diploma for debauchery', claimed one feminist, while the anglophile Mirovich used the example of Britain to draw a link between the abolition of police-controlled brothels and the strength of a constitutional regime. The history of abolition, she said, showed 'that the struggle against evil is inseparably linked with the cultural and political conditions of that country'.[40]

Sentiment at the congress was decisively on the side of abolition and Pokrovskaia's resolution to this effect (supported by all the major feminist societies in St Petersburg and Moscow) was passed with no difficulty. But support for abolition did not imply support for a *laissez-faire* approach towards commercialised vice. Abolitionists and their opponents alike advocated strenuous measures to suppress brothels, houses of assignation and other dens of immorality, and to punish severely the enticement of women and young girls into prostitution. Mirovich even went so far as to propose hard labour for life as a statutory punishment for child seduction.[41]

The effects of the congress were, however, minimal. There was no second congress to follow up the work of the first, as had been planned. Nor was there a rash of legislation in its wake, although the resolutions had been so phrased as to make them suitable for presentation to the Duma. Only three years later did a bill seeking to abolish police supervision see the light of day. Presented to the Duma by the Kadet deputy (and zemstvo doctor), Shingarev, it made little progress through the legislature and the system of regulation was left intact until the Revolution.[42]

If the campaign against regulated prostitution – and against the dual moral standard generally – had little practical success in Russia, the same cannot be said of another area of feminist activity, that which related to education and professional training. Of all the issues which had absorbed the energies of the women's movement over the past half-century, it was this which proved to be of most enduring interest and to have yielded the greatest rewards. In that time, the educational expectations of women from the upper and middle strata of society had been transformed. No longer was there any question that women were mentally and emotionally capable of intellectual exertion: as school pupils, they were subjected to a course of study broadly equivalent to that pursued in boys' gymnasia and, on matriculation, a significant percentage went on to higher education. Although women had enjoyed only a brief two years of admission to university lectures before the education minister banned their further registration, a reasonable substitute existed in the women's higher courses which, by 1910, had been established in ten university cities throughout the Empire. The following year, four of these institutions (in St Petersburg, Moscow, Kiev and Kazan) were effectively transformed into women's universities, when their students were given full rights to enter for state examinations.[43]

Since 1906, women wishing to become doctors had had the choice of two medical institutes (at Moscow as well as the older St Petersburg establishment), and two more such institutes had opened, in Odessa and Kharkov, by 1910. There were, by this time, over 1,400 women doctors in Russia (out of a total of 24,264), a small percentage of the total, certainly, but a significant achievement considering the many obstacles which had been put in their way. And the numbers were rising: by 1912 there were over 2,000 registered women doctors. They tended to specialise in women's and children's medicine; Shabanova, for example, won herself a position of some repute in that field. Otherwise, they were to be found mainly among zemstvo doctors, or holding less prestigious posts in city hospitals.[44]

Fewer opportunities existed for women within the legal profession. The government had explicitly excluded them from it in the mid-1870s, since which time the few women able to obtain legal qualifications abroad had been given no opportunity to practise at home. In 1906, however, law studies were at last opened to women in Russia, both at the higher courses and at universities, despite the government's unaltered opposition to their making professional use of their qualifications. Not unexpectedly, the opening of legal studies brought with it the demand that women be admitted to the Bar (the office of *prisiazhnyi poverennyi*), a demand which was fully supported by many law faculties and practising lawyers. By 1908, a small number of women had been accepted as assistant barristers (*pomoshchniki prisiazhnykh poverennykh*), only to have their appointments overturned by the courts. The following year, a woman was engaged as a defence lawyer in a criminal case but was immediately challenged and prevented from continuing.[45]

Since women's rights to practise law had met with no success in the courts, the issue was now taken to the Duma. A bill introduced in November 1909 was sympathetically received by the Kadets and most Octobrists and was passed in 1912. It had strong defenders in the State Council as well, but their support was not sufficiently persuasive to prevent its final rejection, by a majority of eighteen, early in 1913. A further attempt was made later that same year, but was similarly rejected by the State Council in 1916.[46]

By far the most popular occupation for graduates of the higher courses was teaching, the only profession to which women had had relatively unimpeded access since the 1870s. At the turn of the century, two-thirds of the graduates of the St Petersburg higher courses were going into the profession, a few teaching at the courses themselves and a few more setting up their own schools, but the vast majority teaching in girl's secondary and mixed elementary schools. They were particularly welcome at the latter, not simply because they were deemed to be more suitable than men to teach young children but equally because they could be paid much lower salaries and could not expect any of the rights and promotion prospects which men could claim. But gradually, the numerous restrictions which hampered both their professional activity and their private lives (the most onerous being a prohibition on the right to marry) were being eroded. Though still badly paid and excluded from the more prestigious positions, professional opportunities by 1914 were far wider than they had been twenty years earlier. By 1912 the ratio of female to male teachers in Russian schools was three to two, and in rural schools run by the zemstvos it was three to one.[47]

Despite the undoubted transformation of the educational expectations of women, there were still great problems to be overcome. Quite apart from the numerous bureaucratic obstacles which women all too often encountered in their quest for academic credentials, there remained the unresolved question of the purpose of women's education. Was it primarily to equip them for a professional career, no different from that pursued by their male peers, or was its chief purpose to prepare them for their biological role as mothers? Nikolai Pirogov, over fifty years earlier, had had the latter aim in mind when he wrote his celebrated 'Questions of Life', and his was a point of view which had readily commended itself to two succeeding generations of Russian educationalists. The belief that a career would always assume a subordinate role in a woman's life heavily influenced the policies of the government, inhibiting the development of higher education and consequently affecting the curriculum of girls' secondary schools. Yet at the same time, the aptitude of women in particular professions such as teaching and medicine (both of which were held to be compatible with 'womanly' roles) was increasingly accepted and to such an extent that by 1910 their contribution to those professions had become indispensible.

The incompatibility between these two conceptions of education for women provoked many a dispute in professional and bureaucratic circles, and equally in the women's movement itself. It was by no means a straightforward political issue. Although conservatives (often opponents of women's political enfranchisement) not unnaturally tended to the view that female education must be directed towards the training of mothers, radical feminists did not necessarily take the opposite stand. Some believed that, while a woman wanted to work for her living, she was looking for more than professional or academic advancement on the male pattern. In their view a woman's education should not be identical to a man's: women had specific intellectual and psychological gifts which should be used to the benefit of the community. Only by nurturing the feminine as well as the masculine side of the human personality could society achieve true equality between the sexes.[48]

Whether women's intellectual capacities differed significantly from men's was a question which received due attention at a major congress on women's education organised by the League of Equal Rights in December 1912. A number of speakers interpreted the question in the sense in which it had often been considered over the past half century, namely, the superiority or inferiority of the female intellect compared with the male. While no one at the congress argued that women were inherently inferior to men, some shared the view of the literary critic, S.A. Vengerov (a professor at the St Petersburg higher women's courses), that girls' secondary education did not prepare their minds adequately for further study. However, the majority of speakers did not see this as a fundamental problem. Generally it was held that women compensated for the deficiences of their schooling by their enthusiasm and dedication; any lingering inadequacies would be removed by the establishment of a common curriculum in boys' and girls' secondary schools and by the long overdue admission of women to university.[49]

Two speakers, however, regarded the question as one of intrinsic psychological significance for the women's movement. The historian Aleksandra Efimenko accepted the much-disputed contention that the female intellect excelled in intuitive as opposed to logical thought, but argued that this should be the key rather than the barrier to greater intellectual initiative on the part of women. She felt that by exploiting their own particular qualities, women could achieve more than they did at present, without falling victim to the ambition and 'careerism' which men displayed. Tyrkova developed the theme further, suggesting that 'women's logic', so often dismissed in the past as an irredeemable defect, was in fact a quality to be prized above the intellectual attributes cultivated in men. Women, she felt, were more in touch with their feelings, more aware of the subconscious world of the mind which psychologists were only now beginning to explore. She perceived women's emulation of the male intellect to be no less a threat to contemporary culture than their aping of male sexual morality, a phenomenon which she castigated as 'prostitution not only of the body but, far more dreadful, of the spirit also'.[50]

This first national congress on women's education, which was also the last major congress on a feminist theme to be held between 1908 and the Revolution, was in certain respects the most successful of the three. Like the others, its organisation suffered from the seemingly inevitable delay in receiving official permission and the equally inevitable last-minute rush, in spite of which it managed to present a remarkably coherent summing up of half a century of educational achievements and frustrations. Instead of attempting to illuminate all the facets of women's existence in contemporary society, as the 1908 congress had done, the congress restricted itself to narrower goals. In the process, it touched upon many of the grievances felt by the whole of the educated population of Russia, and brought out the almost universal resentment of an authoritarian educational system whose suffocating influence was felt not only in the classroom but in every sphere of daily life.[51]

One reason for the greater coherence of the congress was the absence of a disruptive Worker's Group. While this undoubtedly made for a certain complacency, even dullness, in the proceedings it did permit the chief target to be easily identified. Despite the profound disagreements which existed on issues such as general versus specialised education, and the classical curriculum versus the modern, the principal enemy of progress was indisputably the government, whose bureaucratic stranglehold on the educational system hindered every effort to bring enlightenment to the people, in place of mere instruction.

It is true that there were radicals among the speakers, like the Menshevik, Kuvshinskaia, who had been a leading participant in the political disputes of the 1908 Congress. On this occasion her speech, on literacy among working-class women, produced little controversy. It was an almost optimistic account of the way in which industrialisation was breaking down old prejudices against female education, despite the constraints of long working hours and inadequate provision of classes. Far from insisting that substantial reform was impossible under the existing social system, she cited the example of Britain to suggest that a shorter working day would lead automatically to a growth in literacy among proletarian women. Whether mass literacy would itself raise the status of women in the factory was less certain: current statistics showed that female literacy did not bring with it higher wages, though in the case of men there was a clear correlation between the two.[52]

More overtly critical of the liberal consensus at the congress was Mariia Shitkina, a garment worker from Petersburg, who followed Kuvshinskaia with a speech on worker's self-education circles. Contradicting speakers from philanthropic organisations (such as the Society for the Care of Young Girls) which provided educational facilities for women, she stated categorically that adult education could be of use to workers only when they themselves organised it and, moreover, that no benefit could accrue to either sex by segregating women's education from men's. But the burden of her speech was, like so many of the contributions to the congress, an attack on the obstructive approach of the government towards private educational initiatives, in this instance towards union-sponsored clubs in industrial districts, which were subject to constant harassment from the police in these years. Though feminists and liberal reformers might quarrel with her dismissive attitude towards their own educational ventures, they could only applaud her castigation of police interference and her demand for civil and political rights.[53]

* * *

By this time the women's movement had begun to emerge from the doldrums. The political temper of the country had changed with the assassination of the prime minister, Stolypin, widespread apathy giving way to an intensification of political activity on both left and right. During 1911, industrial unrest, which had been all but stifled for the past four years, began to grow again. Early in 1912, the massacre of 170 striking workers in the Lena goldfields in Siberia set off a wave of strikes and student demonstrations throughout Russia. For the first time women workers (whose docility had recommended them to employers after the turmoil of 1905) were taking a prominent part in strike activity.

Feminists were not slow to respond to the change in the political climate and greeted the passing of the 'long five-year night' with heightened expectations. Most promising was the renewal of demands for the vote. At the beginning of 1912, the League of Equal Rights sponsored its first major proposal on women's suffrage to be presented to the Duma, a bill giving women equal voting rights in state elections. This was introduced by the Trudovik Bulat in February, with the support of forty deputies, most of whom were either Trudoviks or Kadets. Though as unsuccessful as all previous attempts to obtain women's suffrage, the bill heralded a return (albeit hesitant at first) to active campaigning for political rights.[54]

There was certainly no rush of enthusiasm: no public meetings were organised to promote the bill and an attempt during the election campaign for the Fourth Duma to organise a suffrage meeting in St Petersburg petered out after the Mutual Philanthropic Society dismissed the idea as 'inopportune'. None the less, a new spirit was discernible. What was impossible in the spring was realised in November, when the first joint meeting of feminist groups since the heyday of the liberation movement was held in St Petersburg. To the astonishment of the organisers, it attracted a large audience. A second meeting, promoted by the Women's Progressive Party, followed a month later, again producing a packed hall. Activity continued into the New Year: the Progressive Party planned further meetings, the Mutual Philanthropic Society proposed a course of lectures on local self-government and the Moscow branch of the League of Equal Rights (apparently now recovered from the Mirovich–Raikh schism) announced plans for a second national women's congress to be held at the end of 1913.[55]

Also in the early months of 1913, came the last legislative attempt before 1917 to obtain female suffrage. The occasion was a universal suffrage bill drawn up by the Kadets in a renewed campaign for civil and political rights, which it launched at the end of 1912. The campaign was largely the inspiration of Miliukov who saw it, against strong opposition from a number of his colleagues, as the most urgent task of the party in the coming months. Suitably, therefore, it was Miliukov who presented the bill on 27 February. It was a fine irony that the man whose name had been closely associated with liberal opposition to women's political rights should now be championing their cause.[56]

At what point Miliukov had altered his opinion on the matter is not clear. He always maintained that his objections in 1905 and 1906 had been based solely on practical political considerations; he believed then that to include women in the suffrage formula would alienate the peasant masses, whom his party was anxious to attract. By the time of the 1908 Congress, however, he was prepared to state that circumstances had changed sufficiently to make women's suffrage acceptable, a concession which did not entirely redeem his reputation among feminists. Although he did not say as much, it would be hard to avoid the conclusion that he was prepared, in 1908, to support the principle when there was no longer the slightest possibility of his being able to implement it. But his change of heart also reflects a change of orientation in the Kadet party as a whole. By 1908 the Kadets no longer looked to the peasants as a major source of support, and their radical policy on agrarian reform, so striking in 1905, now lay gathering dust on the shelves. This was still more the case by 1913. They had lost the votes of the peasantry and now held only 9 per cent of all the electoral seats outside the six major cities of the Empire.[57]

It was Miliukov himself who, in the Duma debates on the suffrage bill, most vigorously rebutted right-wing objections that women's suffrage was 'the latest Paris fashion' to be foisted on the peasantry:

> We respect peasant wishes and demands insofar as they express the interests of the peasant masses, their democratic demands. But to copy the peasant view of the world everywhere and in every detail, even when it is based on ignorance and prejudice – that we cannot do. On the contrary we believe that they must be combatted, in the countryside as everywhere.

Women all over the world had shown themselves to be fit to take on political responsibility: in a few countries they had already done so. 'Now', said Miliukov, 'it is our turn, Russia's turn'.[58]

Although the Kadets had more seats in the Fourth Duma than in its predecessor, the suffrage bill was doomed to failure. Rights, Nationalists and Octobrists were all opposed to universal suffrage and the question of whether women should be included did not greatly affect their opposition. The bill was rejected on the second day of the debate by a vote to 206 to 126.[59]

* * *

The reawakening of the feminist movement was not untouched by setbacks and conflicts. Quite apart from lingering feuds within the women's organisations, such as those which bedevilled the existence of the League of Equal Rights, the organisers of meetings and lectures had to contend with the undiminished interference from the police and local authorities, which drove even the most law-abiding to the brink of despair. A typical incident occurred at the very first of the new wave of meetings, when mounted police provoked a near-riot among a crowd of people unable to get into the full hall. Pokrovskaia's response to this incident, which after all was no more nor less than the feminists had learned to expect over the years, is indicative of the new mood. With an asperity which one would hardly have met in her even during 1905, she accused the police of using any excuse to provoke trouble, and she resurrected the old demand of the liberation movement for freedom of association and assembly.[60]

At the same time, feminists had to meet the challenge of the revolutionary women's movement, which was finally taking recognisable shape. Hitherto, attempts to organise working-class women had been sporadic and not notably successful. However, the recovery of revolutionary initiative which accompanied the wave of strikes and protests during 1912 brought with it a re-evaluation of working women's revolutionary potential. For the first time, social–democratic party organisations (and notably the Bolsheviks) began to appeal directly to women in their propaganda, to the consternation of more traditionally-minded party workers. The most successful of their enterprises was International Women's Day, a festival inaugurated by the Socialist International in 1910, but celebrated for the first time in Russia in February 1913, with a series of meetings in five cities of the Empire. The following year the Bolsheviks launched *Rabotnitsa*, the first Russian social–democratic journal aimed specifically at women.[61]

While feminists were glad that working-class women were being taken seriously as a political force, they were far less happy with the prevailing tone of socialist propaganda, much of which was intended to counteract the lure of separate women's organisations and direct working women into the established proletarian movement. This had, of course, been a constant feature of the socialist approach to the women's movement; the difference now was that it was proving effective. Whereas in 1905 women in feminist organisations could claim much of the credit for awakening interest in women's issues among factory workers, they could not do so in 1913, when the initiative lay clearly with socialist women active in working-class politics.

Even so, the divide between socialists and feminists was not absolute. A Menshevik such as Kuvshinskaia found it possible to participate in the 1912 Education Congress, while only a few months later the feminist Margulies (who had organised the radical Women's Political Club in 1906) addressed a socialist meeting on International Women's Day. As late as March 1914, the secretary of the League of Equal Rights, Natalia Stankevich, could see ample scope for co-operation between the two sides. Collaboration was not only possible, she believed, but desirable, be it on particular issues such as maternity insurance, or on the fundamental question of democratic rights. She agreed that the goals of each were distinct, but that did not necessarily put them in a state of conflict. 'The common fate of Russian citizens brings both streams together: repression affects one and the other alike'.[62]

Stankevich took a sanguine view of the future awaiting the women's movement, upbraiding Tyrkova and those who thought like her for their unwarranted pessimism in dismissing the movement's achievements. She had some reason to feel hopeful. The early months of 1914 had seen a rash of public meetings on feminist issues, all of which had drawn large crowds.[63] But where this activity was leading, one can only surmise. From the experience of the preceding decade, it would be hard to feel any confidence in the sustained growth of the movement beyond the immediate future. In the event, the feminist revival came too late. Almost as soon as it was safely launched, world war intervened, bringing a halt to the campaign for equal rights and diverting the attention of feminists into new and patriotic channels.

Notes

1 Raymond Pearson, 'Milyukov and the Sixth Kadet Congress' *Slavonic and East European Review* April 1975, p. 214.

2 *PZhK na 1909 g.* p. 149; *Ustav Obshchestva pod nazvaniem 'Rossiiskaia Liga Ravnopraviia Zhenshchin'* (Spb: 1911); *Soiuz zhenshchin* no. 2 (1909) pp. 17–19.

3 *Ibid.* p. 19.

4 *PZhK na 1913 g.* p. 11; *PZhK na 1915 g.* p. 153.

5 *Zhenskoe delo* no. 23 (1911) p. 18; no. 15 (1911) pp. 17–20. Mirovich did tend to utter rash statements in the heat of the moment, but there is no hint

from her previous behaviour that she harboured anti-semitic feelings.

6 The departure of Mirovich did not displease some of her colleagues. One of them brought to light earlier resentment of her dominating personality when she accused her of having 'usurped' the role of leader in the Russian delegation to the 1906 IWSA congress in Copenhagen. *Ibid.* p. 18.

7 *Otchet o deiatel'nosti Rossiiskoi Ligi Ravnopraviia Zhenshchin za 1913 god* (Spb: 1914) pp. 46–47.

8 *PZhK na 1914 g.* p. 327.

9 Goldberg, *The Russian Women's Movement* pp. 332–6; Knight, *The Participation of Women in the Revolutionary Movement* p. 156.

10 *Gos. Duma III Sessiia IV* vol. ii, col. 2333; *Prilozheniia* vol. iii, no. 266.

11 B.B. Veselovskii, *Istoriia zemstva za sorok let* (Spb: 1911) vol. iv, p. 168. Introduction of the subject in zemstvo assemblies produced mixed reactions, from full support to 'quite cynical mockery'. *Soiuz zhenshchin* no. 1 (1908) p. 17.

12 *Gos. Duma III Sessiia I* vol. i, col. 1423; *Prilozheniia* vol i, no. 101; *Soiuz zhenshchin* no. 3 (1908) pp. 11–12; no. 4 (1908) pp. 1–6.

13 The reform was abandoned after widespread criticism of the government's proposals from the United Nobility and the zemstvos themselves. Geoffrey Hosking, *The Russian Constitutional Experiment. Government and Duma 1907–1914* (Cambridge: 1973) p. 160.

14 *Soiuz zhenshchin* no. 4 (1908) p. 3.

15 For conservative opinion in Britain, see David Morgan, *Suffragists and Liberals. The Politics of Woman Suffrage in England* (Oxford: 1975). Individual Tories did support women's suffrage in the hope that it would strengthen the property-owning electorate against the rising tide of popular democracy. But Morgan argues that it was just because neither major party saw women's suffrage as politically useful that the issue remained unsolved for half a century.

16 Brian Harrison, *Separate Spheres* (London: 1978) pp. 56, 83.

17 The only suffrage bill introduced by the Kadets in the Third Duma would have given the vote to all citizens over 21 in municipal elections. The bill failed. *Gos. Duma III Sessiia I*, vol. ii, col. 4484.

18 *Ibid. Sessiia IV Prilozheniia* vol. i, no. 122.

19 *Ibid. Sessiia IV* vol. ii, cols. 1735, 1626–35, 1968–87; *Zhenskoe delo* no. 9 (1911) p. 3.

20 *Zhenskii vestnik* no. 2 (1913) p. 60. See also no. 5–6 (1911) pp. 119–20.

21 *Svod zakonov Rossiiskoi Imperii* (Spb: 1900) vol. x, pt. 1, arts. 1130, 1132, 1148.

22 William G. Wagner, 'Legislative Reform of Inheritance in Russia, 1861–1914' in William E. Butler (ed.) *Russian Law: Historical and Political Perspectives* (Leyden: 1977) pp. 170, 174; *Gos. Sovet 1911–12 gg. Sessiia VII* cols. 1642–3, 1675, 1684–90, 1712–42; *Gos. Duma III Sessiia V* vol. iv, cols. 2078, 2598.

23 *Svod zakonov* vol. x, pt. 1, arts. 46–60.

24 E. Fleishits, 'Novella semeistvennago prava' *Pravo* no. 14 (1914) cols. 1113–29; *Zhenskii vestnik* no. 7–8 (1909) p. 139.

25 *Gos. Duma III Sessiia III* vol. iv, col. 945; *Prilozheniia* vol. ii, no. 416.

26 *Zhenskoe delo* no. 5 (1911) p. 1. See also *Zhenskii vestnik* no. 1 (1906) p. 27.

27 *Gos. Duma IV Sessiia II* vol. ii, cols. 374, 379. *Gos. Sovet Sessiia VIII* cols.

1195–7, 1202–6, 1214, 1215. The bill also required a man to support his separated wife in case of need, if her behaviour was not responsible for the breakdown of the marriage. Custody of children would be granted to the innocent party. The courts would decide in disputed custody cases.

28 *Ibid.* cols. 410, 411–2.

29 Stites, *The Women's Liberation Movement* p. 363. See Fleishits, 'Novella' cols. 1126–9 and *Zhenskii vestnik* no. 9 (1914) p. 199 for operation of the 1914 law.

30 See *Zhenskii vestnik* no. 9 (1910) p. 171 for Pokrovskaia's criticism of H.G. Wells' novel *Ann Veronica*, whose heroine marries her lover and loses her independence.

31 This lack of inhibition was not unique to Russia. See Angus McLaren, 'Abortion in England, 1890–1914' *Victorian Studies* Summer 1977.

32 A.A. Ginzburg, 'Izgnanie ploda' *Zhurnal Ministerstva Iustitsii* no. 7 (1912) pt. 2, pp. 35–70; *Zhenskii vestnik* no. 4 (1912) pp. 105–6; no. 1 (1914) pp. 1–4. Abortions in one Moscow hospital were 1.5 per 100 live births in 1903, rising to 4.84 in 1907, 6.52 in 1909 and 19.54 in 1910.

33 L. Gorovits, 'K voprosu o nakazuemosti aborta' *Sovremennik* no. 5 (1914) pp. 36–44; E. Zinov'eva, 'V zashchitu prav rozhdennykh' *Sovremennyi mir* no. 8 (1913) pp. 248–56; *Zhenskii vestnik* no. 4 (1914) pp. 102–5.

34 *Trudy pervago vserossiiskago s"ezda po bor'be s torgom zhenshchinami i ego prichinami* 2 vols. (Spb: 1911, 1912) vol. i, pp. 23, 34–42, (hereafter *Trudy . . . 1910 goda*). The convention was ratified in 1910. *Zhurnal Ministerstva Iustitsii* no. 9 (1912) pt. 1, pp. 1–8.

35 The bill (or 'measures to suppress the trade in women for the aims of debauchery') became law on 25 December 1909. *Gos. Duma III Sessiia III* vol. ii, col. 3.

36 *Trudy . . . 1910 goda* vol. i, pp. 132, 179–81, 219–20. The resolutions were later carefully edited to remove virtually all reference to political and civil rights. *Ibid.* vol. ii, pp. 612–618.

37 *Ibid.* vol. i, pp. 135, 149.

38 *Ibid.* vol. i, pp. 76, 169–70.

39 *Ibid.* pp. 201–14. For a similar connection between sexual indulgence and the collapse of society's values see A.S. Isgoev, 'Ob intelligentnoi molodezhi' in *Vekhi. Sbornik statei o russkoi intelligentsii* 2nd. ed. (M: 1909) pp. 97–124. See Stites *The Women's Liberation Movement* pp. 185–90 for 'Saninism' and decadence.

40 *Trudy . . . 1910 goda* vol ii, pp. 499–504, 520–21, 523–5, 537, 541. For an identical view see Alfred Blaschko (a noted German abolitionist) in International Congress of Medicine, *The Dangers of Syphilis and the Question of State Control* (London: 1914) pp. 11–12.

41 *Trudy . . . 1910 goda* vol. ii, p. 608.

42 *Ibid.* p. 336; *Gos. Duma IV Sessiia II Prilozheniia* vol. i, no. 28.

43 Dudgeon, *Women and Higher Education* pp. 302, 304. By 1913 there were at least 373,546 girls in secondary education, 323,477 in Ministry of Education schools. Precise figures are difficult to estimate. In higher education, Ruth Dudgeon finds an increase from 6,700 in 1905/6 to 38,100 in 1913/4. In 1914 women formed about one-third of the total number of students. (Personal communication with the author.)

44 *Zhenskii vestnik* no. 7–8 (1909) p. 160; *Trudy pervago vserossiiskago s"ezda po obrazovaniiu zhenshchin* 2 vols. (Petrograd: 1914, 1915) vol. i, p. 206. In

Britain there were 495 women doctors at the 1911 census. *Englishwomen's Yearbook 1915* (London: 1915) p. 80.

45 *Zhenskii vestnik* no. 12 (1909) pp. 261–3. Women had practised as private attorneys from 1874 until banned in 1876. Up to 1909 they had a limited right to plead in court. See Samuel Kucherov, *Courts, Lawyers and Trials under the Last Three Tsars* (New York: 1953) pp. 155–9 for the difference between barristers and private attorneys. For women and the legal profession see *Trudy . . . po obrazovaniiu zhenshchin* vol. i, pp. 194–204.

46 Valk (ed.) *Sankt-Peterburgskie vysshie zhenskie kursy* pp. 162–3.

47 *Trudy . . . po obrazovaniiu zhenshchin* vol ii, p. 356; Dudgeon, *Women and Higher Education* p. 294.

48 *Trudy 1-go vserossiiskago s"ezda* pp. 512–19.

49 *Trudy . . . po obrazovaniiu zhenshchin* vol. i, pp. 14–19, 66–69.

50 *Ibid*. pp. 1–4, 20–23.

51 See Kuskova's speech on the police surveillance of secondary school pupils. *Ibid*. vol. ii, pp. 215–41.

52 *Ibid*. pp. 425–33.

53 *Ibid*. pp. 433–8.

54 *Zhenskoe delo* no. 1 (1913) p. 1; *Gos. Duma III Sessiia V* vol. ii col. 2163; *Prilozheniia* no. 336. The bill was sent to committee but proceeded no further. *Zhenskii vestnik* no. 5–6 (1912) pp. 113–15.

55 *Ibid*. p. 121, no. 12 (1912) pp. 268–270, no. 2 (1913) p. 60. The congress was never held.

56 *Gos. Duma IV Sessiia I*, vol. i, col. 1799; Hosking, *The Russian Constitutional Experiment*, p. 193.

57 William Rosenberg, *Liberals in the Russian Revolution* (Princeton: 1974) p. 30.

58 *Gos. Duma IV Sessiia I* vol. i, cols. 2068, 2176–7.

59 *Ibid*. col. 2220.

60 *Zhenskii vestnik* no. 12 (1912) pp. 273–4.

61 Goldberg, *The Russian Women's Movement* pp. 336–45; Anne Bobroff, 'The Bolsheviks and Working Women, 1905–20' *Soviet Studies* October 1974, p. 545.

62 N. Stankevich, 'Zhenskii mesiats' *Sovremennik* no. 5 (1914) pp. 124–9.

63 *Zhenskii vestnik* no. 3 (1914) pp. 86–7.

7 Conclusion: War, Revolution and Dissolution

The outbreak of the First World War should have presented the women's movement with a grave moral choice. War was a violation of all that feminists held dear, the triumph of force and nationalist pride over reason and tolerance. Women, Pokrovskaia had claimed during the Russo–Japanese war, were natural pacifists; if that was so, now was their moment to unite in protest against the nation's resort to arms. But women were also wives and mothers of men who had volunteered to fight for their country. If these women refused to support the war, would they not thereby be guilty of disloyalty to their own kith and kin? By failing to come to the aid of their governments, would they not be endangering the lives of those very men whom they wished to preserve from the slaughter?

In the event, few feminists had to make this painful choice. When the great catastrophe occurred, their pacifist conscience seemingly evaporated. This was hardly surprising. The force of public opinion was immensely powerful; in the face of a national emergency, only the most committed pacifists were willing to be branded traitors for the sake of their cause. Feminists everywhere had an especially strong motivation for wishing to appear patriotic, concerned as they were to present themselves as responsible citizens who recognised their obligations as well as their rights. 'Let us prove ourselves worthy of citizenship,' Mrs Fawcett appealed to British suffragists, 'whether our claim is recognised or not.'[1]

In Russia, pacifism had always been a somewhat fragile plant. The peace societies which had mushroomed in Europe and North America in the latter part of the nineteenth century were allowed no counterpart in the Empire, until a Moscow society was established in 1909; a movement which boasted 150 societies all over the world and an international bureau in Berne never found more than a pale echo at home. For a while it seemed that Russian feminists might succeed where men had failed when a Women's League for Peace was founded in 1899, on the occasion of the first peace conference in the Hague. But this too did not thrive and was forced into liquidation after the Boer War.[2]

There is no question that, in 1914, the educated public in Russia was overwhelmingly committed to the Allies' cause, in liberal circles no less than conservative. Anti-war sentiment, strong among the liberal intelligentsia in Russia as in Europe before 1914, dissipated on the outbreak of hostilities – men like Miliukov who had been vilified as traitors by right-wing nationalists became stalwart patriots almost overnight. But this phenomenon was not restricted to middle-class liberals. The greatest defection came from the working masses, on whom the revolutionary parties had been relying to save the world from an imperialist war:

Streets, which yesterday were crammed with the ebb and flow of the striking masses, were now full of patriots. Wave after wave of people made their way to the Winter Palace and sank on their knees before the Tsar.[3]

Even in the revolutionary vanguard there was no unity. The German social–democrats' decision to support their government in the war precipated the wholesale collapse of the Socialist International. Though many Russian socialists were horrified by the German party's capitulation and refused to offer the same support to their own government, a major split took place in their ranks. Patriots were divided from pacifists, and pacifists from the small minority of Lenin's supporters who preached defeatism and worked for the transformation of the European war into a revolutionary war against capitalism. The schism affected women quite as much as men: while Kollontai and Inessa Armand became active campaigners for Lenin's policy, they could not depend on female solidarity to help their cause, either in Russia or in the international socialist movement.[4]

The extent of anti-war feeling in Russia is almost impossible to gauge. Opportunities for public dissent were far fewer there than in any other of the belligerent countries, and there was not the remotest possibility of a non-revolutionary pacifist movement surviving in Russia, as it did in Britain and America throughout the war. Since periodicals and newspapers were regularly censored, they inevitably conveyed a distorted impression of public feeling and it is highly probable that those who, in peacetime, would have voiced pacifist sentiments, now kept their opinions to themselves. Such inhibitions would naturally have worked at least as effectively on women as on men, and while the evidence suggests that the pacifist tendency among feminists totally dissipated with the outbreak of hostilities, there remains the strong possibility that some women, who were not prepared to expose themselves to public obloquy or criminal prosecution, were nevertheless deeply upset by the war.

Even if this were so, there is no doubt that many had no such scruples. *Zhenskoe delo* adopted a tone of elevated patriotism from the start:

The days of endurance impose on every one of us a great duty – to devote our strength to the defence of the fatherland. The nation turns to all its children –

both men and women. At a time when it sends our fathers, husbands, sons and brothers into the line of battle it entrusts us, women, with sacred duties. Sacrifices are inevitable and we know that 'the tears of poor mothers' will flow . . . If the loss of a dear person strikes us too we must not forget that it is a holy sacrifice for our sins, laid on the altar of the fatherland for its future well-being.[5]

Pokrovskaia's response was somewhat more complex. She regarded the war with a mixture of horror and satisfaction, as the suicide of European civilisation. That civilisation, so great in its achievements, had nevertheless contained within it the seeds of its own destruction, namely man's overweaning love of power and physical force. Germany and its Emperor had brought this disaster on Europe, yet Germany was itself a product of European civilisation, which must therefore bear the ultimate responsibility. Only the male half of the population, however, must take the blame; women were absolved. Their role was to lead humanity out of the abyss. 'Only they can annihilate the power of brute force, the mania for world domination which creates slavery and war.' Maybe this war, she felt, with all the suffering which it would bring in its train, would goad women into action to fight for 'true progress and a better future for humanity, for its golden age'.[6]

* * *

If feminists in Russia and abroad failed to present a unified opposition to the war, and in many instances were ardent supporters of their respective governments, this is not to say that support for the war was unanimous. In fact the outbreak of hostilities precipitated a split in the international feminist movement, not (as one might have expected) between rival supporters of opposing countries, but between patriots and pacifists.

Late in 1914, pacifist members of the International Woman Suffrage Alliance, dissenting from their leader's decision to keep the alliance above the strife, called for a meeting of like-minded women at The Hague. The meeting, which took place in February 1915, was a trial balloon for an international congress to protest against the war and discuss measures which might be taken to end it. Response to this brave and rather utopian scheme was mixed. The French feminist movement unanimously condemned any peace initiative made before the defeat of Germany and indignantly refused the invitation. The International Council of Women thought the proposal ill-advised; Emmeline and Christabel Pankhurst revived the Women's Social and Political Union to oppose it. But others were enthusiastic: a delegation was promised from America, 180 British women made preparations to attend and favourable replies came from Germany, Scandinavia and Holland.

The obstacles to the congress were considerable. In Britain the Home

Secretary issued travel permits for only twenty-five (most of whom were then prevented from sailing by the closure of the Channel), while no more than twenty-eight Germans managed to get across the border into Holland. Of all the great powers, only the delegation from the United States encountered little obstruction, and it was an American, Jane Addams, who chaired the congress. The United States, which remained resolutely outside the war until early 1917, was the one major nation where a pacifist movement thrived: in the same year as the Hague congress, Jane Addams founded the Women's Peace Party, which by 1916 had a membership of 25,000.[7]

Once it had assembled, the congress at The Hague issued a formal statement which protested against 'the madness and horror of war, involving as it does a reckless sacrifice of human life and the destruction of so much that humanity has laboured through centuries to build up.' It urged the opening of peace negotiations based on five democratic principles and it concluded by demanding the political enfranchisement of women, since 'the combined influence of the women of all countries is one of the strongest forces for the prevention of war'.[8] The congress established an International Committee of Women for Permanent Peace and arranged for delegations of women to be sent to all the capitals of Europe to present its views to those countries.

One of these delegations duly came to the Russian capital (renamed Petrograd in 1914) and was received by the Minister of Foreign Affairs. It had 'several interesting private talks' with Miliukov, the contents of which were unfortunately never divulged, and was entertained at the home of Shishkina-Iavein, the president of the League of Equal Rights. Whether she fully approved of the peace mission (and the preceding congress) is unclear. Although, like all Russian feminists, she had refused an invitation to The Hague, her refusal did not signify disapproval of the scheme. She made no public disavowal of the congress, as Lady Aberdeen and Mrs Fawcett did, and her willingness to be associated with the delegation which came to Petrograd suggests, at the very least, some sympathy with its aims. Evidently she did not share the hostility of *Zhenskoe delo*, whose editors dismissed the congress as a hare-brained scheme which had been exploited by the Germans, and rejoiced when it failed in its purpose.[9]

At the same time, she was no pacifist. If she supported efforts to bring the war to an end she had no doubts as to the correct behaviour for Russian women so long as hostilities continued. By whatever means available, and with whatever skills they possessed, they must help to keep essential services functioning while men were away at the front and contribute to the alleviation of suffering caused by the war.

Like Shishkina-Iavein, Anna Shabanova took a not unfavourable view of the initiative from The Hague. Though she too declined the invitation to attend, she did so with apparent regret, pleading 'innumerable duties' incurred by 'the disastrous times which the war has brought', and far from dissociating herself from the congress, sent her best wishes for its success. But again like Shishkina-Iavein, she stressed how important it was for women to prove their worth to the nation in its hour of need. As soon as the war broke out she immersed herself in the task of mobilising women for the war effort, both in her professional work as a doctor and as the president of the Mutual Philanthropic Society. Largely on her initiative, the society immediately set up a committee to aid victims of the war, which supervised the sewing of linen for the wounded, fund-raising and a course of lectures on basic nursing skills.[10]

In Russia, as elsewhere, the war emergency opened up a range of new opportunities for women, the most immediately obvious being in the nursing and medical professions. Within weeks of the declaration of war, women were enrolling as Red Cross medical assistants and 'sisters of mercy' and were soon despatched to the front. Of those who stayed at home, many volunteered for work in infirmaries for wounded soldiers which were established under private auspices: one such hospital was set up by the Women's Medical Institute in Petrograd, others by the League of Equal Rights and the Mutual Philanthropic Society.[11]

There was at first no mass mobilisation of women into jobs hitherto reserved for men. In middle-class occupations particularly, old obstacles to female employment continued in force, to the chagrin of feminists who had hoped that the war would destroy lingering prejudices. Many branches of state and public service remained closed, likewise the legal profession, despite repeated representations from women's organisations. But, in manual occupations, the rising number of conscripts for the army compelled employers to turn to female labour, which offered the additional attraction of being cheaper than male. The public's imagination was soon tickled by the sight of women conductors on trams and trains, while in a large number of manufacturing industries the population of women rose with each year of the war. In Petrograd, the proportion of women in industry rose from 25.3 per cent of the total in 1913 to 33.3 per cent by 1917; in the Moscow region (where women had formed a major part of the workforce for decades) the proportion rose from 39.4 per cent in 1914 to 48.7 per cent by the Revolution. In agriculture too, women found themselves doing men's jobs, often being left in sole charge of a family plot when their husbands and sons were conscripted. It has been estimated that by 1916, women formed 72 per cent of the labour force on peasant farms and 58 per cent on landowners' estates.[12]

The increased presence of women in vital services and industries was directed by necessity rather than a spirit of self-sacrifice. Women undeniably performed feats of endurance in the course of their work, but for most, the personal privations were a misfortune to be suffered, not a burden to be shouldered willingly. Feminists, however, appreciated that women's undeniable investment in the war effort was a propaganda weapon which they should fully utilise. There was never any doubt in their minds that they should offer their skills with a clear expectation of reward, and they linked quite explicitly the increased opportunities for public service which the war presented to the attainment of equal rights after the war was won. This was not a cynical calculation. Their contribution to the war was not measured solely by what they intended to get out of it. Those women who volunteered their services did so, without doubt, from a variety of personal motives, but also in the conviction that what they did was necessary. But the more consciously feminist, at any rate, appreciated that just because it was necessary, it should therefore be recognised as such by society. If society was willing to place upon women great responsibilities as citizens, it must be willing to grant them the corresponding rights.

With this in mind, feminist leaders returned to the question of a national women's organisation. For the first months of the war, the equal rights campaign had been pushed aside by the same wave of patriotic euphoria which had seized the political parties and led to the temporary suspension of party politics in the Duma. Military defeat, the increasing dislocation of the domestic economy, maladministration and corruption, all brought a rapid disenchantment with the way in which the war was being prosecuted and a determination on the part of liberals to remove the government's monopoly of the administration of the war. Feminists shared this aspiration, but they had an additional reason for organising, which was to impress upon the political opposition itself the contribution of women to the war and their claim to equal treatment. Not unreasonably, they feared that without their active intervention the claim would go unrecorded.

It was, however, one thing to advocate unity and quite another to achieve it. Neither the existing political conditions nor the relations between women's groups were conducive to the promotion of a national women's union and several attempts came to nothing. Collaboration between feminist groups was at best sporadic. Neither of the two feminist journals had much to say about the other: *Zhenskii vestnik* (published in Petrograd) gave the impression that the city's League of Equal Rights had ceased to function. It did, however, report a conference organised by the Moscow League in April 1915, which discussed women's war work and set up a temporary committee, but achieved little else.[13]

One project, a Women's Economic Union, achieved a modest success. Founded in Petrograd on the suggestion of Pokrovskaia at the end of 1915, it set out to combat food shortages and inflation by providing facilities such as a shop and a restaurant for its members. The union's ultimate goal was to contribute to women's economic independence by establishing a workshop and lectures, but these were never realised. Its one substantial achievement was the creation of a restaurant catering for a mixed clientele of students, workers and office staff. But the union never went beyond its philanthropic beginnings to become the sort of organisation which its founders had envisaged, an organisation like Sylvia Pankhurst's East London Federation of Suffragettes, which set up three 'Cost Price Restaurants', a maternity clinic and day nursery, plus a small factory employing women.[14]

The same months saw the last round in the protracted struggle to obtain government authorisation for a National Council of Women. A refusal was once again all that was forthcoming, but this time Shabanova and her collaborators decided to seek a way round the prohibition. At the end of 1916, the Mutual Philanthropic Society, the Petrograd club of the Women's Progressive Party and a number of other women's groups signed the draft statute of an All-Russian Women's Society (*Vserossiiskoe Zhenskoe Obshchestvo*), which came into existence without official approval at the beginning of 1917. Its formation was, however, hardly more than a symbolic gesture. Even after the February Revolution, when the society transformed itself into a National Council, it contributed little to the women's movement and fixed its first general meeting for the very end of the year. The meeting never took place.[15]

* * *

Even after two and a half years of fighting, there was little evidence that feminists were slackening in their resolve to aid the war effort. So far as one can judge, they all belonged to the same camp which believed that the war should be prosecuted unequivocally and efficiently; their complaints were the common ones of maladministration and lack of will power to defeat the enemy.[16] But by the beginning of 1917, an element of desperation had crept into their pronouncements. Women were helpless to prevent the continued slaughter on the battlefield, at home they had to grapple with constant shortages, rising prices and endless queues in freezing weather for bread and milk. Feminist organisations could do little more. Their limited resources were fully stretched and, besides, they had lost their slender contacts with working-class women, who were the most painfully affected by the crisis. To all appearances, feminists did not participate in the strikes and disturbances which marked the early weeks of 1917. Fully occupied in war work, they offered little encouragement to the growing unrest among the working-class population of the cities. Although Pokrovskaia called on women to unite 'for the improvement of their position and for the good of their homeland' there is very little to suggest that, in this respect, feminist organisations were any more successul in 1917 than in the previous year.[17]

At the end of February popular discontent, which had been simmering ominously over the past two years, erupted in major strikes, food riots and demonstrations in Petrograd. The disturbances were quite uncoordinated and might well have been put down if the troops which had been moved into the city had obeyed orders to shoot, and if the festering crisis in the government had not rendered it impotent to deal with the threat from below. As it was, civil disorder in the streets and factories reacted with a final confrontation between the tsar and the Duma, to precipitate the abdication of Nicholas and the collapse of the imperial regime.

The duality of the February Revolution immediately assumed an institutional form: on the one hand, the provisional government (nominated by moderate leaders of the Duma and led by Kadets and Octobrists); on the other, the Petrograd Soviet (or Council) of Workers' and Soldiers' Deputies. The first attempted to establish itself as the legitimate, if temporary, ruler of Russia; the second intended to represent the interests of the working masses and to control the actions of the government. It was in the context of this 'dual power' that the political and social drama of 1917 was played out.

Coming after the desperation of the preceding months, the overthrow of the tsar was greeted with heartfelt relief. The feminist press was as jubilant as the nation at large: freedom had dawned and with it the will to restore Russia's fortunes. But feminists had their own interests to defend. Soon after its formation, the provisional government had declared a political amnesty and freedom of speech and assembly. Within a week it issued a programme promising a Constituent Assembly and civil equality regardless of class, creed and nationality. But it said nothing about sexual inequality. The reaction of feminists was prompt. The following day, the League of Equal Rights issued a resolution protesting against the omission and launched a propaganda campaign to persuade women to unite for the sake of their political emancipation. They met a ready response from all over Russia. The league's offices were 'besieged' from morning to night, conferences and meetings were held, literature sent out to the provinces. Some meetings were so popular that it was necessary to clear the hall three times for the same speakers.[18]

A fortnight after the campaign was launched, a large procession of up to 40,000 women, led by Vera Figner and Shishkina-Iavein, proceeded from the Petrograd City Duma to the Tauride Palace to lobby the new rulers of Russia. The demonstration, replete with two brass bands playing the Marseillaise, red banners, placards and several 'Amazons on horseback', was reminiscent of the great English suffragette marches which, a decade earlier, had been the envy of Russian feminists. Unlike those earlier demonstrations, this one achieved its objectives almost before the day was out.[19]

The meeting at the Tauride Palace began inauspiciously enough. Neither Chkheidze nor Skobelev (respectively president and vice-president of the Soviet) would make a firm commitment to women's suffrage, and replied that they must first consult their comrades. But the demonstrators made it plain that they would not disperse until a decision had been reached. After a prolonged interval, Chkheidze and the president of the Duma, Rodzianko, came out to the expectant crowd. They were addressed by an eloquent Shishkina-Iavein:

> We have come here to remind you that women were your faithful comrades in the gigantic struggle for the freedom of the Russian people; that they also have been filling up the prisons, and boldly marched to the galleys. The best of us looked into the eyes of death without fear. Here at my side stands V.N. Figner, who has been struggling all her life for what has now been obtained.

Now that the foundations of a 'new, great, healthy and free Russia' were being laid, it was high time, Shishkina continued, that women be unequivocally recognised as full citizens:

> We declare that the Constituent Assembly in which only one half of the population will be represented can in no wise be regarded as expressing the will of the whole people, but only half of it.

Realising, perhaps, that any further temporising would not be tolerated by the crowd, Chkheidze gave a pledge to fight for women's suffrage. The demonstrators were not satisfied:

> We want no more promises of good will. We have had enough of them! We demand an official and clear answer – that the women will have votes in the Constituent Assembly.[20]

Rodzianko, anxious to prove himself a modern democrat, echoed Chkheidze's words and advised the meeting to seek an assurance of support from the prime minister, L'vov. This the leaders did, and the day ended in a mood of rejoicing and self-congratulation. Two days later, a deputation consisting of all the feminist leaders received a firm commitment from L'vov to include women in the proposed electoral law.[21]

Not content with their triumph, feminists were anxious to have the promise in writing. At an all-Russian Congress of Women early in April, Kuskova, now unmistakably in the feminists ranks, called for a special government decree on women's suffrage, a resolution which was overwhelmingly adopted. But the principal aim of the congress was to found a new organisation, and this task proved less simple. As was only to be expected, a group of Bolsheviks attacked the congress for its 'undemocratic' character and attempted to disrupt the meeting by staging a walk-out. The manoeuvre did not have its desired effect, but prompted Menshevik delegates to unite with the feminists. After this upset, another group of delegates withdrew from the congress in protest against a resolution proposed by Mariia Chekhova, which urged the congress to form a general women's association with overtly political aims. But despite the schisms, the congress voted to establish the Republican Union of Democratic Women's Organisations, which came into existence immediately afterwards.[22]

By the end of May, when a special conference set up by the provisional government met to consider the electoral law for the Constituent Assembly, it was clear that the question of women's suffrage had moved out of the realm of controversy. Doubtless, there were still many who put little store by it. Kerenskii reportedly believed that 'so vast a change' would have to wait for a decision from the Constituent Assembly, as did some members of the Soviet.[23] But the special conference shared the view that women had earned their citizenship, and the matter was quickly despatched, leaving the conference to grapple with the more contentious issues of the soldiers' franchise and the position of the former royal family. The electoral law as it finally emerged gave 'Russian citizens of both sexes who have reached the age of twenty by the day of the elections' the right to vote for the Constituent Assembly. Members of the armed forces were also enfranchised; deserters, convicts, the insane and members of the imperial family were excluded.[24]

The degree to which the war and the revolutionary crisis had contributed to the feminists' victory is difficult to assess. As in Britain, the voluntary participation of women in the war effort in Russia was used both by the feminists and their erstwhile opponents as a persuasive argument for female suffrage. But the war did not produce such a favourable outcome in all the belligerent nations (France, for example), and it would seem reasonable to suggest that, rather than being the principal reason for the change in attitude, the war was only a precipitating factor, even a pretext, permitting opponents of women's suffrage (like Asquith in Britain) to accept a long overdue reform without losing face. In Russia, as in Austria and Germany, the issue was complicated by the fact that the regime which eventually granted women's suffrage was not the same as the one which had refused to consider it before the war. Thus, the victory was possibly due more to the radical climate of 1917 rather than to a change in attitude as a result of women's war work. The opinion of a moderate conservative like Rodzianko may not have altered over the preceding three years; he may well have been unconvinced that women had proved themselves in the war. What had altered, however, were the circumstances in Russia, which made opposition to the widest possible measure of enfranchisement politically unacceptable.

In any event, the feminist leaders did nothing during these months to prompt misgivings about women's civic responsibility. They remained firmly committed to keeping Russia in the war and, having won the suffrage battle, put all their forces behind the provisional government in its increasingly desperate efforts to restore Russia's fighting power. The Republican Union of Democratic Women's Organisations, the National Council of Women, *Zhenskii vestnik* and *Zhenskoe delo* all conceived their first duty to be the encouragement of women to take an active part in the defence of the country. They applauded the formation of the Women's Battalions, which they hoped would provide a greatly needed example to men who were shirking their duty, and they proposed a general labour conscription of women. In the summer Shabanova played host to Mrs Pankhurst, one of the many who came to Russia during 1917, with the blessing of the Allied governments, to boost morale and make known the Allies' concern.[25]

But women's organisations were even more helpless than the provisional government to halt the disintegration of established authority and feminists soon began to despair at the internal chaos and military apathy which were threatening the security of that revolution which they had so joyfully welcomed. They had no sympathy with the peace policy of the Soviet: what was needed was 'one heroic effort' on the part of the army, not a policy whose inevitable consequence would be a humiliating separate peace with Germany. In a bitter attack on the Bolsheviks, Pokrovskaia summed up the feminists' aspirations:

> We fervently desire that fraternity, equality and freedom will enter the way of life of the peoples of the whole world and that the Russian revolution will lay the foundations of a new era. We believe that these ideals can be realised only when the people fights for its freedom, guided by ideals and aspirations, but not by coarse material incentives.

Taking issue with *Pravda*, she argued that in the past when mass demands for bread, land and economic change had been the moving force of revolutions, the result had been 'the very defeat of the masses themselves, internecine war, torrents of the nation's blood'. The Bolsheviks, on their own admission, did not want a 'tidy well-intentioned and harmonious revolution'. Instead, Pokrovskaia claimed, they sought one which was 'violent and merciless, paying regard to nothing':

> But such a revolution will not create the people's freedom, rather bind it with new fetters. Thus speaks history. Russia will not on any account repeat the old

lessons; it must trace out new paths to a better future for mankind, making humanity the basis of its actions.[26]

* * *

What feminists thought of the Bolshevik coup must be left largely to the imagination. The sources, as Richard Stites notes, are thin for 1917 overall, but they become almost non-existent after October.[27] Few feminists have left any record of their feelings, or even their activities after the overthrow of the provisional government; their organisations dispersed, their journals ceased publication. We do not know how many of those who had been active in the women's movement emigrated and how many remained in Russia, nor how many of the latter made their peace with the new regime. Certainly, few besides Tyrkova and Kuskova took a very prominent part in the resistance to the Bolsheviks, nor in émigré politics. But one may suppose that the feminists who left Russia shared their fellow émigrés' hostility towards the Bolsheviks and the Soviet state.

Of those who stayed in Russia one can discover very little. Liubov' Gurevich returned to the literary activities which she had pursued earlier in her career. Chekhova and her husband apparently accepted the new regime. Shchepkina continued, at least for a time, to work as a historian. In 1921 she published a history of the women's movement during the French Revolution (to which Kollontai wrote a critical introduction) and four years later was preparing an article on the Union of Equal Rights. But the journal (*Byloe*) for which her article was destined ceased publication in 1926 and the piece never appeared.[28]

About Shabanova, one knows a little more. Already sixty-nine at the time of the Revolution, she continued to work full time as a pediatrician until the mid-1920s (and part time up to her death in 1932). Made president of the Russian National Council of Women early in 1917, she kept up a regular correspondence with Lady Aberdeen, which was interrupted only by the Civil War. Although understandably reticent in her judgement on the new regime, it is quite evident that she was far from reconciled to it. Even after the worst emergencies of civil war and famine, she could find little to commend in her new world and spoke of her work as an escape from 'the troubles of life'. 'I preserve my memories and I dream,' she wrote in 1928. Nonetheless she was not without honour in her own country; her jubilee was celebrated that same year and she was made a 'heroine of labour'. Outwardly, she seemed to have found a niche in Soviet Russia and to have retained her optimism. In an article published in 1927 she wrote, 'A person is old who does not look to the future and does not live with hope.' But in her private correspondence this optimism was lacking.[29]

As for her work for the National Council, that ceased with the Bolshevik coup. Though she retained an honorary position as vice-president of the ICW (as Filosofova had done for many years), she was 'a shepherd without a flock': 'most of the members of the Council have disappeared, dispersed by the revolutionary tempest'. In post-revolutionary Russia, she complained, there was no room for feminists and their achievements were wilfully forgotten.[30]

If Shabanova found conditions hard, her fate was enviable compared to that of Shishkina-Iavein, fellow doctor and feminist. Shishkina's life immediately after the Bolshevik coup is not recorded, but in 1921 a former colleague in the International Woman Suffrage Alliance, Chrystal Macmillan, received a letter from her recounting her plight. Some time previously, the Shishkin-Iavein family had returned to their native Estonia, only to find their former home destroyed. In 1920, just before taking up a professorship in medicine at Dorpat University, Shishkina's husband had died and his widow, as a Russian, was subsequently barred from practising in Estonia. Moving to Bulgaria with her children, she caught typhus and was now 'in the direst need'. Macmillan appealed to readers to send financial aid, but there was no further news of the family.[31]

* * *

The obliteration of the feminist movement by the October Revolution is intensely frustrating for the historian who wishes to learn about the subsequent fate of its participants. But more than that, it distorts the whole history of the women's movement in Russia. Labelled bourgeois by its Marxist opponents, the feminist campaign for political and civil rights was given no credit for shifts in social attitudes and changes in the law. From the Bolshevik standpoint, the feminists had done no more than tinker with the system; equality between the sexes was the exclusive achievement of Soviet rule. Yet it is clear that, whatever the movement's failure between 1905 and the Bolshevik takeover, it had a far from negligible influence. Even under the tsarist regime, the feminists were responsible for some legislative victories, notably changes in inheritance and the married woman's passport. More importantly, they helped to transform public opinion on all aspects of the 'woman question' and they made it impossible for future legislators to ignore women's interests. Above all on the issue which was most dear to them, that of political rights, feminist propaganda was vital. If it had not been for their twelve-year campaign, one can be sure that the call for women's suffrage in March 1917 would have made little impression on the new regime. As it was, the obstacles to enfranchisement were already toppling by the time women's delegations presented their demands to the Soviet and Duma, only weeks after the downfall of the tsar.

One may go further and argue that the feminist movement made a significant impression on social–democracy itself. Such was the abhorrence felt by orthodox Marxists (Menshevik no less than Bolshevik) towards the idea of separate women's organisations, that the potential value of the female proletariat went almost unnoticed for many years. During 1905, women workers were virtually ignored by the social–democratic party organisations and it was only through the efforts of a small number of individuals, such as Kollontai and Kuvshinskaia, Praskoviia Kudelli and Anna Gurevich, that clubs and circles exclusively for working-class women were established between 1907 and 1914. Certainly, these were not an unqualified success. Quite apart from the difficulty of recruiting members in a period of reaction, these 'socialist feminists' had to overcome the indifference of their own party colleagues. It was not only the working-class men who opposed them; even the old revolutionary, Vera Zasulich (who could not have been unaware of prejudice against women), thought Kollontai's work 'irrelevant', while Krupskaia gave little encouragement before 1912.

Nonetheless, if attempts to organise working-class women were only partially successful, they did make it less easy to dismiss the female proletariat as a force impeding the revolution. Just as Father Gapon had realised at the end of 1904, socialist leaders (and notably Lenin) soon began to appreciate that working-class women must be mobilised for the cause, not just for their own good, but to remove what was seen as a powerful obstacle to change. While it would be ridiculous to argue that feminist activity was responsible for this new outlook, it is not at all far-fetched to suggest a strong influence. Not only those social–democrats who had participated in the Union of Equal Rights during 1905, but also unswerving opponents of 'bourgeois feminism' like Kollontai were fully alive to its dangerous attraction. Not for nothing did Kollontai devote so many pages of her 400-page polemic, *The Social Foundations of the Woman Question*, to a demolition of the feminists. At the period when she wrote it (in 1908), the possibility that feminist organisations might 'take over' the female proletariat still seemed a real one, despite the feminists' own regret that they were attracting few working-class women into their movement. Only with hindsight can one see that the feminists stood little chance of appealing successfully to their 'younger sisters'. This was not at all clear at the time.

But even if one gives feminism some credit for changing social attitudes (including revolutionary perceptions of women), one still has to ask whether feminists did not allow themselves to get side-tracked from major issues by their campaign for the vote, not simply in Russia, but wherever the women's movement was strong. There is no doubt that, by the early twentieth century, feminists everywhere were beginning to concentrate on the issue of women's suffrage, and that in many countries it was the most contentious and most publicised aspect of the women's movement before the First World War. In Britain it became almost literally the battleground of feminism between 1906 and 1914.

But the very fact that winning the vote was such a hotly-disputed question suggests that its significance was greater than it appears in retrospect, that it symbolised a fundamental change in relations between the sexes which went way beyond the acquisition of a paper qualification. One has only to read the reports of debates in the House of Commons (or even in the Duma) to realise that men's opposition to female enfranchisement was not generally based on any rational perception of women's abilities, but was intimately related to fears of losing power, in the external world of politics but also in the home. Feminists perceived this, although they rarely developed a coherent theory of women's oppression. Russian feminists, perhaps even less than elsewhere, produced little theoretical writing of their own, though they translated much of what was published abroad. But it is clear from their statements and their campaigning strategy that they saw the franchise as a symbol of citizenship as much as they saw it as a means to achieving further social and political reform.

Nonetheless, for all the passion which went into the campaign for political rights, feminists in Russia did not suffer from tunnel vision. Throughout their campaign they stressed its interrelationship with the political liberation movement against autocracy, and indeed sometimes allowed their own demands to get submerged in the immediate political crisis, as in the autumn of 1905. But from a different perspective too one can see that the vote did not become an exclusive preoccupation. Feminists were deeply interested in other questions – improving the rights of women in the family (for example, the divorce laws), exploring problems in sexual relations, and discussing changing family relationships and the upbringing of children. They explored questions which remain unresolved almost a century later: whether there are innate differences, in psychological make-up and in the conceptualisation of the world, between men and women; whether education should be directed towards fitting women for a public role in society; whether society (in its educational system) undervalues certain qualities which women possess to a greater degree than men.

When one looks at the course of feminism in Russia, one naturally concludes that before 1900 its campaigning energies were directed mainly towards the expansion of educational and employment opportunities for middle-class and gentry women, and that a change in direction occurred in 1905, towards the acquisition of political rights. But one has to bear constantly in mind that most feminists did not see those activities as an end in themselves. They saw education, employment and civil and political rights as a means of establishing their autonomy and their recognition in society as equal citizens. When Tyrkova or Mirovich spoke at suffrage meetings in 1906, they were not denying that anything else in the women's movement had any importance. They were simply concentrating on the issue which seemed most immediate at the time. Four or five years later, when political conditions made the campaign for the vote less straightforward, they spent more time considering other feminist concerns. It was, after all, Tyrkova who warned women against the dangers of becoming carbon copies of men. It was she who asked women to explore their own potential, their intuition and feeling.

If historians in the USSR had been able to admit that non-revolutionary feminism had been of some significance to the solution of the 'woman question' in Russia, one would have gained a very much more honest and accurate picture of the movement. As it is, Soviet historians are only now beginning to treat 'bourgeois feminism' as a serious historical phenomenon and to get away from the biased picture handed down from the feminists' revolutionary adversaries. But it is not only Soviet historiography which has contrived to obscure the history of feminism. Unconsciously the émigrés did the same. It was not that they engaged in wilful distortion, rather that they tended to forget that aspect of their past. Preoccupied with the attempt to explain the catastrophe which had befallen their homeland and, all too often, with apportioning blame, issues which seemed important before 1917 appeared less significant afterwards.

Granted, one would not have expected Miliukov to discuss in more detail his evolution from opponent to advocate of women's suffrage; it was evidently an issue which occupied little of his attention, even in the years when it was still in dispute.[32] But from Kuskova and Tyrkova one might have learned more had political circumstances been different. Tyrkova in particular was far more involved in feminist controversies, as well as feminist organisations like the Mutual Philanthropic Society, than one would ever have guessed from her memoirs. She defended women's suffrage at the Kadets' crucial second congress, she lectured around the country, chaired meetings, spoke at all the major feminist congresses and wrote articles for the feminist press. Only two years before the Revolution, she published a biography of Anna Filosofova, whose secretary she had been during the last years of Filosofova's life. The book was not simply another facet of her literary activity, but a substantial contribution to the history of the women's movement in Russia, and a labour of love.[33] There is not the slightest suggestion that Tyrkova, in 1914 or 1915, had lost interest in feminism. Far from being an indifferent spectator, she criticised Russian women's lack of involvement in feminist issues and in politics generally and urged them to emulate their sisters abroad.

Little of this is evident from her memoirs. Apart from her description of events which were taking place when she returned from exile at the end of 1905, and of the debate at the Kadet congress the following January, she had almost nothing to say about the women's movement. By the early 1950s, when her autobiography was written, the topic had apparently ceased to be of concern to her. The same was perhaps true of the many other feminists, of whom no trace remains.

To some extent, this was a phenomenon observable all over the world. With the franchise won in North America and in most of Europe, the women's movement gained a major victory, but lost momentum. Nonetheless, although the movement fragmented after the First World War, its history could still be written by its former participants. The twenties and early thirties saw, if not a flood, then a constant trickle of memoirs and biographies, particularly in the two principal centres of the suffrage movement, Britain and the United States. Much of the material was highly tendentious, and selective in its coverage. But it existed, and formed the basis for further research. The same could not be said of the Soviet or the émigré press. While the memoirs of 'women of the sixties' were produced in the Soviet Union with relative freedom, one has to scour the bookshelves for more than the baldest account of non-revolutionary women after 1880. The absence of such literature is an eloquent testimony to the disregard with which the women's movement came to be held. The Bolshevik regime had declared feminism redundant. The feminists themselves apparently concurred.

Notes

1 Strachey, *The Cause* p. 338.

2 Shabanova, *Ocherk*, p. 24. 'External circumstances' (i.e. government obstructionism) were largely responsible for Russia's backwardness in the international peace movement. See L.A. Kamarovskii, 'Sovremennyia obshchestva mira' *Russkaia mysl'* no. 10 (1896) pt. 2, pp. 117–39; A. Kropotkin, 'Vsemirnye kongressy mira' *Vestnik Evropy* no. 12 (1909) p. 514.

3 Iu. Martov and F. Dan recording the day after Russia's mobilisation. Cited in Julius Braunthal, *A History of the International* vol. ii (London: 1967) p. 30.

4 See Stites, *The Women's Liberation Movement* pp. 284–7; Clements, *Bolshevik Feminist* ch. 4.

5 *Zhenskoe delo* no. 15 (1914) p. 2.

6 *Zhenskii vestnik* no. 9 (1914) pp. 170–3.

7 Delegates came to The Hague from 150 organisations in twelve countries. There were over 1,000 participants (more than half of them Dutch). Gertrude Bussey and Margaret Tims, *The Women's International League for Peace and Freedom, 1915–1965* (London: 1965); Evans, *The Feminists* p. 226.

8 *International Congress of Women, The Hague, April 28–May 1, 1915. Resolutions Adopted* (Amsterdam: n.d.).

9 *Zhenskoe delo* no. 9 (1915) pp. 1–2; no. 12 (1915) pp. 1–2; *Towards Permanent Peace. A Record of the Women's International Congress held at The Hague, April 28th–May 1st, 1915* (London: 1915) pp. 16, 26.

10 *Zhenskii vestnik* no. 10 (1914) p. 272; *International Congress of Women . . . 1915* p. 220. Shabanova later expressed full agreement with the views of Lady Aberdeen on the 'state of affairs which preoccupy us at the moment.' Lady Aberdeen had been hostile to The Hague congress and one wonders to what extent Shabanova felt her loyalties torn on this issue. Letter to Lady Aberdeen, 1 May 1915, ICW archive.

11 *Zhenskii vestnik* no. 9 (1914) p. 199; *Zhenskoe delo* no. 11 (1915) p. 13.

12 J.L. Keep, *The Russian Revolution. A Study in Mass Mobilisation* (London: 1976) p. 32. Women were first employed on Moscow trams early in 1915. *Zhenskoe delo* no. 10 (1915) p. 17. For women in industry see S.O. Zagorsky, *State Control of Industry in Russia During the War* (New Haven: 1928) pp. 54–5. Minors, prisoners of war and refugees made up the shortfall in manpower. In the Donets mines 75,185 prisoners were employed by early 1917, compared with 12,185 women.

13 *Zhenskii vestnik* no. 7–8 (1916) pp. 102–4.

14 E. Sylvia Pankhurst, *The Home Front. A Mirror to Life in England During the World War* (London: 1932); *Zhenskii vestnik* no. 11 (1915) pp. 192–3; no. 12 (1915) pp. 216–17; no. 3 (1916) p. 143.

15 *Ibid.* no. 9–10 (1917) p. 111.

16 From the context in which the blank spaces occurred, it seems that complaints about inefficiency in the army were as likely to be censored as demands for equal rights.

17 *Ibid.* no. 1 (1917) pp. 1–2. See Dale Ross, *The Role of the Women of Petrograd in War, Revolution and Counter-Revolution, 1914–1921* (Ph.D. Rutgers University; 1973) pp. 115–18; Stites, *The Women's Liberation Movement* pp. 289–91; Bobroff, 'Bolsheviks and Working Women' pp. 556–8.

18 *Izvestiia* 5 March 1917, p. 5; 8 March, p. 5; *Jus Suffragii* 1 November 1917, p. 25.

19 *Ibid.* pp. 25–6; L. Ia. Gurevich, *Pochemu nuzhno dat' zhenshchinam takiia zhe prava kak muzhchinam* (Petrograd: 1917) p. 2; *Izvestiia* 21 March 1917, p. 7.

20 *Jus Suffragii* 1 November 1917, p. 26. I have not been able to find the full Russian original of this speech. See also *Rech'* 21 March 1917, p. 5.

21 Gurevich, *Pochemu nuzhno dat' zhenshchinam* p. 2; *Zhenskii vestnik* no. 5 (1917) p. 71. The delegation included Figner, Miliukova, Pokrovskaia, Tyrkova, Shabanova, Shishkina-Iavein and others.

22 *Russkiia vedomosti* 8 April 1917, p. 5; 9 April, p. 6.

23 Claude Anet, *Through the Russian Revolution: Notes of an Eye Witness from 12 March to 30 May* (London: 1917) p. 96: *Jus Suffragii* 1 November 1917, p. 25.

24 *Zakon o vyborakh v Uchreditel'noe Sobranie, offitsial'noe utverzhdennoe Vremennym Pravitel'stvom 20 iiulia 1917 g.* (Petrograd–Moscow: 1917) paras. 3–10. See K. Arsen'ev, 'Uchreditel'noe sobranie i Petrogradskie raionnye vybory – dve storony medali' *Vestnik Evropy* no. 4–6 (1917) p. 660; A.N. Makarov, 'Zakon o vyborakh v uchreditel'noe sobranie' *Ibid.*

no. 9–12 (1917) pp. 325–43; *Zhenskii vestnik* no. 5 (1917) p. 72.

25 *Ibid.* p. 66; no. 10–11 (1917) p. 112; Stites, *The Women's Liberation Movement* pp. 295–300; E. Sylvia Pankhurst, *The Life of Emmeline Pankhurst* (London: 1935) p. 159–61. Sylvia Pankhurst writes that her mother was still in Russia when the Bolsheviks seized power. In fact, on Tomas Masaryk's advice, she returned home a few weeks before. David Mitchell, *Women on the Warpath* (London: 1966) pp. 65–70.

26 *Zhenskii vestnik* no. 5–6 (1917) pp. 67–9.

27 Stites, *The Women's Liberation Movement* p. 292n.

28 E. Shchepkina, *Zhenskoe dvizhenie v gody frantsuzskoi revoliutsii* (Petrograd: 1921). See also L. Gurevich (ed.) *O Stanislavskom* (M: 1948) preface; M.V. Sedel'nikova, *N.V. Chekhov – vidnyi deiatel' narodnogo prosveshcheniia* (M: 1960). I am grateful to Rochelle Ruthchild for these references.

29 Letter to Lady Aberdeen, 16 December 1928. ICW archive; E.D. Zabludovskaia, 'Odna iz pervykh zhenshchin vrachei-pediatrov v Rossii, A.N. Shabanova', *Pediatriia* June 1957, p. 77.

30 Letter to Anna Backer, 30 August 1921; letter to Lady Aberdeen, 30 August 1921. ICW archive.

31 *Jus Suffragii* June 1921, p. 134; Stites, *The Women's Liberation Movement* pp. 307–8.

32 For Miliukov's brief account of the debate at the second Kadet congress in 1906 see *Vospominaniia 1859–1917* (New York: 1955) vol. i. p. 308.

33 This is vol. i of *Sbornik pamiati Anny Pavlovny Filosofovoi*.

Bibliography

It is difficult in some instances to make a satisfactory distinction between primary and secondary sources. All autobiographical accounts by participants in the women's movement and by leading political figures have been included in the primary sources, even though some were written many years after the events which they were describing. Published material on the international women's movement has been separated from material relating to Russia, but no attempt has been made to distinguish between primary and secondary sources on the international movement.
[M = Moscow; Spb = St Petersburg]

Archival material

1. *London Library collection; Folio 1905*; Miscellaneous documents relating to the Union of Unions and the All-Russian Union of Equal Rights for women.
2. *Public Archives of Canada, Ottawa*: Archives of the International Council of Women.
3. *Fawcett Library, City of London Polytechnic*: Miscellaneous letters and typescript reports relating to the National Union of Women's Suffrage Societies and to the International Woman Suffrage Alliance.

Unpublished theses

Dudgeon, Ruth Arlene Fluck. *Women and Higher Education in Russia 1855–1905* (Ph.D George Washington University: 1975).

Edmondson, Linda Harriet. *Feminism in Russia 1900–1917* (Ph.D. University of London: 1981).

Engel, Barbara Alpern. *From Feminism to Populism: A Study of Changing Attitudes of Women of the Russian Intelligentsia 1855–1881* (Ph.D. Columbia University: 1974).

Goldberg, Rochelle Lois. *The Russian Women's Movement 1859–1917* (Ph.D. University of Rochester: 1976).

Knight, Amy. *The Participation of Women in the Revolutionary Movement in Russia from 1890 to 1914* (Ph.D. University of London: 1977).

Neumark, Noralyn. *The Consciousness of Women in the Russian Women's Movement 1855–1914* (Ph.D. University of Sydney: 1976).

Ross, Dale. *The Role of the Women of Petrograd in War, Revolution and Counter-Revolution 1914–1921* (Ph.D. Rutgers University: 1973).

Stites, Richard. *The Question of the Emancipation of Women in Nineteenth Century Russia* (Ph.D. Harvard University: 1968).

Feminist journals

Zhenskii vestnik Spb (1866–8)
Zhenskoe obrazovanie Spb (1876–91)
Zhenskoe delo Spb (1899–1900)
Zhenskii vestnik Spb (1904–17)
Soiuz zhenshchin Spb (1907–9)
Zhenskoe delo M (1910–17)
Zhenskaia mysl' Kiev (1909–10)
Jus Suffragii Rotterdam–London (1906–25)

Other journals

I have listed only those journals which were used extensively for information. Individual articles from other journals are listed under their authors. Dates refer to years consulted.

Pravo Spb (1898–1917)
Listok osvobozhdeniia Stuttgart–Paris (1904–5)
Osvobozhdenie Paris (1905)
Vestnik Partii Narodnoi Svobody Spb (1906)
Sotsial-demokrat Geneva (1908–9)
Golos sotsial-demokrata Geneva (1908–9)

Newspapers

(Dates are for years consulted)

Novoe vremia Spb (1905–9)
Russkiia vedomosti M (1905–9; 1917)
Rus' Spb (1905)
Novaia Rus' Spb (1908–9)
Novosti Spb (1905)
Rech' Spb (1906–9; 1917)
Slovo Spb (1905)
Nasha zhizn' Spb (1904–5)
Novaia zhizn' Spb (1905)
Izvestiia Petrograd (1917)

Reference works

Bol'shaia entsiklopediia 20 vols. (Spb: n.d.)
Entsiklopedicheskii slovar' Brokgauz-Efron 45 vols. (Spb: 1890–1907)
Entsiklopedicheskii slovar' Granat 7th. ed. vols. i–xxxiii (M: n.d.)
Novyi entsiklopedicheskii slovar' 29 vols. (Spb: n.d.)
Afanas'ev, N.I., *Sovremenniki* 2 vols. (Spb 1909–10)
Beliaeva, L.N., Zinov'eva, M.K., Nikiforov, M.M., *Bibliografiia periodicheskikh izdanii Rossii 1901–1916* 4 vols. (Leningrad: 1958–61).
Boiovich, M.M., (comp.) *Chleny Gosudarstvennoi Dumy* 4 vols. (M 1906–13)
Fidler, F.F. (comp.) *Pervye literaturnye shagi. Avtobiografii sovremennykh russkikh pisatelei* (M 1911)
Kommunisticheskaia Akademiia, *Pervaia russkaia revoliutsiia. Ukazetel' literatury*. (M 1930)
Masanov, I.F., *Slovar' psevdonimov russkikh pisatelei, uchenykh i obshchestvennykh deiatelei* 4 vols. (M 1956–60)
Ukazatel'vazhneishikh sochinenii po zhenskomu voprosu (M: 1907)
Ulianov, N.A., *Ukazatel' zhurnal'noi literatury* 2 vols. (Spb: 1911, 1915)

Primary sources on the Russian women's movement

Abramovich, N. Ia., *Zhenshchina i mir muzhskoi kul'tury* (M: 1913).
Khristina Danilovna Alchevskaia. Poluvekovoi iubilei (1862–1912) (M: 1912).
Amfiteatrov, A.V., *Zhenskoe nestroenie* 3rd. ed. (Spb: 1908).
Ardashev, N., *Velikaia voina i zhenshchiny russkiia* (M: 1915).
Ariian, P.N., (ed.) *Pervyi zhenskii kalendar'* 17 vols. (Spb: 1899–1915).
Arsen'ev, K., 'Uchreditel'noe sobranie i petrogradskie raionnye vybory – dve storony medali' *Vestnik Evropy* no. 4–6 (1917) pp. 660–5.
Bebel, A., *Zhenshchina i sotsializm* (trans. V.A. Posse) (Odessa: 1905).
Bezobrazov, P.V., *O pravakh zhenshchiny* (M: 1895).
Biulleten' pervago vserossiiskago zhenskago s"ezda nos. 2, 6, 7, 9, 10 (Spb: 1908).
Blaschko, Alfred, *Prostitutsiia nachala XX veka* (trans. from German) (Spb: 1905).

Bogdanovich, T., 'Zhenskoe dvizhenie za posledniia piat' desiat let. (Vtoroi mezhdunarodnyi zhenskii kongress)' *Mir bozhii* no. 9 (1903) pt. 1, pp. 204–36.

Davydov, N.V., *Zhenshchina pered ugolovnym sudom* (M: 1906).

Davydova, L., 'Na zhenskom mezhdunarodnom kongresse' *Mir bozhii* no. 8 (1899) pt. 2, pp. 42–60.

Delo o vyborgskom vozzvanii. Stenograficheskii otchet (Spb: 1908).

Delo. Sbornik v pol'zu SPB Zhenskago Meditsinskago Instituta (M: 1899).

D'iakonova, E.A., *Dnevnik 1886–1902* (Spb: 1905).

Dioneo (I.V. Shklovskii), 'Suffrazhistki' *Russkoe bogatstvo* no. 1 (1909) pp. 30–65.

Dolgova, N.P., *Imeiutsia – li osnovaniia dopustit' zhenshchin k uchastiiu v zemskom samoupravlenii?* (Spb: 1913).

Ermanskii, A., 'Vserossiiskii zhenskii s''ezd' *Sovremennyi mir* no. 1 (1909) pp. 103–12.

Evreinova, A.M., 'Ob uravnenii prav zhenshchin pri nasledovanii' *Zhurnal grazhdanskago i ugolovnago prava* no. 3 (1884) appendix, pp. 129–60.

Figner, Vera, *Memoirs of a Revolutionist* (London: 1929). *Studencheskie gody 1872–1876* (M: 1924).

Fleishits, E., 'Advokaty budushchago' *Vestnik grazhdanskago prava* no. 7 (1914) pp. 58–70.

'Novella semeistvennago prava' *Pravo* no. 14 (1914) cols. 1113–29.

'Pervyi vserossiiskii s''ezd po obrazovaniiu zhenshchin' *Vestnik Evropy* no. 2 (1913) pp. 361–5.

Gernet, M., 'Zhenskoe ravnopravie i ugolovyny zakon' *Sovremennyi mir* no. 5–6 (1916) pt. 2, pp. 36–48.

Gertsenshtein, G.M., 'Zhenshchiny-vrachi na poprishche prakticheskoi deiatel'nosti v Rossii' *Mir bozhii* no. 2 (1898) pt. 1, pp. 146–65.

Gessen, I.V., 'Razdel'noe zhitel'stvo suprugov' *Pravo* no. 49 (1911) cols. 2755–67; no. 50 (1911) cols. 2842–51. 'V dvukh vekakh; zhiznennyi otchet' *Arkhiv russkoi revoliutsii* vol. xxii (Berlin: 1937).

Ginzburg, A. *Zhenshchina pered zakonom* (M: n.d.).

Ginzburg, A.A., 'Izgnanie ploda' *Zhurnal Ministerstva Iustitsii* no. 7 (1912) pt. 2, pp. 35–70.

Gizhitskaia, L. (Lily Braun), 'Novaia zhenshchina v literature' *Mir bozhii* no. 1, (1897) pt. 1, pp. 33–45. 'Zhenskoe dvizhenie v Germanii i Anglii' *Mir bozhii* no. 5 (1896) pt. 1, pp. 38–54.

Glebov, P., *Politicheskiia prava zhenshchin v mestnom samoupravlenii* (M: 1906).

Glinskii, B., 'Pervyi zhenskii vserossiiskii s''ezd' *Istoricheskii vestnik* no. 1 (1909) pp. 384–407.

Goikhbarg, A.G., 'Zamuzhnaia zhenshchina kak neravnopravnaia lichnost' v sovremennom grazhdanskom prave' *Pravo* no. 5 (1914) cols. 3540–52.

Gol'tseva, N.A., *Zhenskoe dvizhenie v Soedinennykh Shtatakh* (M: 1906).

Gorovits, L., 'K voprosu o nakazuemosti aborta' *Sovremennik* no. 5 (1914) pp. 36–44.

Gosudarstvennaia Duma: Stenograficheskie otchety 32 vols. (Spb: 1906–17).

Prilozheniia (Spb: 1907–14).

Ukazatel' (Spb: 1907–14).

Gosudarstvennyi Sovet: Stenograficheskie otchety Sessiia VII, Sessiia VIII (Spb: 1912, 1913).

Grave, O.K., *Zhenskii vopros* (Spb: 1907).

Groman, V., (ed.) *Materialy k krest'ianskomu voprosu: Otchet o zasedaniiakh delegatskago s"ezda Vserossiiskago Krest'ianskago Soiuza 6–10 noiabria 1905g.* (Spb: 1905).
Grossman, G., 'Mezhdunarodnyi zhenskii kongress v Berline' *Pravda* no. 7–8 (1904) pp. 179–89.
Gurevich, L.Ia., *9-e ianvaria. Po dannym 'anketnoi komissii'* (Spb: 1905).
(ed.) *O Stanislavskom* (M: 1948).
Pochemu nuzhno dat' zhenshchinam vse prava i svobodu (Spb: 1906).
Pochemu nuzhno dat' zhenshchinam takiia zhe prava kak muzhchinam (Petrograd: 1917). Updated version of above.
G(urevich), L., 'Pamiati N.V. Stasovoi' *Severnyi vestnik* no. 10 (1895) pt. 2, pp. 88–91.
Zhenskii vopros v Gosudarstvennoi Dume (Spb: 1906).
(Gurevich, L.) *Zhenskoe dvizhenie poslednikh dnei* (Odessa: 1905).
Isaev, A.A., *Chego ozhidat' zhenshchine ot sotsializma* (Stuttgart: 1903).
Iuzhakov, S., *Zhenshchina-izbiratel'nitsa. (K voprosu o reforme russkago izbiratel'nago prava.* (M: 1906).
Ivanovich, S., 'Zhenshchina-chinovnik v Rossii' *Novyi zhurnal dlia vsekh* no. 1 (1910) cols. 109–16.
Ivanovich, V., (comp.) *Rossiiskiia partii, soiuzy i ligi* (Spb: 1906).
Kaidanova, O., *Dlia chego zhenshchinam nuzhno ravnopravie* (Kherson: 1917).
Zhenskaia dolia (M: 1906).
Kal'manovich, A.A., *Otchet o zhenskom mezhdunarodnom kongresse 1904g.* (Saratov: 1905).
Pretenzii k zhenskomu dvizheniiu voobshche i k 1-mu vseross. zhenskomu s"ezdu v chastnosti. (Spb: 1910).
Suffrazhistki i suffrazhetki. (Spb: 1911).
Zhenskoe dvizhenie i ego zadachi (Spb: 1908).
Zhenskoe dvizhenie i otnoshenie partii k nemu (Spb: 1911).
Kamarovskii, L.A., 'Sovremennyia obshchestva mira' *Russkaia mysl'* no. 10 (1896) pt. 2, pp. 117–39.
Kamrash, V.G., *Feminizm, ob emansipatsii zhenshchiny* (M: 1902).
Kaufman, A., 'Russkaia kursistka v tsifrakh' *Russkaia mysl'* no. 6 (1912) pt. 2, pp. 63–93.
Kechedzhi-Shapovalov, M.V., *Zhenskoe dvizhenie v Rossii i zagranitsei* (Spb: 1902).
Khvostov, V.M., *Psikhologiia zhenshchin. O ravnopravii zhenshchin* (M: 1911).
Zhenshchina i chelovecheskoe dostoinstvo (M: 1914).
Zhenshchina nakanune novoi epokhi. Dva etiuda po zhenskomu voprosu (M: 1905).
K(irpichnikov) S.D., *Soiuz soiuzov* (Spb: 1906).
Kizevetter, A., 'Pamiati Z.S. Mirovich' *Russkaia mysl'* no. 9 (1913) pt. 2, pp. 140–1.
Kleinbort, L., 'Zhenskie dni' *Novyi zhurnal dlia vsekh* no. 2 (1913) cols. 99–108.
Kokoshkin, F., *Ob osnovaniiakh zhelatel'noi organizatsii narodnago predstavitel'stva v Rossii* (M: 1906).
Kollontai, Aleksandra, 'Avtobiograficheskii ocherk' *Proletarskaia revoliutsiia* no. 3 (1921) pp. 261–302.
'Dva techeniia. (Po povodu 1-oi mezhdunarodnoi zhenskoi sotsialisticheskoi konferentsii v Shtutgarte)' *Obrazovanie* no. 10 (1907) pt. 2, pp. 46–62.
'Novaia zhenshchina' *Sovremennyi mir* no. 9 (1913) pp. 151–185.

Sotsial'nyia osnovy zhenskago voprosa (Spb: 1909).
Konstitutsionno-demokraticheskaia partiia. S"ezd 12–18 oktiabria 1905g. (M: 1905).
Postanovleniia 2-go s"ezda 5–11 ianvaria 1906g. i programma (Spb: 1906).
Postanovleniia 3-go s"ezda 21–25 aprelia 1906g. i ustav partii (Spb: 1906).
Otchet tsentral'nago komiteta konst. dem. partii (partii narodnoi svobody) – za dva goda s 18 okt. 1905g. po okt. 1907g. (Spb: 1907).
Zakonodatel'nye proekty i predlozheniia Partii Narodnoi Svobody 1905–1907gg. (Spb: 1907).
Kropotkin, A., 'Vsemirnye kongressy mira' *Vestnik Evropy* no. 12 (1909) pp. 513–30.
Kudrin, N.E., (N.S. Rusanov), *O ravnopravnosti zhenshchin* (Spb: 1905).
Kuskova, E.D., 'Davno minuvshee' *Novyi zhurnal* nos. 43–5, 47–51, 54 (1955–8).
'Zhenskii vopros', 'Zhenskoe dvizhenie' *Entsiklopedicheskii slovar' Granat* 7th ed. vol. xx, cols. 162–76; supp., cols. 1–38. (M: n.d.).
'Zhenskii vopros i zhenskii s"ezd' *Obrazovanie* no. 1 (1909) pp. 74–99; no. 2 (1909) pp. 33–44.
Kuvshinskaia, E., *Istoriia fabrichnago zakonodatel'stva v Anglii* (Spb: 1912).
Bor'ba rabochikh za politicheskuiu svobodu v Anglii (Spb: 1907).
L.B., 'Iz Anglii. (Novaia zhenshchina)' *Obrazovanie* no. 7–8 (1898) pt. 2, pp. 22–40.
Lapinskii, M.N., *O razvitii lichnosti u zhenshchin* (Kiev: 1915).
Letkova, E., 'Elena Iusifovna Likhacheva' *Russkoe bogatstvo* no. 12 (1904) pt. 2, pp. 202–7.
and Batinshkov, F.D., (ed.), *K svetu. Nauchno-literaturnyi sbornik* (Spb: 1904).
Levinson-Lessing, F. Iu., *O glavneishikh faktorakh zhenskago dvizheniia* (Spb: n.d.).
L(evinson-Lessing) F., 'Materinstvo i umstvennyi trud' *Mir bozhii* no. 9 (1902) pt. 2, pp. 7–16.
Likhacheva, E., *Materialy dlia istorii zhenskago obrazovaniia v Rossii* 2 vols. (Spb: 1899, 1906).
'Zhenskoe dvizhenie za poslednee desiatiletie' *Otechestvennye zapiski* no. 3 (1880) pt. 2 pp. 1–24.
Lot-Borodina, M.I., 'Frantsuzskaia zhenshchina pered litsom voiny' *Russkaia mysl'* no. 9 (1915) pt. 2, pp. 56–70.
Lukanov, P., *Chego trevuiut krest'iane* (Spb: 1906).
Lukhmanova, N., (ed.) *Sputnik zhenshchiny. Nastol'naia kniga dlia zhenshchin* (Spb: 1898).
Makarov, A.N., 'Zakon o vyborakh v uchreditel'noe sobranie' *Vestnik Evropy* no. 9–12 (1917) pp. 325–43.
Maklakov, V.A., *Pervaia Gosudarstvennaia Duma: Vospominaniia sovremennika* (Paris: 1939).
Maksimov, V., *Zakony o razvode* (M: 1908).
Margulies, M.A., 'Po povodu mezhdunarodnago kongressa po voprosu o torgovle belymi nevol'nitsami' *Pravo* no. 17 (1899) cols. 873–4.
Martov, L., Maslov, P., Potresov, A., (ed.) *Obshchestvennoe dvizhenie v Rossii v nachale XX-go veka* 4 vols. (Spb: 1909–10).
Maslova, P.I., *Zhenshchina o zhenshchine* (Spb: 1907).
Matiushenskii, A.I., *Polovoi rynok i polovyia otnosheniia* (Spb: 1908).

Mikhailova, Vera, *Russkie zakony o zhenshchine* (M: 1913).
Miliukov, P.N., *God bor'by* (Spb: 1907).
Vospominaniia (1859–1917) (New York: 1955).
Mill, J.S., *Izbiratel'nyia prava zhenshchin*, (trans. N. Mirovich) (M: 1905).
Mir truda (probnyi nomer 6-go maia 1906g.) (M: 1906).
Mirovich, N. (Z.S. Ivanova) *Iz istorii zhenskago dvizheniia v Rossi* (M: 1908).
'Iz istorii zhenskago obrazovaniia v Rossii XVIII i XIX vv.' *Russkaia mysl'* no. 9 (1900) pt. 2, pp. 62–85.
'Novyi fazis zhenskago dvizheniia v sovremennoi Anglii' *Vestnik Evropy* no. 8 (1909) pp. 810–819.
'O pervom s"ezde russkikh deiatel'nits po blagotvoreniiu i prosveshcheniiu' *Russkaia mysl'* no. 5 (1905) pt. 2, pp. 132–7.
'Otkrytoe pis'mo k chlenam "Soiuza 17-go oktiabria" *Russkaia mysl'* no. 3 (1906) pt. 2, pp. 100–4.
Pervyi vserossiiskii zhenskii s"ezd' *Vestnik Evropy* no. 1 (1909) pp. 411–15.
'Pobeda zhenskago dvizheniia v Finliandii' *Russkaia mysl'* no. 7 (1907) pt. 2, pp. 118–36.
'S"ezdy zemskikh i gorodskikh deiatelei i vopros ob izbiratel'nykh pravakh zhenshchin' *Russkaia mysl'* no. 12 (1905) pt. 2, pp. 164–71.
Vserossiiskii zhenskii s"ezd (M: 1909).
'Zhenshchina i ekonomicheskii vopros' *Obrazovanie* no. 10 (1899) pt. 1, pp. 54–62.
' "Zhenskii parlament" v Londone' *Russkaia mysl'* no. 7 (1909) pt. 2, pp. 124–37.
Zhenskoe dvizhenie v Evrope i Amerike (M: 1907).
Mizhuev, P.G.., 'Zhenskii vopros i zhenskoe dvizhenie' *Obrazovanie* no. 12 (1904) pt. 2, pp. 1–44.
Möbius, P., *Fizioligicheskoe slaboumie zhenshchiny* (trans. from German) (M: 1909).
Mogilianskii, M., 'Smertnaia kazn' v 1908g.' *Pravo* no. 52 (1908) cols. 2926–7.
Nabokov, V.D., 'Mozhet-li zhenshchina vesti zashchitu pred ugolovnym sudom?' *Pravo* no. 46 (1909) cols. 2473–81.
Novik, I.D., *Bor'ba za politicheskiia prava zhenshchin* (M: 1906).
Novikov, A., *Zhenshchina – tovarishch muzhchiny* (Rostov: n.d.).
Obolenskii, L.E., 'Biologi o zhenskom voprose' *Russkaia mysl'* no. 2 (1893) pt. 2, pp. 61–70.
Orlovskaia, M.V., *O zhenskom dvizhenii v Rossii* (Spb: 1911).
Orovich, Ia., *Zhenshchina v prave* (Spb: 1895).
Otchet o deiatel'nosti Rossiiskoi Ligi Ravnopraviia Zhenshchin za 1913 god. (Spb: 1914).
Pankhurst, Christabel, *Strashnyi bich (The Great Scourge)* (trans. A.K. [al'manovich]) (Spb: 1914).
Panteleev, L.F., *Iz vospominanii proshlago* (Spb: 1905).
Pavlov-Silvanskii, N., 'O prave zhenshchin byt' advokatami' *Russkoe bogatstvo* no. 5 (1905) pt. 2, pp. 1–26.
Pember Reeves, W., *Zhenskoe izbiratel'noe pravo* (trans. from English) (Kiev: 1905).
Petrazhitskii, L.I., *O pol'ze politicheskikh prav zhenshchin* (Spb: 1907).
Pimenova, Emiliia K., *Dni minuvshie. Vospominaniia* (Leningrad-Moscow: 1929).
P(imenova), E., 'Na zapade' *Obrazovanie* no. 5–6 (1896) pt. 2, pp. 120–26.

Pirogov, N.I., 'Voprosy zhizni' *Morskoi sbornik* no. 9 (1856) pt. 3, pp. 559–97.
Pirstorf, Iu., *Zhenskii trud i zhenskii vopros* (trans. from German) (Spb: 1905).
Pisareva, E., *Pamiati Anny Pavlovny Filosofovoi* (Spb: 1912).
Pokrovskaia, M.I., 'Peterburgskie rabochie i ikh ekonomicheskoe polozhenie. Zametki i nabliudeniia vracha' *Vestnik Evropy* no. 3, (1899).
Vrachebno-politseiskii nadzor za prostitutsiei sposobstvuet vyrozhdeniiu naroda (Spb: 1902).
Zashchitniki i protivniki ravnopraviia zhenshchin v pervoi Gosudarstvennoi Dume (Spb: 1907).
Polianskii, A. (ed.) *Russkaia zhenshchina na gosudarstvennoi i obshchestvennoi sluzhbe* (M: 1901).
Portugalov, G.M., 'O zhenskom iuridicheskom obrazovanii' *Pravo* no. 46 (1904) cols. 3176–81.
Rapoport, S.I., 'Bor'ba zhenshchin za prava. (Pis'mo iz Anglii)' *Mir bozhii* no. 6 (1905) pt. 2, pp. 64–75.
'Stroiteli angliiskoi zhizni. (Ocherk reform i sotsial'nykh dvizhenii.) Zhenskoe delo' *Sovremennyi mir* no. 1 (1908) pt. 1, pp. 90–109.
Ravnopravie zhenshchin. Tretii s"ezd soiuza ravnopravnosti zhenshchin. Otchety i protokoly (Spb: 1906).
Rossiiskoe Obshchestvo Zashchity Zhenshchin v 1913g./v 1915g. (Petrograd: 1914, 1916).
Russkaia zhenshchina, *K krest'iankam i rabotnitsam* (M: n.d.).
Ruttsen, L., *Ravnopravnost' zhenshchin* (M: 1907).
Sankt-Peterburgskie vysshie zhenskie kursy za 25 let 1878–1903. Ocherki i materialy (Spb: 1903).
Sbornik 'Izvestii krest'ianskikh deputatov' i 'Trudovoi Rossii' (M: 1906).
Sbornik na pomoshch ' uchashchimsia zhenshchinam (M: 1901).
Sbornik pamiati Anny Pavlovny Filosofovoi 2 vols. (Petrograd: 1915).
Shabanova, A.N., *Ocherk zhenskago dvizheniia v Rossii* (Spb: 1912).
'Vospominaniia o zhenskom mezhdunarodnom kongresse v Berline' *Novoe slovo* no. 2 (1896) pt. 2, pp. 82–93.
Sh(abanova) 'Zhenskie vrachebnie kursy. Iz vospominanii byvshei slushatel'nitsy' *Vestnik Evropy* no. 1 (1886) pp. 345–57.
Shashkov, S.S., *Ocherk istorii russkoi zhenshchiny* (Spb: 1872).
Shchepkina, E.N., *Iz istorii zhenskoi lichnosti v Rossii* (Spb: 1914).
'Pamiati dvukh zhenshchin-vrachei' *Obrazovanie* no. 5–6 (1896) pt. 1, pp. 92–137.
'Vospominaniia i dnevniki russkikh zhenshchin' *Istoricheskii vestnik* no. 8 (1914) pp. 536–55.
Zhenskoe dvizhenie 1905 goda v otzyvakh sovremennykh deiatelei (Spb: 1905).
Zhenskoe dvizhenie v gody frantsuzskoi revoliutsii (Petrograd: 1921).
'Zhenskoe naselenie Peterburga' *Obrazovanie* no. 5–6 (1897) pp. 218–32.
Shokhol', K., 'K voprosu o razvitii vysshago zhenskago obrazovaniia v Rossii' *Zhurnal Ministerstva Narodnago Prosveshcheniia* (August 1912) pp. 153–95; (March 1913) pp. 1–36; (July 1913) pp. 1–58.
'Pravovoe polozhenie zhenshchin-vrachei' *Pravo* no. 19 (1912) cols. 1079–81.
Shtakenshneider, Elena, *Dnevnik i zapiski 1854–1886* (Moscow-Leningrad: 1934).
Sinaiskii, V.I., *Lichnoe i imushchestvennoe polozhenie zamuzhnei zhenshchiny* (Dorpat: 1910).

Sobolev, M., 'Zhenskii trud v narodnom khoziaistve XIX veka' *Mir bozhii* no. 8 (1901) pp. 71–99.
Sputnik izbiratelia na 1906g. (Spb: 1906).
Stankevich, N., 'Zhenskii mesiats' *Sovremennik* no. 5 (1914).
Stasov, Vladimir, *Nadezhda Vasil'evna Stasova* (Spb: 1899).
Sviatlovskii, V., *Professional'noe dvizhenie v Rossii* (Spb: 1907).
Svod zakonov Rossiiskoi Imperii vol. iii (Spb: 1896); vol. x (Spb: 1900).
Svod zakonov Rossiiskoi Imperii ed. A.A. Dobrovol'skii 16 vols. (neofitsial'noe izdanie) (Spb: 1913).
Tiutriumov, I.M., (ed.) *Grazhdanskoe ulozhenie. Proekt vysochaishe uchrezhdennoi redaktsionnoi komissii po sostavleniiu grazhdanskago ulozheniia* 2 vols (Spb: 1910).
Tkhorzhevskii, S.I., *Vseobshchee, ravnoe, priamoe i tainoe izbiratel'noe pravo* (Petrograd: 1917).
Trudy pervago vserossiiskago s"ezda po bor'be s torgom zhenshchinami i ego prichinami, proiskhodivshago v S-Peterburge s 21 po 25 aprelia 1910 goda (Spb: 1911, 1912).
Trudy 1-go vserossiiskago s"ezda po obrazovaniiu zhenshchin, org. Rossiiskoi Ligoi Ravnopraviia Zhenshchin V S-Peterburge (Petrograd: 1914, 1915).
Trudy pervago vserossiiskago zhenskago s"ezda pri Russkom Zhenskom (Vzaimno-Blagotvoritel'nom) Obshchestve v S-Peterburge 10–16 dek. 1908 goda (Spb: 1909).
Tsebrikova, M., *Katorga i ssylka* (Geneva: 1890).
'Neskol'ko myslei o zhenskom vospitanii' *Russkaia mysl'* no. 4 (1902) pt. 2, pp. 19–43.
Pis'mo Imperatoru Aleksandru (London: 1894).
Tyrkova-Williams, A.V., *Chego zhdat' ot resheniia zhenskago voprosa* (M: n.d.).
From Liberty to Brest-Litovsk (London: 1919).
Na putiakh k svobode (New York: 1952).
Osvobozhdenie zhenshchiny (Petrograd: 1917).
'Pervye shagi. Pervyi zhenskii vserossiiskii s"ezd' *Novyi zhurnal dlia vsekh* no. 1 (1909) cols. 113–22.
'Pervyi zhenskii s"ezd' *Zarnitsy* no. 2 (1909) pt. 2, pp. 172–209.
To, chego bol'she ne budet (Paris: 1954).
Ustav Obshchestva pod nazvaniem 'Rossiiskaia Liga Ravnopraviia Zhenshchin' (Spb: 1911).
Vakhtina, M., *Rol'zhenshchiny v istoricheskoi evoliutsii i drugie doklady* (Spb: 1911).
Vasilevskii, L.M., *Zhenskii vopros* (Spb: 1906).
Vekhi. Sbornik statei o russkoi intelligentsii 2nd. ed. (M: 1909).
Vengerova, Zinaida, 'Feminizm i zhenskaia svoboda' *Obrazovanie* no. 5–6 (1898) pp. 73–90.
Veselovskii, B.B., *Istoriia zemstva za sorok let* 4 vols. (Spb: 1909–11).
Vodovozova, E.N., *Na zare zhizni* 2 vols. (Leningrad: 1964).
Vol'kenshtein, O.A., 'Itogi pervago vserossiiskago zhenskago s"ezda' *Russkaia mysl'* no. 2 (1909) pt. 2, pp. 146–53.
Komu i zachem nuzhno vseobshchee izbiratel'noe pravo (Spb: 1906).
Monarkhiia ili respublika (Petrograd: 1917).
Neprikosnovennost' lichnosti i zhilishcha (Petrograd: 1917).
Osvobozhdenie zhenshchiny (Petrograd: 1917).
Zhenshchina-izbiratel'nitsa (Rostov-on-Don: 1906).

Volkova, A.I., *Vospominaniia, dnevniki i stat'i* (Nizhnii-Novgorod: 1913).
Zakon o vyborakh v Uchreditel'noe Sobranie. (Petrograd-Moscow: [1917]).
Zemskii s"ezd 6-go i sl. noiabria 1904g. Kratkii otchet (Paris: 1905).
Zinov'ea, E., 'V zashchituv prav rozhdennykh' *Sovremennyi mir* no. 8 (1913) pp. 248–56.

Secondary sources on the Russian women's movement

Alston, P.L., *Education and the State in Tsarist Russia* (Stanford: 1969).
Anet, Claude, *Through the Russian Revolution. Notes of an Eyewitness* (London: 1917).
Artiukhina, A.V., (ed.) *Zhenshchiny v revoliutsii* (M: 1959).
Atkinson, Dorothy, Dallin, Alexander and Lapidus, Gail Warshofsky, (ed.) *Women in Russia* (Stanford: 1977).
Bater, James, *St Petersburg, Industrialization and Change* (London: 1976).
Bennigsen, Alexandre, Quelquejay, Chantal, *Les mouvements nationaux chez les musulmans de Russie* (Paris–The Hague: 1960).
La presse et le mouvement national chez les musulmans de Russie avant 1920 (Paris–The Hague: 1964).
Bilshai, V.L., *Reshenie zhenskogo voprosa v SSSR* (M: 1956).
Black, J.L., 'Educating Women in Eighteenth-Century Russia; Myths and Realities' *Canadian Slavic Papers* vol. xx, no. 1 (March 1978) pp. 23–43.
Bobroff, Anne, 'The Bolsheviks and Working Women, 1905–1920' *Soviet Studies* vol. xxvi, no. 4 (October 1974) pp. 540–67.
Borman, A.V., *A.V. Tyrkova-Vil'iams po ee pis'mam i vospominaniiam syna* (Louvain–Washington: 1964).
Botchkareva, Marie, *Yashka* (New York: 1919).
Broido, Vera, *Apostles into Terrorists* (New York: 1977).
Bryant, Louise, *Six Red Months in Russia* (London: 1919).
Bulanova, O., 'Doch' dekabrista. (Iz semeinoi khroniki)' *Byloe* no. 5 (1925) pp. 163–87; no. 6 (1925) pp. 20–37.
Butler, William E., (ed.) *Russian Law: Historical and Political Perspectives* (Leyden: 1977).
Byrnes, Robert F., 'Pobedonostsev on the Instruments of Russian Government' in E.J. Simmons (ed.) *Continuity and Change in Russian and Soviet Thought* (Cambridge, Mass.: 1955).
Chermenskii, E.D., *Burzhuaziia i tsarizm v pervoi russkoi revoliutsii* 2nd. ed. (M: 1970).
Clements, Barbara Evans, *Bolshevik Feminist: the Life of Aleksandra Kollontai* (Bloomington, Indiana–London; 1979).
'Kollontai's Contribution to the Workers' Opposition' *Russian History* vol. ii, pt. 2 (1975) pp. 191–206.
Crisp, Olga, *Studies in the Russian Economy before 1914* (London: 1976).
Curtiss, J.S., 'Russian Sisters of Mercy in the Crimea 1854–1855' *Slavic Review* vol. xxv (March 1966) pp. 84–100.
Darlington, T., *Education in Russia*. Board of Education Special Reports on Educational Subjects, vol. xxiii (London: 1909).
Dunham, Vera, 'The Strong Woman Motif in Russian Fiction' in C.E. Black (ed.) *The Transformation of Russian Society* (Cambridge, Mass: 1960).
Edmondson, Linda, 'Russian Feminists and the First All-Russian Congress of Women' *Russian History* vol. iii pt. 2 (1976) pp. 123–49.

Elwood, Ralph Carter, *Russian Social-Democracy in the Underground. A Study of the RSDRP in the Ukraine 1907–1914* (Assen: 1974).

Engel, Barbara Alpern, 'Women Medical Students in Russia, 1872–1882' *Journal of Social History* vol. xii, no. 3 (Spring 1979) pp. 394–414.

and Rosenthal, Clifford N., (ed.) *Five Sisters. Women Against the Tsar* (New York: 1975).

Farnsworth, Beatrice, *Aleksandra Kollontai. Socialism, Feminism and the Bolshevik Revolution* (Stanford: 1980).

Ferro, Marc, *La révolution de 1917. La chute du tsarisme et les origines d'Octobre* (Paris: 1967).

La révolution de 1917. Octobre: naissance d'une société (Paris: 1976).

Filippova, L.D., 'Iz istorii zhenskogo obrazovaniia v Rossii' *Voprosy istorii* (February 1963) pp. 209–18.

Galai, Shmuel, *The Liberation Movement in Russia 1900–1905* (Cambridge: 1973).

Gerschenkron, Alexander, *Economic Backwardness in Historical Perspective* (Cambridge, Mass–London 1962).

Grave, B.B. (ed.) 'Kadety v 1905–1906gg.' *Krasnyi arkhiv* vol. xlvi, no. 3 (1931) pp. 38–68; vol. xlvii–xlviii, no. 4–5 (1931) pp. 112–39.

Grishina, Z.V., 'Pervyi vserossiiskii zhenskii s"ezd' *Vestnik Moskovskogo Universiteta* series ix, no. 5 (1976) pp. 55–67.

Zhenskie organizatsii v Rossii (*1905g. –fevral'/mart 1917g*. Avtoreferat dissertatsii na soiskanie uchënoi stepeni kandidata istoricheskikh nauk (M: 1978).

Hans, Nicholas, *History of Russian Educational Policy 1701–1917* (London: 1931).

The Russian Tradition in Education (London: 1963).

Harper, S.N. 'Exceptional Measures in Russia' *Russian Review* vol. 1, no. 4 (1912) pp. 92–105.

Hayden, Carole Eubanks, 'The Zhenotdel and the Bolshevik Party' *Russian History* vol. iii, pt. 2 (1976) pp. 150–73.

Healy, Ann Erickson, *The Russian Autocracy in Crisis, 1905–1907* (Hamden, Conn: 1976).

Hollingsworth, Barry, 'The British Memorial to the Russian Duma 1906' *Slavonic and East European Review* vol. liii, (October 1975) pp. 539–57.

'The Society of Friends of Russian Freedom. English Liberals and Russian Socialists 1890–1917' *Oxford Slavonic Papers* new series iii, (Oxford: 1970) pp. 45–64.

Holt, Alix, (ed.) *Alexandra Kollontai. Selected Writings* (London: 1977).

Hosking, Geoffrey, A., *The Russian Constitutional Experiment. Government and Duma 1907–1914* (Cambridge: 1973).

Hutchinson, J.F., 'Science, Politics and the Alcohol Problem in post-1905 Russia', *Slavonic and East European Review* vol. lviii, no. 2 (April 1980) pp. 232–54.

Johanson, Christine, 'Autocratic Politics, Public Opinion and Women's Medical Education during the Reign of Alexander II, 1855–1881' *Slavic Review* vol. xxxviii, no. 3 (September 1979) pp. 426–43.

Johnson, W.H.E., *Russia's Educational Heritage* (New York: 1969).

Kalinychev, F.I., (ed.) *Gosudarstvennaia Duma v Rossii v dokumentakh i materialakh* (M: 1957).

Keep, John L., *The Russian Revolution. A Study in Mass Mobilization* (London: 1976).

Knight, Amy, 'The Fritschi: A Study of Female Radicals in the Russian Populist Movement' *Canadian-American Slavic Studies* vol. ix, no. 1 (Spring 1975) pp. 1–17.

Kucherov, Samuel, *Courts, Lawyers and Trials Under the Last Three Tsars* (New York: 1953).

Lapidus, Gail Warshofsky, *Women in Soviet Society. Equality, Development and Social Change* (Berkeley: 1978).

Lebedeva, O.S., *De l'emancipation de la femme musulmane* (Lisieux: 1900).

Levin, Alfred, *The Second Duma. A Study of the Social Democratic Party and the Russian Constitutional Experiment* (New Haven: 1940).

The Third Duma: Election and Profile (Hamden, Conn: 1973).

McNeal, R.H., *Bride of the Revolution, Krupskaya and Lenin* (London: 1973).

'Women in the Russian Radical Movement' *Journal of Social History* vol. v no. 2 (Winter 1971) pp. 143–61.

Meehan-Waters, Brenda, 'Catherine the Great and the Problem of Female Rule' *Russian Review* vol. xxxiv, no. 3 (July 1975) pp. 293–307.

Meijer, J.M., *Knowledge and Revolution: the Russian Colony in Zurich 1870–1873* (Assen: 1955).

Monter, Barbara Heldt, '*Rassvet* (1859–1862) and the Woman Question' *Slavic Review* Vol. xxxvi, no. 1 (March 1977) pp. 76–85.

Nevinson, Henry W., *The Dawn in Russia or Scenes in the Russian Revolution* (London–New York: 1906).

Norman, Anita, 'Ariadna Tyrkova-Williams, November 26, 1869–January 12, 1962' *Russian Review* vol. xxi, no. 3 (July 1962) pp. 277–81.

Pares, Bernard, *Russia and Reform* (London: 1907).

Pearson, Raymond, 'Milyukov and the Sixth Kadet Congress' *Slavonic and East European Review* vol. liii, no. 13, (April 1975) pp. 210–29.

Pomper, Philip, *Peter Lavrov and the Russian Revolutionary Movement* (Chicago: 1972).

Ransel, David L., (ed.) *The Family in Imperial History. New Lines of Historical Research* (Urbana–Chicago–London: 1978).

Rashin, A., *Naselenie Rossii za sto let (1811–1913 gg.)* (M: 1956).

Riha, Thomas, *A Russian European. Paul Miliukov in Russian Politics* (Notre Dame–London: 1969).

Rosenberg, William, *Liberals in the Russian Revolution* (Princeton: 1974).

Sablinsky, Walter, *The Road to Bloody Sunday* (Princeton: 1976).

'Samoderzhavie i izbiratel'nye prava zhenshchin' *Krasnyi arkhiv* vol. vi, no. 79 (1936) pp. 26–33.

Satina, S., *Education of Women in Pre-Revolutionary Russia* (New York: 1966).

Serditova, S.N., *Bol'sheviki v bor'be za zhenskie proletarskie massy 1903g. – fevral' 1917g.* (M: 1959).

Seton-Watson, Hugh, *The Decline of Imperial Russia* (London: 1952).

Snow, George E., 'The Peterhof Conference of 1905 and the Creation of the Bulygin Duma' *Russian History* vol. ii, pt. 2, (1975) pp. 149–60.

Steinberg, I., *Spiridonova – Revolutionary Terrorist* (London: 1935).

Stepniak-Kravchinskii, S., *Underground Russia* 2nd. ed. (London: 1883).

Stites, Richard, 'M.L. Mikhailov and the Emergence of the Woman Question in Russia' *Canadian Slavic Studies* vol. iii, no. 2 (Summer 1969) pp. 178–99.

'Women's Liberation Movements in Russia, 1900–1930' *Canadian-American Slavic Studies* vol. vii, no. 4 (Winter 1973) pp. 460–74.

The Women's Liberation Movement in Russia. Feminism, Nihilism and Bolshev-

ism, 1860–1930 (Princeton: 1978).
'Zhenotdel: Bolshevism and Russian Women, 1917–1930' *Russian History* vol. iii, pt. 2 (1976) pp. 174–93.

Surh, Gerald D., 'Petersburg's First Mass Labor Organization: The Assembly of Russian Workers and Father Gapon' *Russian Review* July 1981, pp. 241–62; October 1981, pp. 412–41.

Valk, S.N., (ed.) *Sankt-Peterburgskie vysshie zhenskie (Bestuzhevskie) kursy 1878–1918* 2nd. ed. (Leningrad: 1973).

Wallace, D. Mackenzie, *Russia* 2 vols. (London: 1877).

Whittaker, Cynthia, 'The Women's Movement during the Reign of Alexander II: A Case Study in Russian Liberalism' *Journal of Modern History* vol. xlviii, no. 2 (June 1976). On Demand Supplement.

Williams, Harold Whitmore, *Russia of the Russians* (London: 1915).

Zabludovskaia, E.D., 'Odna iz pervykh zhenshchin vrachei-pediatrov v Rossii, A.N. Shabanova' *Pediatriia* (June 1957) pp. 71–8.

Zagorsky, S.O., *State Control of Industry in Russia during the War* (Yale: 1928).

Zelnik, R.E. 'The Sunday School Movement in Russia 1859–1862' *Journal of Modern History* vol. xxxvii (June 1965) pp. 151–70.

Zhikhareva, A., 'Anna Sergeevna Miliukova. Zhiznennyi put' ' *Poslednii novosti* 5 April 1935, p. 2; 7 April 1935, p. 2.

Primary and secondary sources of the international women's movement

Anthony, K., *Feminism in Germany and Scandinavia* (New York: 1915).

Banks, J.A. and Olive, *Feminism and Family Planning in Victorian England* (Liverpool: 1964).

Blackburn, Helen, *A Record of Women's Suffrage* (London: 1902).

Blewett, Neal, 'The Franchise in the United Kingdom 1885–1918' *Past and Present* no. 32 (1965) pp. 27–56.

Branca, Patricia, *Silent Sisterhood. Middle-Class Women in the Victorian Home* (London: 1975).

Bussey, Gertrude and Tims, Margaret, *The Women's International League for Peace and Freedom, 1915–1965 A Record of Fifty Years' Work* (London: 1965).

Cambridge Women's Studies Group, *Women in Society* (London: 1981).

Condorcet, le marquis de, *Oeuvres de Condorcet* 12 vols. (Paris: 1847).

Dangerfield, George, *The Strange Death of Liberal England* (London: 1935).

Davidoff, Leonore, 'Mastered for Life: Servant and Wife in Victorian and Edwardian England' *Journal of Social History* vol. vii, no. 4 (Summer 1974) pp. 406–28.

Davies, Margaret Llewelyn, (ed.) *Life As We Have Known It, by Cooperative Working Women* (intr. Anna Davin) (London: 1977).

Eisenstein, Zillah R., *The Radical Future of Liberal Feminism* (New York–London: 1981).

Englishwoman's Yearbook 1915 (London: 1915).

Evans, Richard, *The Feminist Movement in Germany 1894–1933* (London: 1976).
The Feminists (London: 1977).

Fawcett, Millicent Garrett, *Women's Suffrage. A Short History of a Great Movement* (London–Edinburgh: 1912).

Flexner, Eleanor, *Century of Struggle. The Woman's Rights Movement in the United States* (New York: 1973).
Gilman, Charlotte Perkins, *Women and Economics* (Boston: 1898).
Greg, W.R. *Literary and Social Judgments* (London: 1868).
Grimes, Alan, P., *The Puritan Ethic and Woman Suffrage* (Oxford–New York: 1967).
Grimshaw, Patricia, *Women's Suffrage in New Zealand* (Auckland–Oxford: 1972).
Harper, Ida Husted, (ed.) *History of Woman Suffrage* vols. v and vi (New York: 1922).
and Anthony, Susan B., (ed.) *History of Woman Suffrage* vol. iv (Rochester, New York: 1902).
Harrison, Brian, *Separate Spheres* (London: 1978).
Hause, Steven C. and Kenney, Anne R., 'The Limits of Suffragist Behavior: Legalism and Militancy in France, 1876–1922' *American Historical Review* October 1981, pp. 781–806.
Hobsbawm, E.J. *The Age of Capital 1848–1875* (London: 1975).
Hufton, Olwen, 'Women and the Family Economy in Eighteenth-Century France' *French Historical Studies* no. 9 (1975–6) pp. 1–22.
'Women in Revolution 1789–1796' *Past and Present* vol. 53 (1971) pp. 90–108.
International Congress of Medicine, *The Dangers of Syphilis and the Question of State Control* (London: 1914).
The International Congress of Women: London 1899 7 vols. (London: 1900).
International Congress of Women, The Hague, April 28–May 1 1915, Resolutions Adopted (Amsterdam: n.d.).
International Council of Women, Quinquennial Meeting Canada 1909 (London: 1910).
Report on the Quinquennial Meetings Rome 1914 (Karlsruhe: n.d.).
Reports for 1904–1905/1905–1906/1906–1907/1907–1908 (Aberdeen: 1905–1908).
Women in a Changing World: the Dynamic Story of the International Council of Women since 1888 (London: 1966).
Women's Position in the Laws of the Nations (Karlsruhe: 1912).
Der Internationale Frauen-Kongress in Berlin 1904 (Berlin: n.d.).
International Woman Suffrage Alliance, *Report Second and Third Conference* (Copenhagen: 1906).
Report of the Fourth Conference (Amsterdam: 1908).
Report of the Fifth Conference and First Quinquennial, London, England (London: 1909).
Report of the Sixth Congress, Stockholm, Sweden (London: 1911).
Report of the Seventh Congress, Budapest, Hungary (Manchester: 1913).
Kaplan, Marion A., *The Jewish Feminist Movement in Germany*. (Westport, Conn: 1979).
Kempf, Beatrix, *Suffragette for Peace. The Life of Bertha von Suttner* (London: 1972).
Kraditor, Aileen Sema, *The Ideas of the Woman Suffrage Movement* (New York: 1971).
Laslett, Peter, *The World We Have Lost* (New York: 1960).
and Wall, Richard (ed.) *Household and Family in Past Time* (Cambridge: 1972).

Liddington, Jill and Norris, Jill, *One Hand Tied Behind Us. The Rise of the Women's Suffrage Movement* (London: 1978).
Lipinska, M., *Histoire des femmes médecins* (Paris: 1900).
Lytle, Scott, H., 'The Second Sex (September 1793)' *Journal of Modern History* vol. 27 (1955) pp. 14–26.
Marwick, Arthur, *Women at War: 1914–1918* (London: 1977).
Maurois, André, *Lélia. The Life of George Sand* (trans. Gerard Hopkins) (New York: 1953).
Mayreder, Rose, *A Survey of the Woman Problem* (London: 1913).
McGregor, O.R., 'The Social Position of Women in England 1850–1914: A Bibliography' *British Journal of Sociology* (March 1955), pp. 48–60.
McLaren, Angus, 'Abortion in England 1890–1914' *Victorian Studies* (Summer 1977) pp. 379–400.
Metcalfe, A.E., *Woman's Effort. A Chronicle of British Women's Fifty Years' Struggle for Citizenship* (Oxford: 1917).
Mill, J.S. *The Subjection of Women* (1869) (London: 1970).
Mitchell, David John, *The Fighting Pankhursts* (London: 1967). *Women on the Warpath* (London: 1966).
Mitchell, Juliet and Oakley, Ann, (ed.) *The Rights and Wrongs of Women* (Harmondsworth: 1976).
Morgan, David, *Suffragists and Liberals: The Politics of Woman Suffrage in England* (Oxford: 1975).
Neff, Wanda F., *Victorian Working Women* (New York: 1929).
Neumann, R.P., 'The Sexual Question and Social Democracy in Imperial Germany' *Journal of Social History* vol. vii, no. 3 (1974).
Newsome, Stella, *The Women's Freedom League 1907–1957* (London: 1960).
O'Neill, W.L., *Everyone was Brave: A History of Feminism in America* (Chicago: 1971).
The Woman Movement. Feminism in the United States and England (London: 1969).
Ostrogorski, M., *The Rights of Women* (New York: 1893).
Packe, Michael St. John, *The Life of John Stuart Mill* (London: 1954).
Pankhurst, E. Sylvia, *The Home Front. A Mirror to Life in England During the World War* (London: 1932).
The Life of Emmeline Pankhurst (London: 1935).
The Suffragette Movement. An Intimate Account of Persons and Ideals (London: 1931).
Pinchbeck, Ivy, *Women Workers and the Industrial Revolution 1750–1850* (London: 1930).
Report of the International Council of Women assembled by the National Woman Suffrage Association, Washington, D.C., United States of America, March 25 to April 1, 1888 (Washington: 1888).
Report of the First International Woman Suffrage Conference held at Washington, U.S.A. (New York: 1902).
Rosen, Andrew, *Rise Up Women! The Militant Campaign of the Women's Social and Political Union 1903–1914* (London–Boston: 1974).
Rover, Constance M., *Women's Suffrage and Party Politics in Britain 1866–1914* (London–Toronto: 1966).
Rowbotham, Sheila, *Hidden from History* (London: 1973). *Women, Resistance and Revolution* (London: 1972).
Schirmacher, K., *The Modern Woman's Right Movement* (New York: 1912).

Schreiber, A., Mathieson, M., *Journey Towards Freedom. Written for the Golden Jubilee of the International Alliance of Women* (Copenhagen: 1955).
Schreiner, Olive, *Woman and Labour* (London: 1911).
Slaughter, Jane and Kern, Robert (eds.) *European Women on the Left* (Westport, Conn.–London: 1981).
Stanton, T. (ed.) *The Woman Question in Europe. A Series of Original Essays* (London: 1884).
Stone, Lawrence, *The Family, Sex and Marriage in England 1500–1800* (London: 1977).
Strachey, Ray, *The Cause. A Short History of the Women's Movement in Great Britain* (London: 1928).
Tilly, Louise A. and Scott, Joan W., *Women, Work and Family* (New York: 1978).
Towards Permanent Peace. A Record of the Women's International Congress held at The Hague April 28th–May 1st, 1915 (London: 1915).
Vicinus, Martha, (ed.) *Suffer and Be Still. Women in the Victorian Age* (Bloomington, Indiana–London: 1972).
Wardle, Ralph M., *Mary Wollstonecraft. A Critical Biography* (Lincoln, Nebraska: 1966).
Weininger, O., *Sex and Character* (trans. from German) (London: 1906).
Who's Who at the International Congress of Women (London: 1899).
Wollstonecraft, Mary, *A Vindication of the Rights of Women* (1792) (London: 1970).
The Woman's [later *Workers'*] *Dreadnought* (London: 1914–24).
Woodham-Smith, Cecil, *Florence Nightingale* 2nd. ed. (Harmondsworth: 1955).
The World's Congress of Representative Women (Chicago: 1893).
Young, G.M., *Victorian England. Portrait of an Age* (Oxford: 1960).
Zeldin, Theodore, *France 1848–1945* vol. 1; *Ambition, Love and Politics* (Oxford: 1973).
Zimmern, Alice, *Women's Suffrage in Many Lands* 2nd. ed. (London: 1910).

Index